TACKLING SOCIAL EXCLUSION

John Pierson

communitycare

First published 2002
by Routledge
2 Park Square, Milton Park, Abingdon, Oxon OX14 4RN

Simultaneously published in the USA and Canada
by Routledge
270 Madison Ave, New York, NY 10016

Transferred to Digital Printing 2005

Routledge is an imprint of the Taylor & Francis Group, an informa business

Typeset in Sabon by Bookcraft Ltd, Stroud, Gloucestershire
Printed and bound in Great Britain by TJI Digital, Padstow, Cornwall

British Library Cataloguing in Publication Data
A catalogue record for this book is available from the British Library

Library of Congress Cataloging in Publication Data
Pierson, John, 1944–
Tackling social exclusion / John Pierson.
p. cm. (Social work skills series ; 3)
Includes bibliographical references and index.
1. Social service. 2. Marginality, Social. 3. Poor. I. Title. II. Series.

HV40 .P535 2001
361–dc21 2001048302

ISBN 10: 0-415-25682-8 (hbk)
ISBN 10: 0-415-25683-6 (pbk)

ISBN 13: 978-0-415-25682-7 (hbk)
ISBN 13: 978-0-415-25683-4 (pbk)

TACKLING SOCIAL EXCLUSION

The concept of social exclusion is a central part of government policy and is rapidly moving to the centre of practitioner activity. *Tackling Social Exclusion* lays out the approaches to practice for social work and allied occupations in their efforts to combat social exclusion. It examines the meaning of social exclusion and the common elements of practice needed to avert it while recognising that social work is a wide and diverse profession as well as a voluntary activity that performs many tasks within different settings. Chapters show the practice and skills needed to support a variety of situations, including working with families and children excluded through poverty, distressed urban neighbourhoods, racism, refugees and asylum seekers.

Tackling Social Exclusion is a practical handbook. It will be invaluable for local authority social workers and social care professionals, a wide range of voluntary and nonprofit organisations, as well as youth workers, advisers and advocates, community development practitioners and the probation service. Other social care providers involved with government initiatives such as Sure Start, youth offending teams and the New Deal for Communities with their emphasis on 'joined-up' action will also find much to interest them.

John Pierson is a Senior Lecturer in the Institute of Social Work and Applied Social Studies at the University of Staffordshire. He is the co-author and co-editor with Joan Smith of the *Dictionary of Social Work* and of *Rebuilding Community: Policy and Practice in Urban Regeneration* (2001).

the social work skills series

published in association with *Community Care*

series editor: Terry Philpot

the social work skills series

- builds practice skills step by step
- places practice in its policy context
- relates practice to relevant research
- provides a secure base for professional development

This new, skills-based series has been developed by Routledge and *Community Care* working together in partnership to meet the changing needs of today's students and practitioners in the broad field of social care. Written by experienced practitioners and teachers with a commitment to passing on their knowledge to the next generation, each text in the series features: *learning objectives; case examples; activities to test knowledge and understanding; summaries of key learning points; key references; suggestions for further reading.*

Also available in the series:

Managing Aggression
Ray Braithwaite
Consultant and trainer in managing aggression at work. Lead trainer and speaker in the 'No Fear' campaign.

Commissioning and Purchasing
Terry Bamford
Former Chair of the British Association of Social Workers and Executive Director of Housing and Social Services, Royal Borough of Kensington and Chelsea

To the memory of my friend Eddie Glendon
1947–2000

My eyes looked for him everywhere, and he was not there … Nor could they now tell me, 'look, he is on the way', as used to be the case when he was alive and absent from me.

Augustine

CONTENTS

FIGURES

CASE STUDIES

ACKNOWLEDGEMENTS

I am grateful for the help and advice that I received from many quarters while writing this volume. In particular Terry Philpot, the series editor, provided me with guidance and encouragement – not the first time he has given me his generous support. Martin Thomas of the Institute of Social Work and Applied Social Studies, Staffordshire University, deserves thanks for his flexibility and assistance in sorting out sabbatical arrangements. Moira Taylor at Routledge has my gratitude for her editing of the manuscript and ready advice that made the end result much more readable. I also pay tribute to the two anonymous reviewers who pointed out certain weaknesses in draft that I hope I have dealt with.

Social exclusion is a large topic. Without the help of friends, colleagues and informants in the field who have supplied me with valuable perspectives and practice approaches this volume would not have been written. I would like to thank:

Bob MacLaren, formerly of Cheshire Social Services and now with Wrexham Social Services; Sally Hesketh and Anne Cunningham of the Park Family Centre, Ellesmere Port; Mike Wolfe, of the Citizens' Advice Bureau in Stoke-on-Trent; Judith Penrose of Oxfordshire Social Services; Jonathan Hayes of the Shaftesbury Society; Neil Jameson of the Citizens' Organising Foundation; Ben Witney of Staffordshire Education Authority; Saheed Ullah of Tower Hamlets Social Services and Mike Hughes of Barnardos.

INTRODUCTION

> [Social exclusion is] a shorthand label for what can happen when individuals or areas suffer from a combination of linked problems such as unemployment, poor skills, low incomes, poor housing, high crime environments, bad health and family breakdown. Different people will take the term to mean different things – many see it as another term for multiple deprivation, social disadvantage or poverty. Others prefer to talk about the need positively to promote social inclusion. In broad terms, however, social exclusion is taken to mean more than *material lack of income*.
>
> (Scottish Office 1998: 2)

The idea of social exclusion has become fundamental to everyone working with people in the major public services – health, social services, education, neighbourhood renewal, housing and the police. In a short space of time it has become as widely used as 'poverty' or 'inequality' and indeed has sometimes come to replace the latter. Many innovations in welfare services are now being propelled by this one concept. Reducing social exclusion, whether of specific groups such as young people who have dropped out of school, or lone parents on low income, has become an over-arching goal with wide appeal across the political spectrum.

Yet compared with health services or education, social work has been slower to embrace both the concept and the new approaches that need to be adopted, such as working through broad partnerships, and developing anti-poverty strategies. This has left a partial vacuum which other services and agencies have been quick to exploit, even though tackling social exclusion should come naturally to the social work mission. Matters are now changing, however, as social work begins to realise the possibilities in such work. The aim of this book is to help social workers of all kinds come to grips with the implications and to explain what specifically social workers should do to tackle social exclusion in their practice.

What does tackling social exclusion actually mean for social work practice? The term is now used so widely by government and the media that it is in danger of losing its clarity. Social workers might argue that they are already working with socially excluded people. They might say, 'Aren't adults with mental health problems or children with disability excluded? Don't they face stigmatisation, material deprivation and lack of opportunities that cut them off from mainstream society? And haven't we been working to overcome these barriers for many years?'

To some extent this is true, but when social work explicitly focuses on social exclusion, as we shall see, it also takes on a new way of doing things in its approach to social problems. Perhaps most importantly the concept of social exclusion alters the way social workers think about society and in particular the consequences for practice of the sharp inequalities that exist, whether of income, social supports, access to services, or health and wellbeing. It re-orders its practice priorities toward 'preventive work' and building community supports and away from the highly procedural assessment of risk with individual users and their families.

This textbook rests on the conviction that it is crucial for social workers of every description to understand the meaning of social exclusion and its implications for practice. Social exclusion is important for three reasons:

- It describes a range of social problems in a coherent way.
- It is at the centre of government social policy.
- It suggests particular approaches to overcoming a specific set of complex, inter-linked social problems.

A brief word on the terms 'social work' and 'social worker'. As used here social work is a 'big tent'. Under it fit those designated as social workers with local authority or voluntary agencies, social-care workers of every description, advice workers, youth workers, youth justice workers, probation officers, care managers, community support workers, education welfare officers, education social workers, home-care workers and social workers with primary care groups. In an age of specialisation, we too easily forget that these tasks all involve social work skills, even if the professional designation varies.

In combating exclusion it is important to remember that roles and tasks are blurring still further. A multitude of new hybrid jobs explicitly to tackle social exclusion are being created; they have new titles but incorporate social work activity all the same. Among them are personal advisers for the Connexions scheme, re-ablement officers in the health service working with older people, Sure Start project workers, housing plus outreach workers, Supporting People project workers, neighbourhood management team workers and project workers for New Deal for Communities. Then too there is the growing number of staff working with local organisations – housing associations, community centres, cultural resource centres and advice centres. All deal with aspects of social exclusion and all draw on social work components – assessing, giving advice, building networks, marshalling resources. They too are in the big tent.

Tackling social exclusion thus introduces new challenges for social work and confirms old ones. For the student learning about social work and the experienced practitioner alike, that challenge will be met through gaining awareness of new interpretations of social and individual problems, a new sense of responsibility for the role and the ability to take on initiatives to develop and transform practice.

But the core of social work practice prepares it well for these new challenges. While social work shares certain elements of professional organisation with medicine, law or teaching Bill Jordan has noted that it is different in this one important respect: it exerts its influence on individuals, families and communities through informal negotiation

(Jordan 2000). Social workers are distinguished from other professionals by their willingness and capacity to move away from their formal roles and by meeting people in their own, natural settings. This provides informality and the means for negotiating solutions to problems rather than imposing them. Jordan (1987) has also argued that a unique quality of social work is found in the close attention it pays to individuals' own understanding of their situation and to the informal processes by which client or user and social worker broker a solution. This unique way of working provides social work with many opportunities for tackling exclusion and promoting inclusion of their service users.

THE STRUCTURE OF THE BOOK

The chapters are designed to provide an introduction to a particular dimension of social exclusion that social workers will encounter. The first three chapters lay foundations. Chapter 1 introduces you to the concept of social exclusion itself, how it is defined and measured and the arguments between different perspectives over what it really signifies. Chapter 2 brings social work into the picture by discussing those values, approaches and skills that are relevant to tackling exclusion. The aim here is to prepare you for practice by grounding you in those perspectives that help make sense of the tasks ahead. Chapter 3 lays out the five building blocks for practice: maximising income, strengthening networks, developing partnership for holistic practice, increasing the participation of users and residents and finally the importance of small areas or neighbourhoods.

Chapters 4, 5 and 6 each focus on a broad group of users – families with young children, young adults and excluded adult users. Recognising that many social workers practise within broad specialisms, these chapters each aim to establish links between that work and reducing the exclusion of users.

The last three chapters look at structural and organisational changes that approaches to social exclusion require. Chapter 7 introduces a dimension that may be unfamiliar to many contemporary social workers: neighbourhood development work. The chapter lays out what social workers have to do in specific localities to help entire neighbourhoods escape exclusion. Chapter 8 examines the powerful role that racism has played and continues to play in enforcing exclusion upon a range of ethnic groups. In particular, it examines ways of overcoming institutional racism in service agencies and ways of tackling hate groups and bias among users. Chapter 9 concludes by discussing how organisations can adapt to the holistic practice required and specifically how certain structures, such as neighbourhood management teams, can promote the many-sided attack on exclusion.

CHAPTER 1

WHAT SOCIAL EXCLUSION MEANS

OBJECTIVES

By the end of this chapter you should:

- Understand the concept of social exclusion and the different ways it is defined.
- Know which groups in society are excluded and why.
- Begin to think about how social work practice can reduce the social exclusion of those you work with.

This chapter begins with an overview of the concept of social exclusion and the different meanings that people find in it. For all its widespread use any discussion of social exclusion raises controversy and these controversial aspects are considered next. The chapter then explores in more detail some of the components of social exclusion using case studies to draw these out as clearly as possible for the reader. The aim here is to provide practitioners and managers in the field with a workable understanding of what social exclusion is. The final section of the chapter explains why tackling social exclusion, and promoting social inclusion, are key social work tasks for the twenty-first century.

INTRODUCING THE CONCEPT OF SOCIAL EXCLUSION

Any discussion of social exclusion inevitably raises contentious issues and strong feelings, principally because people with quite different points of view find different meanings in the concept. At stake are deeply held views about society and the causes of social problems. Here are some of the points that emerge in such discussions:

- The concept of social exclusion is vague but government likes it because it downplays the reality of poverty and lets government off the hook of having to do anything about it.
- Social exclusion is caused by people excluding themselves from society through their own actions and delinquent moral values that are different from the mainstream.
- Work provides the most effective way of overcoming social exclusion because it provides social connections and higher levels of income than benefits, and so there should be strong encouragement and even compulsion, for all – including disabled people and lone mothers – to take on paid employment.
- Focussing on poverty means only looking at income as the basis for quality of life; social exclusion by contrast focuses more on social *relations* and the extent to which people are able to participate in social affairs and attain sufficient power to influence decisions that affect them.

Are such assertions right? In fact every one of the above points sparks sharp debate and strong feelings. For example, on the third point, advocates and representatives of disability organisations would strongly contest what they regard as the pressure that the government has applied to disabled people to find work. As for the second point, those who have worked for anti-poverty organisations would argue that the term social exclusion is a distraction, even an excuse, for not having to focus on the high levels of child and adult poverty in Britain. Although you will not be able to resolve this one way or another for now, as you accumulate practical experience you will begin to develop your own understanding of what the experience of exclusion is like, what defines it and the ways in which you may be able to counter it.

ACTIVITY 1.1: DEVELOPING AN UNDERSTANDING OF SOCIAL EXCLUSION

In your practice you will encounter the term social exclusion frequently and with different shades of meaning. To help give you a better idea of what social exclusion means for people read the three case studies on the next page and make a note of those aspects of their lives that you think contribute to their exclusion.

CASE STUDY 1: AN ASYLUM SEEKER

A young male asylum seeker arrived from Nigeria. Although his passport indicated he is 21 he is in fact 15 years of age. His mother accompanied him and also sought asylum. Both mother and son were detained for a period at Campsfield House near Oxford where they found conditions difficult and were the subject of abuse from other detainees and staff. A short-lived attempt at a hunger strike by the boy's mother, to call attention to their plight, ended when she was threatened with removal to prison. After six weeks mother and son were moved to a west London borough where they had friends. They were there for two weeks after which they were moved, with only 24 hours' notice, to social housing in Stoke-on-Trent.

CASE STUDY 2: A DISAFFECTED YOUTH

A white male of 16 was arrested for causing affray on a large social housing estate on the edge of Brighton; he was also charged with stealing and taking away a car. He had been caught with three others of his age after joy-riding through the streets of the estate with the police giving chase.

CASE STUDY 3: A POOR NEIGHBOURHOOD

The North Peckham estate, where Damilola Taylor was killed in late 2000, shares the deprivation found on a great many urban neighbourhoods in Britain's inner cities. It has a high minority and immigrant population. Half the residents receive some form of benefit and 62 per cent of the children live in families that receive Income Support. A quarter of the adults who live on the estate are unemployed or considered too disabled to seek work. At the school Damilola attended 12 per cent of the pupils are refugees or asylum seekers and nearly 40 per cent speak English as a second language.

The estate is also subject to urban renewal that aims to alter the very texture of the area. To that end hundreds of apartments in crumbling buildings have been torn down and replaced with attractive single-family houses with gardens and front parking areas. This has had some unintended consequences: housing values have increased by as much as 50 per cent and the project has also resulted in huge disruptions with hundreds of people being moved out of old homes into temporary accommodation before final relocation in new homes.

Before reading any further, think about what social exclusion feels like for those in the case studies. In the first the boy and his mother as asylum seekers reveal the stark features of total exclusion. Although asylum seekers are sometimes mixed with refugees in popular imagery, the tabloid press portray them not as 'invited' as refugees who are recognised under international convention. Their reason for seeking asylum in the UK may stem from oppression on the basis of gender, forced environmental migration or flight from severe economic hardship. These are very different circumstances – at least in the public and the media mind – from those of, say, refugees under the Geneva Convention of 1951 who are fleeing well-founded fears of persecution for reasons of race, religion or nationality.

The circumstances of asylum seekers graphically illustrate the various forces that shape exclusion: barriers to the jobs market, thin or non-existent support networks of their own, extreme difficulties in obtaining the safety-net benefits of the welfare state, children facing poverty and marginalisation in the school system. Although it is difficult to assert that one group of people is 'more excluded' than another, asylum seekers' experience demonstrates exclusion's raw power more than most.

The second case study highlights a very different kind of an excluded individual – what sociological and government parlance call 'disaffected youth'. The government's Social Exclusion Unit has focused particularly on this age group – as well as young offenders, teenage mothers, truants and those excluded from school and young rough sleepers are also grouped in this category. Local and central government have invested heavily to curtail the disorder and crime that disaffected youth cause in local communities. Enforcing certain norms of behaviour, reparation for victims and placing heavy responsibility on their parents for ensuring discipline – all are done in the name of fighting social exclusion.

The third case study gives a different perspective entirely: how an entire local area can suffer exclusion. Derelict or over-crowded housing, abandoned public spaces without 'eyes on the street', non-existent local shops and commerce, collapse of local community activity, and poor schools all combine to exclude the residents living there. These so-called 'neighbourhood effects' become a prime target for measures to combat exclusion.

ORIGINS OF THE CONCEPT

The concept of social exclusion has an interesting history. It originated in France in the 1970s to describe the condition of certain groups on the margins of society who were cut off both from regular sources of employment and the income safety nets of the welfare state. *Les exclus* lacked the substantial rights of *les citoyens*, either in practice because they were victims of discrimination – such as disabled people – or because they were not citizens of the state, such as asylum seekers. Nor did they have access to or connections with those powerful institutions that might have helped them gain voice such as the trade unions or residents' associations. It is important to remember that the concept of social exclusion arose in France and not in Britain or the United States, both of which have substantially different political cultures. In France in particular there has long been an emphasis on citizenship and social cohesion reflecting a strong nation (Canaan 1997).

From France the term gained wide currency in the social policy of the European Union particularly in the Maastricht Treaty of 1996. When the Labour Party came to power in the UK in 1997 it swiftly adopted the concept for its own. From the start the Labour administration saw how its range of social goals could be presented in terms of reducing social exclusion. As a first important step it set up the Social Exclusion Unit in the Cabinet Office to ensure that all departments co-ordinated their efforts.

In the transition from Europe to the UK social exclusion has become a more flexible concept. While the Labour government's policies for reducing social exclusion have amalgamated with earlier strands of welfare policy in the UK, particularly around individual eligibility, means testing and targeting resources, the importance of what is new should not be underestimated. Achieving inclusion for all people and groups in mainstream society has wide appeal across the political spectrum. For the left it suggests a greater push toward equality with focus on tackling deprivation and lack of rights, for the right it suggests shaping a more cohesive, unified society uniting behind a strong national regime.

SOCIAL EXCLUSION: CONTROVERSY AND DEBATE

As used in the UK the concept of social exclusion is sufficiently fuzzy to allow very different understandings of society and social problems to exist side by side. As practitioners, you will find that social exclusion is interpreted differently and that these different interpretations frequently relate to different political points of view. For instance there are those using the term who prefer to focus more on the threat that the socially excluded *themselves* present to social cohesion and mainstream society. But there is also the view that social exclusion should primarily concern the poverty and disadvantage that people suffer in the midst of an otherwise wealthy society, only by making the UK more equal in wealth and personal resources will the scourge of exclusion finally be overcome.

The three strands of social exclusion

In an influential text Ruth Levitas uncovers three different interpretations or 'discourses' within discussions on social exclusion (Levitas 1998).

1 RED: the redistributionist discourse which has as its prime concern those living in poverty and the social forces that make this happen. RED includes within these concerns the extreme extent of inequality in Britain. Those holding this view argue that only through the redistribution of wealth across society as a whole, through taxation, benefits and services, will poverty and inequality be eradicated in Britain. It is especially critical of the idea that individual attitudes, for example toward work, or that moral and cultural attributes are in any way responsible for exclusion of groups or individuals.

2 MUD: the moral underclass discourse which concentrates on individual delinquency and lapses in attitudes and morality. Proponents extend this argument to whole neighbourhoods or social groups. For example they will view low-income neighbourhoods as falling prey to criminalised behaviour or as lacking a work ethic. MUD is also a gendered discourse; it highlights what it regards as moral weakness in which gender plays an important role. It pinpoints, for example, the behaviour of absentee fathers who evade child-support responsibilities, young male offenders, and young teenage women who have children outside a stable relationship. Proponents argue that the excluded in effect exclude themselves by engaging in certain

behaviours such as drug addiction, crime and having children out of wedlock. This position is found frequently among those who argue that there is an 'underclass' in society that has become detached from mainstream social institutions, adopts anti-social behaviour and has values that seem to justify this behaviour.

3 SID: a social integrationist discourse whose primary focus is on paid work and entrance into the labour market. Social integration and cohesion of society in general is achieved through paid work. Levitas argues that this discourse is uppermost in the policy and practice of the Labour government that came to power in 1997. Although it shares some of the features that RED would also identify it tends to equate social exclusion with exclusion from the labour market (Levitas 1998).

ACTIVITY 1.2: THE DIFFERENT MEANINGS OF SOCIAL EXCLUSION

Below are three texts each of which reflect one of the three discourses associated with social exclusion discussed by Levitas above. Try to identify which one exemplifies RED, MUD and SID as discussed above.

1 'It turns out that the cliches about role models are true. Children grow up making sense of the world around them in terms of their own experience. Little boys don't naturally grow up to be responsible fathers and husbands. They don't naturally grow up knowing how to get up every morning at the same time and go to work. ... And most emphatically of all, little boys do not reach adolescence naturally wanting to refrain from sex, just as little girls don't become adolescents naturally wanting to refrain from having babies. ... That's why single-parenthood is a problem for communities, and that's why illegitimacy is the most worrisome aspect of single-parenthood' (Murray 1996: 31).

2 'Welfare has to work with the changing labour market, giving people incentives and support to maximise their opportunities and thereby their rewards from work. Welfare should openly reward good behaviour and it should be used to enhance those roles which the country values. Those individuals who wish to buck the system and oppose the verities of civilised life should not be encouraged. Welfare should be given a central role guaranteeing universal citizenship in an age of stakeholder democracy' (Field 1996: 9–10).

3 'Britain remains a highly divided country with grotesque extremes of income and wealth. Until the cause of these disparities are addressed, the work of the Social Exclusion Unit could seem at best to be marginal, at worst a political smokescreen ... . Social inclusion is no more than an organised attempt by the state to incorporate people at the margins into this flexible and global labour market, characterised by insecurity, low wages and poor conditions, a task made politically more urgent by the growing numbers of those currently excluded' (Craig 2000: 6).

When thinking about social exclusion it is important to have all three strands in mind, although of course you will rarely encounter them in pure form as above. But in considering the policies you are having to carry out and even more importantly when reflecting on your own practice, knowing which strand is uppermost provides a key signal for what your practice is formally being asked to achieve.

A broad definition of social exclusion

One of the themes of this book is that practitioners have more latitude than they might imagine in responding to policy direction from central government. The fact that social exclusion means different things to different people allows for greater flexibility in practice than you might have first thought.

A good example of this can be found in the work of the new multi-agency youth offending teams which illustrates perfectly the contradictions and dilemmas for practitioners in aiming to reduce social exclusion. The formal duties of the youth offending teams under the Crime and Disorder Act 1998 are to reduce crime and social disorder in local areas caused by 'disaffected youth'. This stated mission reflects the social integrationist strand and something of the moral underclass view, with law enforcement, the restoration of community safety and preservation of moral order uppermost. Other objectives such as diverting young people from the criminal justice system or enabling and funding disadvantaged young people to pursue training opportunities are lower priorities and yet practitioners on the ground have been able to achieve precisely these objectives in their work (Bailey and Williams 2000).

With these different tendencies and arguments in conflict it is difficult to formulate a reliable definition of social exclusion that is workable in practice. Reflecting the contradictory nature of the way in which social exclusion is used in policy and practice we adopt the following definition:

> Social exclusion is a process that deprives individuals and families, groups and neighbourhoods of the resources required for participation in the social, economic and political activity of society as a whole. This process is primarily a consequence of poverty and low income, but other factors such as discrimination, low educational attainment and depleted living environments also underpin it. Through this process people are cut off for a significant period in their lives from institutions and services, social networks and developmental opportunities that the great majority of a society enjoys.

Of course practitioners do not have the luxury of endless debates over definitions and perspectives. They are charged by their agency policy at local level and by central government to undertake certain responsibilities. In short it is their task to recognise it and tackle it. For this, social workers are as well fitted as any of the helping professions. Social workers have long been familiar with the effects of social exclusion on individuals and families for a century or more: family breakdown, mental and physical ill-health, educational under-achievement, unemployment and loss of self-esteem.

In coming to grips with exclusion sophisticated ways, however, have recently been developed to ascertain its extent in a particular area and with particular groups of service users. For example, researchers from the New Policy Institute (Howarth *et al.* 1999) have developed indicators that show the degree of exclusion suffered by children and young people, adults, older people and whole communities. Their careful research into social exclusion has shown that these are the most reliable and effective signposts for social exclusion taking place. For children and families the indicators they use are:

- the number of children living in workless households
- low-birth-weight babies
- accidental deaths
- low attainment at school
- permanent exclusion from school
- births to girls conceiving under 16
- the number of children aged 10–16 in young offender institutions.

In using such indicators it is important not to confuse 'causation' with 'correlation'. Indicators do not identify the 'causes' of social exclusion and still less do not provide the basis for blaming individuals or families. They are merely quantifiable signposts – ways of estimating the degree of exclusion within a particular area.

Exclusion also occurs at the level of neighbourhood or community. The signposts of exclusion at this level include, among others, overcrowded housing, low levels of voluntary or community activity, a high percentage of residents without a bank or building society account and high levels of burglaries among others (ibid.: 10). For neighbourhoods as for families social exclusion has devastating effects. Certain long-term trends gather pace: the withdrawal of services as well as commercial and financial outlets, the concentration of vulnerable groups such as lone parents in housing and a rise in the incidence of social disturbances. Social workers are less familiar now with the skills for tackling the social problems of whole neighbourhoods than they used to be. For social work to tackle social exclusion at this level means drawing on some of that earlier tradition and developing new approaches in practice within neighbourhoods.

THE COMPONENTS OF SOCIAL EXCLUSION

We have thus far discussed the different meanings within the concept of social exclusion, begun to think about what being socially excluded actually means for different people and neighbourhoods through short case studies, and formulated a working definition of social exclusion as a process. This section follows up your first thoughts on the process of exclusion by examining its different components in greater depth.

Of the important forces that drive the process of social exclusion forward five stand out:

- poverty and low income
- lack of access to the jobs market
- thin or non-existent social supports and networks
- the effect of the local area or neighbourhood
- exclusion from services.

When they intertwine and reinforce one another, these five components work to exclude people from the norms and standards of wellbeing that the great majority have. Tackling social exclusion and promoting its opposite, social inclusion, means developing approaches to practice that address each of these domains: maximising options for income, strengthening social networks, tackling the quality of life in neighbourhoods and making services more accessible. Let us examine each more closely.

Poverty and low income

The most potent element in the process of social exclusion is poverty and low income. Any social work practice that aims to reduce exclusion cannot avoid this central fact. Many commentators, both in government and out, now refer to 'poverty and social exclusion' to ensure that this is understood. Indeed a family with a reasonable income, or a local neighbourhood with reasonable median income, will usually have ready resources to overcome barriers and exclusions that they may encounter.

We can define poverty in two different ways: as *absolute* or *relative* poverty.

Absolute poverty is defined by a fixed standard below which individuals and families experience complete destitution and so cannot meet even minimum needs for food and shelter. The United Nations Development Programme uses such a standard for measuring poverty in the developing world fixed at one (US) dollar a day. Below that income threshold families face severe malnutrition and dangerous levels of ill-health. Absolute standards have the virtue of allowing us to calculate poverty across different countries. Thus UNDP estimates fairly accurately that within the developing world 30 per cent of all children under five are malnourished (UN 1995).

Relative poverty refers to the lack of resources needed to obtain the kinds of diet, participate in the activities and have the living conditions and amenities that are widely approved and generally obtained by most people in a particular society. A person who suffers this form of poverty has resources so seriously inferior to those commanded by the average individual or household that they are, in effect, excluded from ordinary living patterns and social activities.

The work of Peter Townsend (1979) in particular helped us to the understanding that the basic standards of living which most people enjoy are implicitly defined within each society. These standards have not only to do with income but also consumer purchases, levels of health and wellbeing, and access to goods and services. Those investigating relative poverty look at the ways in which individual and family life is affected by the experience of deprivation. The notion of relative poverty focuses on the degree to which people are prevented from sharing the living standards, opportunities and norms of wellbeing that society as a whole has created for itself. In this sense it is an important forerunner to social exclusion.

The concept of relative poverty implies that as society becomes more sophisticated and affluent so does what an individual or family requires. Information and communication technology (ICT) presents a good example. Twenty-five years ago computer operations were specialised functions performed on huge, room-sized machines by small numbers of highly trained operators. In a relatively short time skills in ICT have moved from the margin of economic activity to its core. Add its research and educative functions and its social networking value through email and it becomes a central tool that impacts on individuals. Families with no access to or knowledge of ICT have

DEFINITIONS OF POVERTY

Absolute poverty

- 'a condition characterised by severe deprivation of basic human needs, including food, safe drinking water, sanitation facilities, health, shelter, education and information. It depends not only on income but also on access to services'.

(UN 1995: 57).

Relative poverty

- 'the poor shall be taken to mean persons, families and groups of persons whose resources (material, cultural and social) are so limited as to exclude them from the minimum acceptable way of life of the Member State in which they live'.

(EEC 1985)

another dimension in which they are poor – this is now referred to as 'information poverty' which did not exist even fifteen years ago.

The notion of relative poverty raises a key question: what does society deem as the standard for deciding who is poor? What are 'the necessities of life'? Determining the norms of society is a crucial part of coming to understand what it is that people are being excluded from when they are poor.

One of the most influential studies that has attempted to answer that is 'Breadline Britain', which through several rigorous public surveys established what the British people considered to be necessities as they have changed since the 1980s. The surveys showed that the public hold wider-ranging ideas about the necessities of life than expert opinion might have thought. In those surveys people of all ages and walks of life move well beyond the basic necessities to acknowledge that social customs, obligation and activities form a platform for needs (Howarth *et al.* 2000: 14).

There is a striking consensus over many items deemed 'necessities', that is those things that all adults should be able to afford and which they should not have to do without. For example, in the most recent of these surveys, 95 per cent thought beds and bedding were necessary (although interestingly 4 per cent thought they were unnecessary!) while 94 per cent thought heating to warm the living areas of the home was necessary. Others items deemed necessary by the vast majority (with percentages in brackets) were things like two meals a day (91), a refrigerator (89), fresh fruit and vegetables daily (86), money to keep the home in a decent state of decoration (82) and a washing machine (76) (Howarth *et al.* 2000).

The same consensus however does not always exist over what is *not* necessary. There is disagreement, especially over a range of items that are new, technological and labour-saving.

ACTIVITY 1.3: THINKING ABOUT POVERTY

Before reading any further look at the list of items on the next page which have been taken from the most recent survey, mentioned above. They have been scrambled to give you the chance of testing your opinion of what constitutes absolute necessity against the results of the public survey. Which of the following would you define as 'necessities', that is 'items which you think all adults should be able to afford and which they should not have to do without' (list the items in order of importance):

- two pairs of all-weather shoes, television, holiday away from home once a year, dictionary, car, carpets in living room, microwave oven, daily newspaper, regular saving of £10 per month, an evening out once a fortnight, visits to friends and family, visits to the children's school, a leisure activity, having a telephone, small amounts of money to spend on self weekly, dressing gown, coach or train fare to visit friends and family every three months.

Access to the jobs market and paid employment

While unemployment has longed been viewed as a principal factor in causing poverty, our awareness of its many effects has become considerably more sophisticated since the 1980s. In this, understanding the concept of exclusion *from the labour market* has assisted greatly.

Those with low levels of skills face the toughest barriers to entering or re-entering the job market. A large group of the unemployed in the UK, white male working-class youth, is perceived by gatekeepers as disruptive, aggressive and unwilling to adapt to social and business norms just as inner-city black youth are in the US (Wilson 1996; Power 1999).

This mismatch has arisen in part because of the increased requirement for 'soft skills' – skills that relate to motivation, teamwork and problem-solving reflecting the move toward services and retail, team-production processes, together with emphasis on quality of service (Giloth 1998: 5). The emerging service economy itself does not provide orderly advancement (as did the earlier manufacturing economy) because of the gulf between high-wage, high-skill jobs at one end and low-wage, low-skill work at the other. Some economists argue that skills in the technical sense are less critical to employability than attitude, and that the notion of 'soft skills' is simply a way of denoting the willingness to learn and to accept the disciplinary requirements of most workplaces.

One strand of government policy applies both enticement and pressure on various groups of people to prepare for and seek work more actively. These various 'New Deals' are for groups with an insecure or disadvantaged relationship to the labour market such as 18–24-year-olds, the long-term adult unemployed, people with disabilities and lone parents. The programmes aim at 'enhancing employability' of such groups both through training and work readiness. Through work they are to lift themselves out of poverty and also enjoy the connections and further opportunities that employment provides.

This emphasis in government policy on the jobs market and finding work presents practitioners with another possible conflict over values. How much 'encouragement', some would say compulsion, should be applied to people of working age to find a job? This is a particularly acute question for those adults that social workers often serve – disabled people, people with mental health problems or lone parents. Each group has a range of requirements to be met and barriers to overcome before they can readily find work. Many social workers would feel uncomfortable in being part of a wider policy goal of pressuring people into work. They would share the redistributionist perspective which accepts that many individuals are not able to work for whatever reason and should be supported through adequate levels of benefits.

But the matter of work readiness is not always clear cut. It has to be acknowledged that having work does in general provide levels of remuneration higher than most state benefits. Work provides social interaction and networks that are extremely difficult to find anywhere else. It also facilitates contact with relatively powerful institutions such as trade unions or professional associations. As a result certain groups that social workers help are in fact pressing for greater access to the jobs market. Young adults leaving care need training schemes, adults with a learning disability want supported employment as we shall see in Chapter 5.

While the Employment Service has a clear lead in delivering aspects of the various New Deal programmes, social workers will find it impossible to avoid assessments of work readiness and training and education across the whole range of users who find barriers between themselves and the labour market. This may take an indirect form, as with local partnership arrangements responsible for delivery of the various New Deal programmes or work with specific individuals such as persons with a learning disability seeking supported employment. This crucial role is clarified further in subsequent chapters.

Of course being in work does not automatically bring rewards for users. Jobs, particularly in the service sector such as restaurants or telephone call centres, pay low wages, are often casualised (that is, are part time and without security) and are stressful occupations. Nor does joblessness automatically bring exclusion. Great numbers of individuals and households are jobless – some 43 per cent of adults have no paid work and 1 in 3 live in a household without paid work (Howarth *et al.* 2000). We have to be cautious therefore in assuming that 'labour market inactivity' automatically excludes since a large proportion of the population would fall into that category.

Social supports and social networks

A third component of social exclusion is the weakness in social networks experienced by groups, families or individuals. 'Network poverty' deprives users of social supports and informal help that we all need to participate in community life and to enjoy the standards of living shared by the majority of people. Social workers have informally recognised this to be the case for some while. For example since the implementation of the Children Act 1989 they have preferred to place children with relatives and as near to home as possible rather than in a children's home or with distant foster parents, thus preserving the childs's natural networks. But this focus on networks has been intermittent and often of low priority. For instance in social care for older people social workers have reduced the commitment to 'non-care' activites – luncheon clubs, specialist transport services and befriending activities which has undermined the network-enhancing role of social care practice (6, P 1997).

Mastering what networks are and how they thrive is therefore an essential element when tackling the social exclusion of users. Fortunately our understanding both of the importance of social networks and how they function has developed considerably in the last twenty years. There are various ways of describing and measuring the characteristics of networks.

One helpful distinction is to think of networks for 'getting by' and those 'for getting ahead'; they are very different and perform very different functions.

Networks for getting by

These are the close, supportive networks embedded in everyday relationships of friends, neighbourhood and family. When we think of the social supports offered by extended families and friends or by close-knit communities, these are networks for getting by. They can supply gaps in childcare, look after a person when they are ill, provide small loans and cash to make ends meet and participate in family celebrations or rites of passage.

As social workers we are vitally interested in how these networks are viewed by the people with whom we are working. They may be seen as affirmative, nurturing or accepting or as antagonistic and inaccessible. At their very worst they can be sources of heavy responsibility, aggression and scapegoating. Understanding how such networks function helps us to better understand the distinctive characteristics of socially excluded and isolated individuals and families (Briggs *et al.* 1997).

Networks for getting ahead

These networks provide crucial information for individuals and families on jobs, education, training and on a range of options for advancing individual interests. In many ways they are the opposite of networks for getting by but can achieve so much more. Mark Granovetter has summed up this kind of network in the phrase the 'strength of weak ties' (Granovetter 1973). The 'weak ties' he refers to are found outside the immediate neighbourhood and family and friends; they are occasional and episodic in nature and are more tenuous than a close personal relationship. They may be based on 'someone who knows someone' about a job possibility or on the links obtained through a skills agency half a city away which a person visits only occasionally (Briggs *et al.* 1997).

Weak ties can be very powerful in providing information and opportunities for self development. Here's why: the contemporary jobs market has become extremely formidable for those from poor urban neighbourhoods.

It has become far more complex for any one individual to negotiate as job descriptions are more fluid and firms, which have focused on 'core competencies', have hived off entry-level jobs to other organisations which were once routes to secure positions. It is increasingly clear that excluded individuals, whether through low income or discrimination, no matter how highly motivated, cannot on their own reconstruct and negotiate a city's map of job connections. Finding a job is no longer an individual transaction where a person simply acquires skills and then joins a job queue, where they are individually assessed without other factors being taken into consideration.

Increasingly the networks to which low-skilled workers and prospective employers belong fail to intersect.

Creating new networks or bolstering existing ones offers a fertile field for practice as we shall see in the next chapter. Network mapping, capitalising on existing strengths within networks for getting by, creating new networks around existing points of service such as family centres and schools, or by using mentors and volunteers, are all approaches which social workers should be developing. They are particularly important when working with individuals that employment gatekeepers view stereotypically as ill-equipped for the jobs market, such as young males – black and white – as well as disabled and older people.

Importance of neighbourhood

Since the 1980s we have learned an immense amount about the power of 'place', of local area and neighbourhood on the lives of those that live there. We know that conditions of poverty and exclusion interact and reinforce each other in particular geographical locations to create a qualitatively different set of conditions that make it virtually impossible for individuals or families to escape these negative 'neighbourhood' effects. This dynamic of poor schooling, vulnerable families and low income is found throughout the UK, largely on social or council housing estates on the edges of our towns and cities but also in over-crowded, low-income areas of mixed tenancy and owner-occupiers.

When we refer to 'neighbourhoods' we are not trying to evoke a cosy well-defined area where the residents all know and support each other in frequent face to face transactions. Far from it. In working with poor and excluded neighbourhoods we use that term simply to refer to a recognisable vicinity, perhaps with established boundaries like a main highway or the edge of an estate, that a majority of residents themselves would acknowledge. The *built environment* of a neighbourhood or local area – such as the quality of the housing, the existence or not of leisure facilities and the road system – is of course important to the quality of life, but we have come to understand from the range of research since the 1980s that the *social fabric* is even more important to understanding the level of exclusion in a locality. By social fabric we mean the social connections between people, the strength of local organisations and associations and the extent and vibrancy of local activity whether commercial or civic. These may be stronger, weaker or even non-existent but knowing something of these relationships is fundamental to practice.

In working with poor neighbourhoods, increasing levels of *participation* – whether in local organisations and institutions, decision-making affecting the locality or in public services themselves – becomes an important goal. There are three reasons why: first, raising levels of participation ensures that the felt needs of local residents and not the interests of service providers or policymakers gets heard. Second, participation can build skills and confidence that make people more effective in articulating their needs and demands. Third, as local residents learn to participate more effectively, the experience of this helps develop skills for further successful collaborations in solving problems (Ferguson and Stoutland 1999: 51).

That is the theory at least. There are also considerable practical barriers to participation by local residents, especially in poor neighbourhoods. In the next chapter we shall look in more detail at this crucial element of practice.

DISTRESSED HOUSING ESTATES

In her research on distressed social housing estates, Anne Power has done as much as anyone to reveal the intensifying effects of exclusion in particular areas. In *Dangerous Disorder,* which she wrote with Rebecca Tunstall in 1997, the authors report on their findings from thirteen areas where there had been serious disorder.

> 'There was a vacuum within the estates which tough boys sought to fill – too little work, too little cash, too few adult male workers and fathers, too many buildings, too many young boys outside any system. There was too little for these boys to do and too many useless places for them to attack. The vast majority of estates in difficulty had some empty property, abandoned land and unsupervised areas, inviting vandalism, fires, gangs, hideaways and other forms of trouble. Empty property was a signal that their community was worthless to the outside. But empty property gave boys room for destruction. The damage caused further abandonment with the consequent weakening of controls.'
>
> (Tunstall and Power 1997: 46)

Exclusion from services

Closely allied to the importance of locality in the social exclusion of individuals, families and groups is the lack of access to basic services. By services we mean the whole range of private and public, in-home and out-of-home services which individuals, families and groups continually draw on for a variety of purposes. In-home services include everything from electricity to care for those who need it; out-of-home services include transport, post office, doctor and hospital facilities or those such as day care for children. In poor or disadvantaged neighbourhoods there are often barriers to obtaining such services beyond the means of any one individual or family to surmount. Take the example of what the withdrawal of financial services can mean for neighbourhoods and those that live there. Withdrawal of financial services from certain areas badly affects groups already experiencing other forms of exclusion. Kempson and Whyley (1998) estimate that 7 per cent of households in Britain do not use financial services while a further 20 per cent have highly restricted use.

ACTIVITY 1.4: REDLINING

Whole neighbourhoods have experienced 'redlining' by mortgage lenders and insurance companies. The practice is so named because financial services companies literally draw a red line around certain areas where they refuse to lend, insure or provide even basic banking services. Choose a social housing estate where you or your team work and find out which financial services are and are not provided. Don't forget to consider services such as extending credit to families or individuals, counters for cashing benefit cheques and services to small shops or businesses. It is important to examine the informal services that people might come into contact with such as credit unions, or loan sharks.

Focusing on social exclusion requires looking hard at how social work services themselves are currently delivered and finding ways for increasing access to them. To take one example: a report from the Joseph Rowntree Foundation (Howarth *et al.* 1999) notes that around 25 per cent *fewer* households with people aged 75 or older in them are being helped to live at home by social services compared with five years ago. The reasons for this are complex and have to do with cutbacks in local authority resources for home help and home care, the charging policies that local authorities have introduced for home care and the attraction of free health care in hospital. This means that services such as home care, respite care to relieve regular family carers occasionally, meals services and day-care centres are all contributing less than they were to maintaining older people at home.

The example raises a number of questions that would require some answers if you were involved in their delivery. Can people now not afford such services? Are they simply not offered as widely as before? Are there other barriers in place that prevent their being used? Shaping practice to combating social exclusion brings with it the commitment to examine access to your own service and to think of ways of increasing the involvement and participation of those who use them. As we shall discover there are two important ways to overcome such barriers. The first is *decentralising* services, bringing their point of delivery closer to the people they serve. This combines with more local user involvement in shaping those services, to correspond more closely with what people on the ground need and want. The second is to *integrate* services so that they work more closely in collaboration. Hence the importance of constructing partnerships involving different agencies and local organisations such as residents' or tenants' groups and of 'joined-up action' on the ground where users can turn to local one-stop shops to seek the services they require.

ACTIVITY 1.5: REFLECTING ON WHAT SOCIAL WORK CAN CONTRIBUTE TO TACKLING SOCIAL EXCLUSION

Before going on to the next chapter read the list below of social problems that the Department of Social Security in *Opportunity for All* (DSS 1999) associates with social exclusion.

- lack of opportunities for work
- lack of opportunities to acquire education and work-related skills
- childhood deprivation

- families disrupted through high levels of conflict, separation or divorce
- barriers to older people living active lives
- inequalities in health
- poor housing
- poor neighbourhoods
- fear of crime
- groups disadvantaged through poverty or discrimination.

If you are a practitioner think of your current set of job responsibilities and decide which of the social problems listed above you and your team could tackle. You might want to categorise those problems according to whether you and your team's job specifications would have scope for tackling those problems on your own or in collaboratiosn with others. If you are a social work or social care student pick out those skills and competencies that you think could be applied to reducing the exclusion of various service user groups.

KEY POINTS

- Social exclusion is a process which deprives individuals, families, groups and neighbourhoods from obtaining the resources for participation in social, economic and political acivity that the great majority of society enjoys. These resources are not just material but have to do with the quality of social interaction. Social exclusion undermines or destroys channels of access for support and opportunity.
- The five main components driving the process forward are
    - poverty and low income
    - barriers to the jobs market
    - lack of support networks
    - the effects of living in extremely poor or distressed neighbourhoods
    - lack of access to good-quality services.
- Social exclusion presents a number of interlinked problems for social workers to deal with, in the form of individuals with depression and poor mental health, families under stress, children living in poverty, and older people cut off from activities and social engagement. Perhaps the biggest challenge for social workers in tackling social exclusion is to develop approaches that deal with these problems on a neighbourhood or community level.

KEY READING

Catherine Howarth, Peter Kenway, Guy Palmer and Romina Miorelli, *Monitoring Poverty and Social Exclusion* (New Policy Institute and the Joseph Rowntree Foundation, 1999). This volume lays out in detail the range of indicators for picking up social exclusion in the groups of users and the communities you work with. Although highly factual the information is provided in colourful graphs which are easy to interpret.

Janie Percy-Smith (ed.) *Policy Responses to Social Exclusion – towards inclusion?* (Open University Press, 2000). Each chapter is written by an academic authority and provides a good explanation of what the Labour government has done to address social exclusion since it came to power in 1997.

Gerald Smale, Graham Tuson and Daphne Statham, *Social Work and Social Problems: working towards social inclusion and social change* (Macmillan, 2000). The authors describe how in practice social workers can move from supplying short-term aid to long-term development work and social change.

CHAPTER 2

SOCIAL EXCLUSION

Perspectives and approaches to practice

OBJECTIVES

By the end of the chapter you should:

- Know the key professional values that underpin your work to reduce exclusion
- Be able to examine your own values and attitudes toward poverty, deprivation and exclusion
- Be familiar with those social work approaches which have the greatest scope for tackling exclusion
- Understand the specific skills most effective in tackling exclusion.

Tackling social exclusion requires holistic, joined up approaches which means bringing the main public services together through partnerships to focus on key forces of exclusion: low income, health inequalities, low educational attainment, constricted opportunities for women and race discrimination. This presents you with a number of challenges as a social worker because recent trends such as care management, with its focus on financial assessment and narrow interpretation of needs, and the heavy emphasis on child protection have only reinforced social work's reliance on specialisms and crisis-oriented work (Audit Commission 2000; Barr *et al.* 2001).

This chapter is designed to help you prepare for practice dedicated to reducing social exclusion. It aims to do this by discussing the values, approaches and skills which are useful for guiding your practice development. At the same time you are encouraged to examine your own values and attitudes which are crucial to motivation.

SOCIAL WORK VALUES AND ATTITUDES TOWARDS POVERTY AND INEQUALITY

Social work is a distinctive profession because of the emphasis it has placed on values. Values represent the profound aspirations of professional commitment, 'held aloft as the ultimate and, perhaps, never wholly attainable ends of policy and practice' (Clark 2000). While values can be thought of as attributes of persons, professions and organisations they are less fixed than we might presume. As Clark puts it they are 'the ongoing accomplishments of knowledgeable and reflective human intelligences immersed in a social world' (ibid: 360).

Social work values emerged from a wide range of beliefs, theories, religious affiliations and moral and political understandings. Although social work educators and professional associations refer to values as if they were well established, there are contending strands which make it difficult to find a unified set of values for the whole profession. To make the picture more complicated beliefs and values are very closely intertwined; indeed, values have been regarded as well-entrenched core attachments and sentiments which result in deep beliefs (Lipset 1996). This interconnection between values and beliefs means that we have to acknowledge that values may be resistant to change and immune to evidence concerning practice outcomes.

Social work has worked with predominantly poor people since its inception in the second half of the nineteenth century. One constant thread of this practice is the 'pathologising' of poor people, that is viewing users' poverty as the result of the poor person's perverse choices, for example spending too much on alcohol and tobacco (or drugs), being apathetic towards work and failing to recognise family responsibilities. This deep-seated belief prompts the practitioner to examine personal expenditure and to offer guidance on users' moral conduct and led to one of the earliest (and still potent) assessment categories: the deserving and the undeserving poor (Jones 1999). The dominant casework tradition tried to secure good personal habits such as thrift, sobriety and hard work through developing the personal relationship with the social worker and to achieve individual and family change with techniques such as counselling combined with compulsory interventions sanctioned by law (Pearson 1989). Social work's professional values were then built up around the notion of the user as an individual and the centrality of the worker's relationship with that individual. A Catholic priest, Father Biestek (1961), codified these in a number of principles:

- individualisation and the uniqueness of each individual
- purposeful expression of feelings
- controlled emotional involvement
- acceptance
- non-judgemental attitude
- client self-determination
- confidentiality.

Although much criticised as putting too much emphasis on the individual relationship between client and practitioner (Pearson 1989; Jones 1998) such principles have continued to be influential on how social workers view their work and themselves.

WHAT ARE VALUES?

The evidence for the existence of a distinctive and coherent set of normative professional social work values is extremely tenuous; and the actual range and content of social workers' personal and professional values can be conjectured from the professional literature but is not evidenced by any significant body of empirical social research. The identification of social work values can therefore be no more than approximate, provisional and inherently controversial. In broad terms, the values of social work are clearly rooted in Christian ethics blended with modern Western secular liberal individualism. They share their origins with the dominant Western tradition of morality.

(Clark 2000: 360)

How effective they are in grounding practitioners to combat social exclusion and disadvantage is an open question which readers should keep in mind.

Clark finds four broad principles present in social work values:

1. The worth and uniqueness of every person: all persons have equal value regardless of age, gender, ethnicity, physical or intellectual ability, income or social contribution. Respect for individuals is active and needs to be positively demonstrated rather than just assumed.
2. Entitlement to justice: every person is entitled to equal treatment on agreed principles of justice that recognise protection of liberties, human needs and fair distribution of resources.
3. Claim to freedom: every person and social group is entitled to their own beliefs and pursuits unless it restricts the freedom of others.
4. Community is essential: human life can only be realised interdependently in communities and much of social work aims to restore or improve specific communities.

(Clark 2000)

USERS ARE SMARTER THAN YOU THINK

Some users have long understood social workers' undying interest in depth psychology, complicated relationships and empathy as the platform from which they launch their work. Clients could sometimes work this to their advantage. 'Tailgunner' Parkinson, a probation officer known for his capacity to pierce social work's pretensions, captured this three decades ago in a short article entitled simply 'I give them money'. In it he wrote, 'Clients tried to talk about the gas bill, workers tried to talk about the client's mother. Perceptive clients got the gas bill paid by talking about mother'.

(Parkinson 1970, cited in Dowling 1999)

One strand of social work values developed around the notion of the uniqueness of each individual, self determination and the empathy that practitioners should bring to their work. To these fundamental values were later added a more explicit political commitment to counter discrimination and oppression. Radical social work and later forms of anti-oppressive practice added a set of social commitments (Langan and Lee 1989; Dominelli 1998). The notion of empowerment provided a fresh platform: enabling people without power to have more control over their lives and greater voice within institutions; extending a person's ability to take effective decisions; and helping people to regain their own lives (Braye and Preston-Shoot 1995: 48).

Your own beliefs about poverty

Professional values are only as effective as the practitioner makes them. For that reason personal values are extremely important too. Your personal beliefs about poverty are based in part on your own upbringing and your experiences but also on how familiar you are with what it is like to be poor, your understanding of society and social structure and what motivates individuals in conditions of scarcity. In the realm of values and beliefs it is easy to lose the complexity of *why* a person, family or neighbhourhood is poor. Yet beliefs and values have a large influence on the way we understand explanations of poverty. For example, if you believe that people are themselves largely responsible for what happens to them in life you quite likely will also think that people are poor because of personal failures for which they bear responsibility. Conversely if you believe in equal opportunity for everyone you may focus on the barriers that limit opportunity as a cause of poverty.

ACTIVITY 2.1: UNDERSTANDING THE REALITY OF POVERTY

Here is a thought experiment. Imagine you are attending a three-day conference and that on the second day that you have just settled in to your seat comfortably waiting for proceedings to begin. The chairperson comes to the podium to open the conference. Her first words are: 'The management have asked me to inform you that unfortunately a number of rooms in the hotel where you have been staying have been burgled and handbags, wallets and other personal items have been stolen. Management tell me they are pursuing the matter as urgently as they can and they ask that you not return to your rooms at this time since it would only hamper investigations.'

- What would your first reaction be?
- What would you actually do?
- Would you be able to concentrate on the conference as it went ahead?
- What would happen to the networking, conviviality and relationship building that you have been engaged in?

Now assume you are a parent on your own, living on Income Support, with two small children and you have just been told that your benefit book will be delayed in getting to you. Do you see similarities with the scenario above?

(Wolfe 2001)

ACTIVITY 2.2: YOUR BELIEFS ABOUT POVERTY

To begin to clarify your views on individual responsibility and poverty consider the following short scenarios.

1 Carol is a 26-year-old lone mother of African Caribbean origin with a 20-year-old male partner and a two-year-old son. Social workers have received reports that she leaves her son unsupervised for two or three hours at a time. Her partner is a van delivery driver who is away a good deal of the time. Carol and her son live entirely on Income Support and other benefits.

2 Mr Ullah has lived in England since 1963. He left his wife and family in Bangladesh to come here to work. He lived and worked in a number of English towns in the textile and steel industries – Birmingham, Manchester, Kirklees and Bradford. His family did not arrive in England until 1987 when his wife and children joined him. Before that he returned regularly to visit them. When they arrived they applied to an inner London authority for rehousing. Eight years ago Mr Ullah was severely disabled by a stroke. His teenage children help out sometimes with his care but he has no home care from social services. Mrs Ullah herself is a diabetic and a smoker. One of his grown children always has to be present when he sees his doctor or other professionals as Mr Ullah speaks no English. The family receive benefits but find it continuously hard to make ends meet.

What do you think are the main reasons for each family's low income? To what degree do you think the following are responsible for the family's predicament:

- personal or individual choices and actions
- cultural and moral attitudes of within the family or neighbourhood in which they live
- 'structural pressures' such as the impact of social class or the jobs market on their lives?

ACTIVITY 2.3: CCETSW'S VALUE REQUIREMENTS

The former Central Council for Education and Training in Social Work sought to blend both old and new values. Below are listed Central Council's value requirements for social work practitioners. Which of these do you think are most applicable to tackling social exclusion? The requirements are that practitioners should:

- Identify and question their own values and prejudices, and their implications for practice
- Respect and value uniqueness and diversity, and recognise and build on strengths
- Promote people's rights to choice, privacy, confidentiality and protection, while recognising and addressing the complexities of competing rights and demands
- Assist people to increase control of and improve the quality of their lives, while recognising that the control of behaviour will be required at times in order to protect children and adults from harm
- Identify, analyse and take action to counter discrimination, racism, disadvantage, inequality and injustice, using strategies appropriate to role and context
- Practise in a manner that does not stigmatise or disadvantage individuals, groups or communities.

Thus both professional and individual values may combine to distance practitioners from anti-poverty work. Poverty is too often seen as the inevitable backdrop to service provision, the responsibility of other workers and agencies. This is despite evidence showing that poverty remains the single factor most widely associated with social work contact and that disabled and older people in particular are failing to claim nearly £2 billion in entitlement (see Becker 1997; Whiteley 1997).

Even where local authority social service departments have direct control of important resources, whether grants for children in need, direct payments to disabled people, or payments to care leavers and foster carers, they use these powers variably and without clear reasoning or as part of an anti-poverty strategy. This limited engagement in anti-poverty initiatives means that local authority social service departments have little accumulated experience in tackling poverty as the central pillar of social exclusion (Dowling 1999; Jones 1999; McLeod 2000).

This attitude receives reinforcement from social work organisations themselves in which the hierarchy of skill locates the experienced social worker at the top undertaking 'complex' work particularly in child protection. Nor is anti-poverty work seen as part of the restructured role of community care manager and purchaser of care. Welfare rights work, on the other hand, if done at all, is carried out frequently by undertrained staff or assistants. In those few Diploma in Social Work programmes that stress the importance of obtaining full and accurate benefits for users students show less commitment and less dedication to acquiring expertise and skills than in virtually every other area of the work (Wolfe 2001).

USEFUL PERSPECTIVES

Because social exclusion is a relatively new concept no single social work theory maps out the pathway for combating it. The importance of poverty, social networks, locality, partnerships and participation – several theories have addressed one or other of these components of exclusion but none has addressed them in their combination. Some groundwork, however, has been laid. The aim of this section is to familiarise you with those existing perspectives that help clarify social exclusion and prompt you to get to grips with particular kinds of social problems.

Anti-oppressive practice

Anti-oppressive practice merges the separate struggles that social work undertook against discrimination into a single coherent approach. Feminism, anti-racism and disability campaigns have all contributed to this approach as has gay and lesbian thinking. It locates the sources of oppression and disadvantage in social structure and focuses on how powerful groups retain dominance by exploiting existing political institutions, language and everyday 'common sense' which goes unchallenged because it seems universal.

Oppression arises from the extreme imbalance of power. Confronting such pervasive power is the key element that binds the experiences of the oppressed together. Certain groups are dominant in society, such as white or able-bodied people, those with wealth, and men. As a result such groups are able to construct institutions (from the family to parliament) that promote and expand their own interests while preserving their political and social power. The point is that this process of domination

DEFINITION OF ANTI-OPPRESSIVE PRACTICE

Anti-oppressive practice embodies a person-centred philosophy [and] an egalitarian value system concerned with reducing the deleterious effects of structural inequalities upon people's lives; a methodology focusing on both process and outcome; and a way of structuring relationships between [practitioner and user] that aims to empower users by reducing the negative effects of hierarchy ...

(Dominelli 1993: 24)

will appear natural and an aspect of what is to be expected rather than as something that has been socially constructed. For example, the difficulties that we 'naturally' associate with being disabled (lack of employment opportunity, barriers to mobility) actually arise not from the physical impairment a person has but from the elaborate social attitudes that able-bodied people have constructed around those impairments and which disadvantage and oppress people who have impairments.

A social work practice that is anti-oppressive begins with this awareness that barriers to full human development are socially and politically created. Part of any social work assessment therefore should uncover these ideological constructs and stereotypes, and the barriers that restrict service users' freedom to act should be challenged through workers' alliance with users. Social workers strive then to improve the material level of resources for oppressed groups, work to amplify their power, and challenge dominant groups' oppression of the marginalised (Fook cited in Payne 1997: 232). Braye and Preston-Shoot (1995) argue that in working with people who are oppressed, it is not sufficient to increase their say in decisions; the sources of their oppression must also be challenged. For the individual practitioner engaging in anti-oppressive practice Dalrymple and Burke link three levels: augmenting the practitioner's own sense of power, acknowledging the connection between personal problems and existing power structures, and undertaking social and political action (Dalrymple and Burke 1996).

While anti-oppressive practice clearly has much to offer in contesting exclusion it has certain limitations. First, it often pays scant attention to poverty, the power of social class and the means for improving income. Jordan has written that the principles of anti-oppressive practice 'fail to capture the essential element in most service users' oppression – exclusion and marginalisation stemming from poverty'. By focusing on 'oppression' in relations between men and women, white and black, able and disabled, young and old, social work fails to address the fact that it is itself deeply implicated in the oppression of users. This is because it fails to tackle the fundamental source of social injustice for users – their poverty (Jordan 2000: 49–50).

Second, anti-oppressive practice is suspicious of notions of neighbourhood and community because it regards them as masking difference and therefore as sources of oppression. But 'neighbourhood' as we shall see is precisely where many initiatives to tackle social exclusion are unfolding. Third, anti-oppressive practice places a premium on language as the medium through which oppressive ideologies are cemented in place and the social work practice it promotes requires close examination of language to reveal the extent of oppression. Thus its main emphasis seems to be in the arena of challenging others' use of language – whether that of other agencies, professions or community groups. As a consequence, social work appears to believe that it has a greater understanding of oppression than other professions, services and agencies, making negotiation with prospective partners difficult through a reluctance to compromise (Pierson 1999).

An ecological approach

The ecological framework provides a holistic way of looking at the connections between family, neighbourhood and society and how each level is affected by the others (Bronfenbrenner 1979). It offers a powerful guide to showing how you can map out the interconnections through which social exclusion occurs.

Bronfenbrenner looked at an individual's environment as a set of structures nesting within structures through which it is possible to picture how institutional decisions, social attitudes and market operations promote or curtail the opportunities and wellbeing of individuals (Figure 2.1). Individuals develop within the:

- micro-system of home and family
- meso-system of school, neighbourhood and other local institutions such as churches, clubs and associations
- exo-system through which more distant but powerful institutions and practices bear on the individual's life. For a child such institutions may be the parent's workplace (and its level of pay and working conditions), the conduct

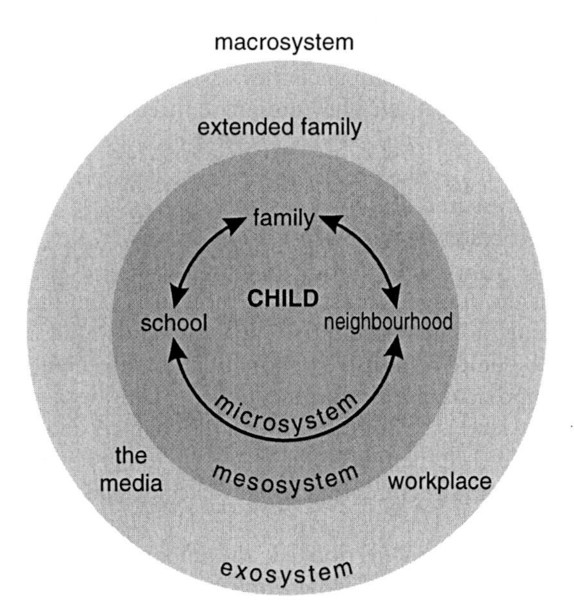

FIGURE 2.1 Bronfenbrenner's ecological system of human development

of local agencies such as youth clubs or something as everyday as the local public transport system. For a young adult it may be how information regarding job opportunities or skills training is transmitted. For a person with disability it may be the attitudes of local employers or the supported employment opportunities or more skills training.

Finally there is the macro-system – a sweepingly large field embracing the cultural, political, economic, legal and religious context of society. It includes social attitudes and values which, although not always articulated in daily life, nevertheless have a huge impact on individuals. For example our images and opinions on gender, older people, HIV, crime and punishment emerge often from the macro-system (Jack and Jack 2000).

The ecological approach has several qualities that are useful in attacking social exclusion.

1. It is holistic. It understands that human development is a product of interaction of forces with a powerful role played by the macro-system so that it attunes social workers to be concerned with the interactions between levels. It also encourages the broader appreciation of the way that social environments impact on different individuals and groups (Jack and Jack 2000).
2. It stresses that the individual's perception of these interactions and the social pressures with which they have to contend are best understood and explained by that person.
3. It underscores the importance of social supports and the social links within communities as fundamental to individual development.

Germain and Gitterman's 'life model' applies the ecological model to problem assessment in social work. In their hands the ecological approach emphasises the life processes of adaptation and reciprocal interaction between people and their social and physical environments. As a consequence they assert that people's problems must be confronted at more than one level. They designate three interrelated areas of living:

- life transitions
- environmental pressures
- interpersonal processes.

The social worker is encouraged to assess the three areas simultaneously in order to find ways of increasing the client's adaptive capacities and at the same time re-shaping the environment to be more responsive (Germain and Gitterman 1980).

The ecological approach compels the practitioner to consider a range of factors across community and family level. As you read through the chapters and in particular consider the case studies its will be helpful to keep these levels in mind: for example, for creating a basic map of the forces and structures that socially excluded people have to contend with (see for example Chapter 3.) The ecological approach will highlight a range of responses that might otherwise have been overlooked: the importance of income and concrete resources such as childcare and employment opportunities, and better co-ordinated services around health, education and housing. It also highlights the changes that can only be achieved by community building where the capacities of local people and neighbourhood organisations are developed (see Jack and Jack 2000: 97, 100).

Community social work

The premise of community social work is that people in difficulty most often receive help from other individuals within their social network. In this understanding of the assets of networks, community social work sees social services as peripheral to many people's lives. For example the care of vulnerable adults is largely undertaken in the community by family, relatives or friends and not by public services. Equally the anti-social activities of young people are controlled informally at local level without the intervention of the criminal justice system. Community social work recognises this and works to bolster those networks or to bring new networks to life where they are insufficient to provide help. Rather than focus only on an individual client and their immediate family it recognises that social problems arise in part through a malfunctioning social network (Hadley *et al.* 1987; Darvill and Smale 1990).

The work of the principal proponents of community social work, especially that of Gerald Smale, offers solid grounding for a practice dedicated to reducing social exclusion. Its main concerns are still acutely relevant: the emphasis on social problems, interest in networks, the need to 'go local', formation of partnerships and the requirement for practitioners to be 'bridge builders' between service systems and different interest groups (especially those without resources).

In framing its practice community social work avoids the alternative of intervention in the 'community' or with the 'individual'. Community social work teams see *both* as legitimate, each requiring planning and resources, and engage in a whole spectrum of activities. The spectrum of work includes:

- direct intervention – work carried out with individuals, families and their immediate networks to tackle problems that directly affect them.

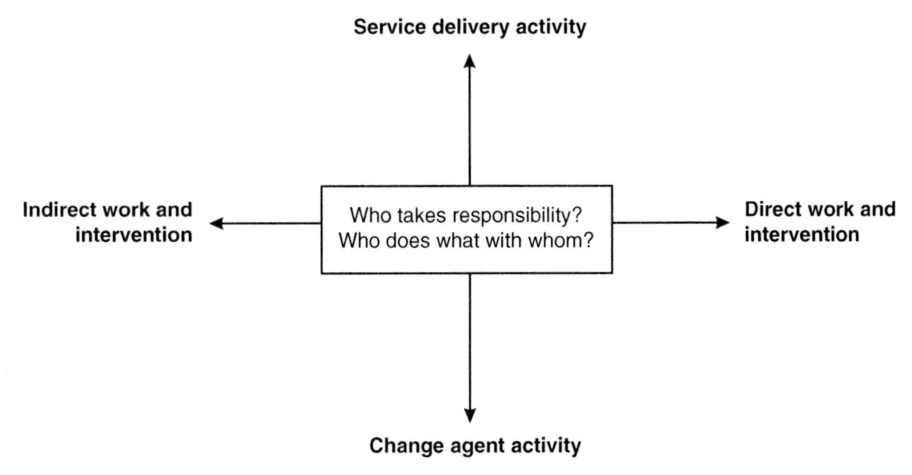

FIGURE 2.2 Community social work map

- indirect intervention – work with wider community groups and other professionals and agencies to tackle problems which affect a range of people including the individuals involved in the direct work.
- change agent activity – this seeks to change the ways that people relate to each other that are responsible for social problems whether at individual, family, or neighbourhood levels. Change agent activity has to do with reallocating resources, such as staff time and money, in different ways to tackle social problems. This includes making such resources available to neighbourhood residents and organisations and joining with other agencies in holistic solutions.
- service delivery activity providing services that help maintain people in their own homes, to reduce risks to vulnerable people, and to provide relief for overloaded parents and carers. This includes making resources available to community organisations for this purpose.

(Smale *et al.* 2000)

Smale *et al.* (2000) use these co-ordinates to construct a 'map' to help you describe what community-oriented, multi-pronged social work looks like. On it you can locate where any one piece of your work falls (Figure 2.2).

ACTIVITY 2.4: EARLY YEARS BILINGUAL SUPPORT SERVICE

About 4 per cent of the London Borough of Merton's population are asylum seekers or refugees with the largest groups being Tamils, Congolese, Ugandans and Somalis. The borough has now established a bilingual support service for families with young children. Its six staff are all bilingual and work in three areas: home/school liaison, classroom support and helping children who are experiencing psychosocial problems.

Although this description of the service is brief, from what you know where would you place it on Smale *et al.*'s 'map'?

PRACTICE IS PREVENTIVE

Practice that tackles social exclusion is 'preventive' practice; that is, a practice that aims to direct resources and intervention towards addressing early signs of social difficulties or social problems before they accelerate and intensify into emergencies that require vastly greater resources in terms of time, energy and money. The notion of 'preventive work' is not wholly satisfactory, first because it raises the question preventing what? Second, it suggests that it is a kind of optional extra as if social work is not really social work until it is reacting to harm or imminent crisis. Gerald Smale *et al.* (2000) use the better phrase 'development work' as distinguished from 'curative' or crisis work through which social work only offers aid in times of emergency.

Child protection services provides the best example of how the heavy emphasis on risk swallows up resources for preventive work. Despite the well-known association between specific environmental stressors and child abuse, child protection systems are triggered by circumstances of imminent danger to the child or after harm has been done. Two reports, *Seen but not Heard* (Audit Commission 1994) and *Messages from Research* (Dartington Research Centre 1995), describe in detail how social workers with children and families could use resources more effectively if they got out from under the shadow of reactive protective work. Nevertheless, such a shift in resource allocation has proved stubbornly difficult.

One widely acknowledged model for understanding the relationship between curative and preventive practice is Pauline Hardiker's, which she developed for work with children.

Practice designed to tackle social exclusion in Hardiker's model in general flows up along the diagonal aiming to embrace larger numbers of people through its range of collaborative interventions. But this is not exclusively the case, and those practitioners who clearly work around risk or engage in casework should also be able to see how their practice fits in tackling social exclusion. As we shall see there are acute consequences of exclusion which draw on counselling and therapeutic skills. Social exclusion has consequences of self-esteem, mental health problems, violence. Many of the initiatives discussed later in this volume are aware that social deprivation causes immense stress and has personal consequences.

SOCIAL WORK SKILLS FOR TACKLING EXCLUSION

Trevithick argues that 'skill' in social work is difficult to define because it overlaps with other key terms with which it is used interchangeably, such as 'intervention' and 'competence'. Hence trying to isolate 'skills' from other techniques and approaches can be at best a provisional task. Trevithick defines skill broadly: it 'denotes the degree of knowledge, expertise, judgement and experience that is brought to play within a given situation, course of action or intervention' (Trevithick 2000: 21). For her, skill involves reaching sound judgements on how to work best in a particular environment. Among her list of 50 skills many have to do with interviewing; among these she includes planning and preparing for interview, creating rapport, knowing the different types of questions – open, closed and circular – and when to use them,

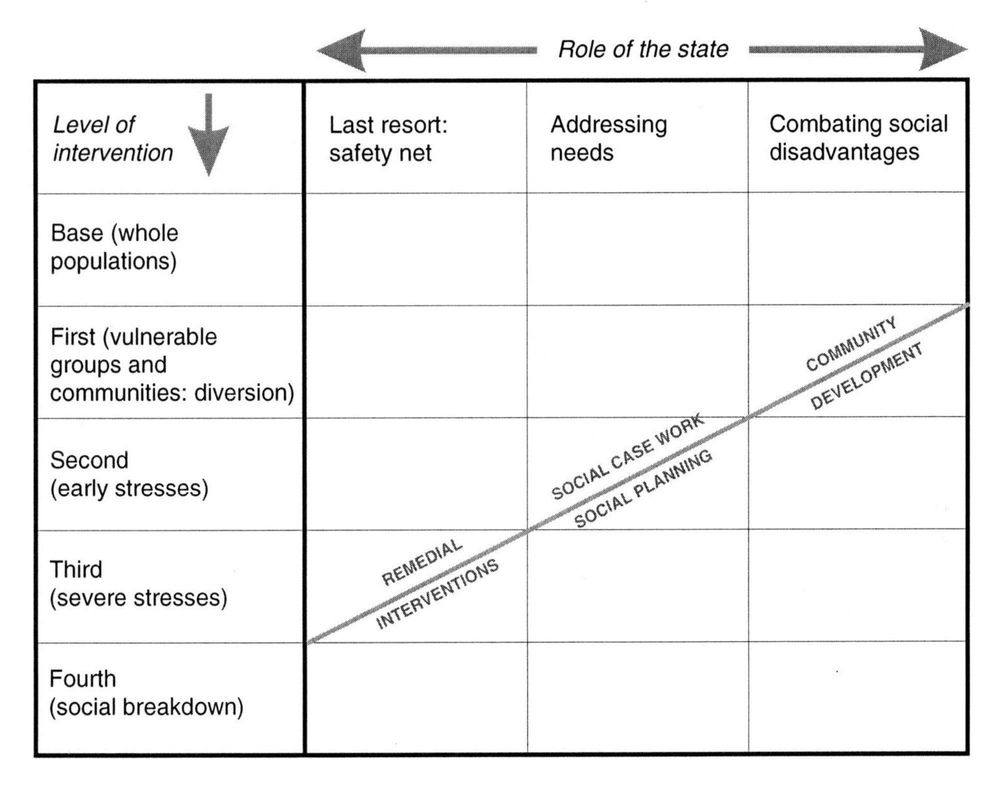

FIGURE 2.3 Hardiker's model: locating preventive practice

In Hardiker's model the first level includes services for vulnerable groups and indeed whole communities. Social work intervention aims to enable vulnerable children and families to draw on universalist and community-based resources wherever possible. These include: providing advice, guidance and facilitating connections to supports from within other services and making sure a range of contact points and signposting in health centres, libraries, churches, temples, schools, leisure and community centres is available.

The second level embraces services that target stresses such as those experienced by families in temporary crisis or difficulties. It broadly points to the kinds of services families with 'children in need' require or community care for vulnerable adults. Social work approaches here include short-term work, task-centred methods and placements, with families drawing on resource centres or short-term breaks and local networks. The aim is to restore personal and social functioning.

The third and fourth level of service targets families undergoing serious stress including the risk of significant harm, family breakdown or compulsory entry into care or custodial systems. Such family problems may be well established and crises may be severe including homicide, sexual abuse, cruelty to children, grievous bodily harm or prolonged neglect. The aim of intervention at this level is to mitigate these difficulties and to restore family functioning and links between family members.

(adapted from Hardiker 2000)

clarifying and summarising, providing advice and information and offering encouragement and validation. But she includes many others such as modelling and teaching others social skills training, counselling skills, containing anxiety and mediation skills (ibid.).

In the following section we consider those key skills that are particularly pertinent to practitioners in combating social exclusion.

Communication skills

Communicating with people is the bedrock of social work practice aiming to reduce social exclusion. All the building blocks discussed in the next chapter rely in one form or another on communication. How you communicate, what objectives you have in mind and in what situations you find yourself having to communicate are all critical factors you have to consider. In practitioner manuals these skills are often subsumed under the heading 'interviewing' as if there were a set of techniques to follow. Interviews in general are conversations initiated by the social worker for a specific purpose, for example assessment, providing advice, gathering information or explaining to users a particular statute or agency policy.

ACTIVITY 2.5: COMMUNICATING – WHAT, WHERE AND TO WHOM

Consider the following situations. You are:

- talking to a 15-year-old boy about his family circumstances
- having a drink with colleagues after work
- in a meeting with some 30 residents from the local neighbourhood about how to make services more responsive to their needs
- asked to write a report on the social care needs and priorities in your team's area
- in a meeting with some 30 residents from the local neighbourhood and you have been asked at the last minute to chair the meeting
- given ten minutes at a multi-agency forum to convince those present to undertake a particular project.

All the above are tasks in communication. Arrange them in the order of the difficulty that each would present for you, starting with the most difficult. Why are they difficult? What makes the easy ones easy? What do you need to do to improve your communication skills in the difficult situations?

Listening

Social workers have to be good listeners, and be able to absorb and respond to what users and their families are saying. Often listening is part of a therapeutic endeavour, reflecting back to the user what the practitioner has heard so that the person can respond and react to their own statements. In working to reduce social exclusion with service users the emphasis in communication shifts in a somewhat different direction. Remember that your mission is developmental, often locally based and preventive. A key objective of this work entails gathering experiences and information on exclusion in the area from the experts: those who are excluded. You listen to users' and local residents' accounts in order to hear histories, make links between what may appear to be only individual problems, gather information on networks, become aware of neighbourhood issues, find out where users' strengths and resources are and where those of the neighbourhoods are.

This might best be described as *listening to stories*, or 'gathering stories' in Cedersund's phrase (Cedersund 1999), where the focus of listening becomes the experiences, obstructions and hardships that a person or family has encountered. The value of stories is that they have many sides to them and may be told and heard in different ways depending on the life experiences of those telling them and those listening. Stories, as Parton and O'Byrne argue, are also a way of creating beliefs in that they impose a coherence on a person's life experience and have a unique power for 'setting forth truth claims' (Witten 1993 cited in Parton and O'Byrne 2000).

Getting people to tell 'their' story acts as a way of bringing elements of their life to awareness – yours, theirs and others. One of the elements of a story that you are looking for is 'local knowledge'. We may think of local knowledge as *partisan* knowledge, because the person who holds it has a passionate interest in a particular outcome (Scott 1998). As you become more familiar with the range of stories of the people you are working with local knowledge linking issues will emerge. This is the keystone of what we will refer to in Chapter 7 as 'relational organising', which borrows much of social work's emphasis on relationship building, and the patience and empathy that that requires, but applies it to community development objectives.

Listening to stories means departing from the question and answer format of the standard interview. In stories knowledge, according to Parton and O'Byrne is 'ready-made to be listened to, needs no proof and [is] capable of creating an obedience that makes reframing or reinterpretation difficult later' (2000: 49). But while stories, in particular 'family stories', may be used to maintain traditional authority – men over women, parents over children – that is not their sole function. Drawing on White (1996) and others Parton and O'Byrne examine the effect of 'externalising conversations' which seeks to re-politicise experience. Externalising conversations facilitates the 'naming' and 're-naming' of the dominant forces in people's lives, inviting them to identify the influences of oppressive 'truths' and the practices associated with them. 'In being assisted to evaluate these influences, people are encouraged to establish alternative stories or "preferred identity claims and alternative preferred practices of self and relationship"' (White 1996 cited in Parton and O'Byrne 2000: 84).

Practitioners addressing the experience of social exclusion should be interested in externalising conversations. To begin this process they may ask questions about the social fabric of people's lives, what they have done and achieved, what they hope to achieve, the history of their family. For example, they could ask: how did you come to be living here? What was it like living through a period of racial harassment? I noticed a couple of neighbours calling in for advice – they seem to respect you a great deal. Do you think that's the case? You obviously had to fight for your child's dignity – that must have taken a lot of courage at times.

The practitioner's task is to see how social exclusion as a process is *experienced*. When you are talking to specific groups of users and citizens, the emotions, stresses, decisions and behaviours that people engage in become an important part of the equation. For example: it is one thing to observe and deal with the barriers that exclude refugee children from mainstream society; it is another to hear directly about the trauma and loss of their separation, perhaps from family, certainly from home country. This capacity to hear first hand the experiences of deprivation and hardship has always characterised social work from its beginnings although it has not always known how to respond effectively.

Excluded individuals will not necessarily see themselves as 'victim' or 'oppressed'. But their stories often do describe the hidden injuries of disadvantage. Overt divisions between social classes used to be obvious and observable; disadvantage, poverty and lack of opportunity were directly linked to a person's position within the class structure and could be described and understood as such. Now, as Richard Sennett has explained, the hidden injuries of disadvantage have produced a 'crisis in self-respect' because social difference appears as a question of character and personal responsibility when it is not (Sennett 1993; *Guardian* 3 February 2001). This personalised sense of defeat in a winner–loser culture is another aspect of what practice has to deal with.

ACTIVITY 2.6: MR ULLAH'S STORY

Reflect on the information concerning Mr Ullah on page 23. Write a list of questions that you would ask to encourage him and his wife to relate their story.

Focusing on strengths not weaknesses

Historically, social work has tended to base its practice on a person's or family's deficits and weaknesses. The complexities of personal, cultural, physical and environmental adversities have been reduced to narrow compartments of diagnostic or assessment schemes and responded to accordingly. Instead of asking what is wrong with this individual, this family or this neighbourhood we can ask 'What strengths do users have that have helped them cope so far? What are their aspirations, talents and abilities? What social, emotional and physical resources are needed to support their growth and wellbeing?'

Saleeby (1992) outlines three assumptions of the strengths perspective:

- Every person has an inherent capacity for regeneration and transformation.
- This power is a potent form of knowledge that can guide personal and social change. Accepting and honouring the personal experiences of others creates the basis for knowledge exchange. Thus, 'Dialogue among equals replaces hierarchical knowledge structures so no individual or group has a monopoly on knowledge or its attendant power' (Saleeby 1992).
- When people's capacities are respected and supported they are more likely to act on their strengths.

Negotiating skills

Negotiation is a process of communication between parties that takes place over a period of time during which the parties involved are trying to reach an agreement that both sides find acceptable. They may have interests in common and be able to reach an agreement that meets at least some of these interests. They may have no common ground to speak of, in which case the negotiation will fail. In this communication each party brings information to try and educate the other, lays out what it wants to see in a final resolution and brings pressure to bear to have those interests realised (Shell 1999; Wolfe 1999). The parties may be individuals, organisations or nations (in which case it is called diplomacy). Fisher and Ury write 'Whether a negotiation concerns a contract, a family quarrel, or a peace settlement among nations, people routinely engage in positional bargaining. Each side takes a position, argues for it, and makes concessions to reach a compromise' (Fisher and Ury 1982: 3).

Social workers are distinguished from other helping professionals, for example lawyers, doctors, teachers or nurses, precisely by their willingness to forsake the formal responsibilities of their role to undertake informal negotiation. In this way they work with ordinary people in their natural settings, using the informality of their methods as a means of negotiating solutions to problems rather than imposing them (Jordan 1987; Parton and O'Byrne 2000: 33). Much of this negotiating involves dealing with conflicting interests among family members or with conflict between individuals and various agencies, or in securing agreement from users to pursue a jointly negotiated plan, whether through task-centred work or a written agreement.

In tackling social exclusion the informal negotiating role of social workers expands into new arenas and becomes more formal. As social worker you may now be involved in negotiating:

- With other agencies – in constructing a partnership in which resources are pooled and sacrifices of 'turf' inevitable.
- In acting as advocate or representative on behalf of a user or a neighbourhood group.
- In support of users or local residents who are entering into their own negotiations and for whom you are providing back-up support as they deal with project funders, various public authorities, elected councillors or technical experts.
- In community development work with political or corporate authority on behalf of neighbourhood organisations.

Approaches to negotiation

In their classic work on negotiation Fisher and Ury (1982) present a set of techniques to help you through virtually any negotiation:

Separate the people from the problem. Treat your negotiating partner with respect even if you reject their position totally: nothing will be gained by rejecting, criticising or otherwise insulting the person who holds a position that you cannot accept. If you do that you close off avenues for future agreements. Equally it is to be expected that people will get angry, depressed, fearful, frustrated or offended in the process of negotiation. They confuse their perceptions with reality or fail to interpret what you say in the way you intend. Whatever else you are doing at any point in negotiation you should ask yourself 'Am I paying enough attention to the people problem?' (Fisher and Ury 1982: 19). This does not mean trying to please the other party by making offers that will elicit a pleasant response. Negotiation is not about maintaining pleasant responses but neither is it about character assassination or demonisation of the other party.

Focus on interests and not positions. A negotiating position is often concrete and explicit but behind every negotiating position lie the deeper, perhaps unexpressed, intangible interests of the different parties. For example, agency representatives negotiating a collaborative service agreement for hospital after-care may fight stubbornly for a certain task to be included, when in fact they care less about the task itself than insuring a continuing role in the joint work going forward. Figuring out what these interests of the other parties are is often just as important as knowing what your interests are. To do this Fisher and Ury suggest the simple technique of putting yourself in the other party's shoes. Examine each position its representatives take and ask why they reach that particular position as well as why they have *not* taken certain other decisions.

Invent options for mutual gain. In many areas of public life much can be achieved by understanding the self-interest of others and focusing action around shared interests. As Stokes and Knight put it, 'When people are acting together in common self interest, significant power can be exerted. When people are kept apart and their self interest is managed by others, powerlessness results' (Stokes and Knight 1997: 14).

Techniques such as brainstorming, seeking preferences and weighting them according to importance, inventing multiple agreements with different strengths, and dovetailing or reconciling deeper interests all assist in this endeavour.

Establish objective criteria. These are used to define or measure negotiated outcomes in a way that is separate from the subjective or personal feelings of the various parties. Broadly, such criteria either have to do with fair standards for judging outcomes or fair procedures for resolving conflicts. Fair standards, for example, may be rules for evaluation, targets for distributing resources, or specified outcomes for a project as a whole or for the individual parties to the process. Developing such criteria is a task to be undertaken early on in the negotiating process so it is helpful to prepare in advance, working through alternative standards beforehand so as to gauge their impact on your case (Fisher and Ury 1982: 88).

ACTIVITY 2.7: WHAT KIND OF NEGOTIATOR ARE YOU?

Richard Shell (1999) identifies five types of negotiating personality which are, in descending order of aggressiveness: competitors, problem-solvers, compromisers, accommodators and conflict avoiders. He poses this simple thought experiment to see which style you are most inclined to:

Imagine you are one of ten people, all of whom are strangers, sitting around a big table in a conference room. Someone suddenly comes into the room and makes this offer: 'I will give a prize of £1000 to each of the first two people who can persuade the person sitting opposite to get up, come around the table and stand behind his or her chair.' What would you do and what tactics would you use?

Advocacy skills

Advocacy seeks to represent and secure the interests of relatively powerless users when dealing with powerful service organisations, the media or in coping with repressive public attitudes. Advocacy takes several forms:

- self-advocacy in which people with similar experiences of social exclusion, for example discrimination arising from a physical or learning impairment, form an organisation to alert the public, pressure service officials and politicians and mobilise for increased resources;
- citizen advocacy;
- practitioner advocacy on behalf of users or local resident groups.

You may be involved in facilitating the first two forms through information, advice or resources, but it is the last that you will be carrying out yourself. Neil Bateman (2000) has laid down six principles for effective advocacy:

1 Always act in your client's best interests. This principle is easily overlooked when facing multiple and competing pressures from managers in your own organisation or other agencies. It means constantly reminding yourself of the person on whose behalf who you are acting.
2 Always act in accordance with your client's wishes and instructions. This is fundamental: the advocate's actions have to be driven by the client's wishes and instructions. Developing what Bateman calls an 'instructional relationship' is an important first step. Within this the advocate can identify facts, options and remedies but will listen for the client's instructions.
3 Keep the client properly informed. The client must know all essential facts related to her or his situation without being deluged by information. Equally the client must be kept informed of all actions taken on their behalf. Accountability is impossible otherwise.

4 Carry out instructions with diligence and competence. If you offer to do something make sure you do it – but know your limits and do not undertake that for which you are not prepared or competent.
5 Act impartially and offer frank, independent advice. This means being able to say uncomfortable things to representatives from other organisations (or your own) and not being beholden to the other side. A co-operative relationship based on partnership with the other side is not appropriate and can lead to a breach of advocacy principles.
6 Maintain the rules of confidentiality. Clients must feel completely secure in the knowledge that what they say remains confidential.

(Bateman 2000)

ACTIVITY 2.8: ACTING AS ADVOCATE

A worker in an advice centre sees Mrs Ullah. She says she would like some help in finding somewhere else to live. She describes the family circumstances and adds that the maisonette where they currently live is damp and the stairs are very difficult for her husband to negotiate. The Ullahs have found the housing association officer extremely intimidating and do not want to upset him. After she leaves, the advice worker concludes that the local authority would never be able to re-house them and writes a stinging letter to the officer of the housing association, in effect delivering an ultimatum about the damp and threatening pursuit of compensation.

What principles of advocacy has the worker violated?

Community work skills

Twelvetrees has defined community work as 'the process of assisting ordinary people to improve their own communities by undertaking collective action' (1991: 1). Community work enables people to develop collective responses to common problems that confront them. These may be large or small – a street lamp that the council has failed to repair over many months, an entire estate without a doctor or a bank, the lack of adequate transport for older people at an under-funded day centre. A range of practitioners, activists and volunteers now engage in community work at least as part of their role, including community support workers, community development workers attached to family centres or local care initiatives, social workers and youth and community workers.

In addition the requirements for funding for many of the recent initiatives aiming to reduce exclusion and to promote neighbourhood renewal have an explicit community dimension. Because of this emphasis on locality, social service agencies are rapidly adopting a community perspective and deploying staff with skills in neighbourhood work.

Formal social work training, however, has shown less interest in community work recently, which is all the more perplexing since it embraces the one set of skills capable of intervening at the 'structural level' and working at neighbourhood level. Dixon and Hoatson (1999) describe how community work has been marginalised within social work training in English-speaking countries since the 1980s. This has produced a paradox whereby social work committed itself to combating oppression in its value base at the same time as dispensing with the one important element needed to bring that work into focus: skills for community and neighbourhood engagement.

Dixon and Hoatson are very clear as to what has been lost. Community work provides:

- Effective strategies for creating personal change through social action by bringing people together to support each other, to identify need, educate, build skills and confidence. The practitioner needs skills that take up individual troubles and link them to community problem-solving.
- Skills and frameworks to strengthen networks of residents, service providers and interest groups in the locality.
- Means for building locally based 'communities of interest' around service provision, based on values of participation and collective practice.
- Knowledge about how to mobilise numbers of people whether through social action campaigns or social movements.

(Dixon and Hoatson 1999: 4)

Community work has a long association with working for groups that are disadvantaged and contending with discrimination. It does this by:

- Seeking to create links and liaisons between groups and individuals within a locality, around issues of common concern on a basis of mutual respect, whilst recognising diversity and differences
- Promoting the development of alliances and the recognition of collective action by encouraging people to reflect and act together in order to achieve common goals, and influence decision-makers
- Acknowledging the specific experience and contribution of all individuals in communities, to enable people to enhance their capacity to play a role in shaping and determining the society of which they are part
- Recognising that the unequal distribution of power is both a personal and political issue, and that community work has a responsibility for linking the personal learning which empowers people, through to the collective learning and action for change which empowers communities.

Community work approaches are important not only because of their skills in working with people collectively but also because they are compelled to adopt a strengths perspective rather than focus on needs and deficits. This is quite simply because in seeking to mobilise and empower local groups, train their leaders and build local organisations, community workers must start with assets and local capacities. As a result there is often tension between community workers and community organisers on the one hand and professionals such as social workers on the other, who focus on needs and how the service can meet those needs – a tension that can be productive.

COMMUNITY WORK SKILLS

- developing community profile, assessing resources, gathering stories about problems and predicaments
- facilitating the establishment of groups and sustaining them
- working productively with conflict within and between groups or organisations
- negotiating with other agencies, politicians and other power-brokers who hold influence such as city officials
- supporting groups and organisations in obtaining funding and other resources
- evaluating particular projects and the effective use of resources

(Twelvetrees 1991)

KEY POINTS

The chapter explores values, approaches and skills needed to tackle social exclusion.

❑ The impact of values – both personal and professional – is deep and long lasting. With regard to poverty, social work has long held some ambivalence: it has always worked closely with poor people but tended to see their poverty as a result of personal weakness.

❑ Anti-oppressive practice, the ecological approach and community social work each in their own way guide the practitioner both to a better understanding of exclusion and more effective practice respsonses.

❑ Key skills for redressing exclusion include listening and communicating, negotiating, advocacy and community work.

KEY READING

Smale, G., Tuson, G., and Statham, D. *Social Work and Social Problems: working towards social inclusion and social change* (Macmillan, 2000). This indispensable text argues that individual difficulties often reflect wider social problems, which requires the social worker to intervene at a neighbourhood level.

Dowling, M. *Poverty: a practitioner's guide* (Venture Press, 1998). There are very few books on social work and poverty. This is one and it has the virtue of being short and aimed directly at practitioners.

Clark, C. *Social Work Ethics: Politics, Principles and Practice* (Macmillan, 2000). Clark stresses the contingent, evolving nature of values rather than as fixed dogma.

Trevithick, P. *Social Work Skills: a practice handbook* (Open University Press, 2000). Trevithick explains the entire range of skills the contemporary social worker requires.

CHAPTER 3

FIVE BUILDING BLOCKS FOR TACKLING EXCLUSION

OBJECTIVES

By the end of the chapter you should:

- Become familiar with the building blocks for practice that tackle social exclusion and promote inclusion
- Be able to review your own role and responsibilities in light of the practice required to reduce exclusion
- Build your own knowledge base on concepts crucial to social exclusion such as the importance of neighbourhood and social networks.

This chapter introduces you to the building blocks for practice which social workers need in order to work with socially excluded individuals, groups and neighbourhoods. The building blocks are generic: that is, they apply across all the various kinds of social work. Some may be familiar to you, others will be new and require you to think creatively about your role and responsibilities; still others have emerged from recent initiatives by government and non-governmental bodies, and from research about how the process of social exclusion works.

The practitioner tackling social exclusion is more flexible, more locally focused and more collaborative with other services. This ensemble of practice approaches and new knowledge-base, when combined with some of the skills described in the previous chapter, creates a new perspective linking social work with social justice.

The five building blocks are:

1. Maximising income and securing basic resources
2. Strengthening social supports and networks
3. Working in partnership with agencies and local organisations
4. Creating channels of effective participation for users, local residents and their organisations
5. Focusing on whole neighbourhoods.

MAXIMISING INCOME AND WELFARE RIGHTS

In this section we look at different strategies for maximising the income for the people you work with through benefits or advice on employment and skills acquisition. As explained in Chapter 2 the majority of those who use social work services are poor, and we know that poverty is at the heart of social exclusion. Any practitioner who wants to tackle social exclusion has to focus relentlessly on maximising the income of those with whom they work and extending that work to a whole area. Social workers are in as good a position as any to assist users and local people in examining at regular intervals the various means to improve their income levels. Practice begins with this realisation and commitment.

ACTIVITY 3.1: WHAT DO YOU AND YOUR TEAM KNOW ABOUT MAXIMISING INCOME OF USERS?

With three or four colleagues run through this checklist on the state of your current preparation for maximising income.

- Does your team – and do you individually – focus on the income of users and consider with them at regular intervals options for how they might raise the level of that income?
- Do you have an up-to-date reference book on benefits such as the Child Poverty Action Group's *Welfare Benefits Handbook*?
- Is money advice provided to users through another agency or by a member of staff such as an advice worker who is not part of your team?
- Who in your agency is responsible for discussing money matters and benefits with users?
- If you are in a local authority social services department, how do you implement your department's charging policy? For example do you attempt to 'water it down' by reporting a low figure for user income? Do you routinely consider user eligibility for other benefits?
- Do you consider yourself well-informed on the range of benefits that users might claim?
- Does your agency have an anti-poverty strategy? Has it joined a benefits take-up campaign with other agencies?

Knowing the benefits system

Poor people do not need social workers in order to obtain benefits, but when in contact with families and individuals you should be able to point them on the right path. The benefits system is complicated with annually changing rates and the introduction of new, often targeted benefits. This should not deter you. Broadly your rule should be: *Social workers should know enough to help users to get what should be theirs – but not be expert at the level of detailed knowledge* (Thomas 2001). You do not have to acquire the knowledge and detail necessary, for example, for appearing at tribunals: realistically this role could only be expected of a full-time welfare rights officer. But you should be able to recognise when a focus on a user's income improvement is essential and know enough about the benefits system to be able to:

- Go through the range of the user's possible entitlements to determine whether they are claiming all that they can;
- Secure back payments of principal benefits if it can be demonstrated that a claimant should have had a benefit earlier.

The structure of benefits is explained in several excellent handbooks which you are strongly encouraged to consult. These include the Child Poverty Action Group's *Welfare Benefits Handbook* (2000), *Welfare Benefits* by Keith Puttick (2000) and Mike Wolfe's *Debt Advice Handbook* (2000), all of which are clear and well laid out.

To begin with, you should be familiar with the basic division between means-tested and non-means-tested benefits.

Means-tested benefits

To claim a means-tested benefit a claimant does not have to have made any previous contribution but their income and capital must be sufficiently low for them to qualify. This usually means the practitioner becoming involved in a detailed investigation of the user's means that is, income of all descriptions and accumulated savings or capital. The main means-tested benefits are:

- Income Support
- income-based Jobseeker's Allowance
- housing benefit
- council tax benefit
- health benefits
- working families' tax credit and disabled person's tax credit.

Income Support and Jobseeker's Allowance (income based)

Income Support (IS) provides a minimum source of income for those who are not required to be available for work and whose income, including that from other benefits, is below an officially defined minimum. IS can help those over 18 as well as some 16- or 17-year-olds.

Because it is geared to cover certain designated 'needs' it varies from person to person depending on what these needs are. Those eligible for IS include:

- disabled claimants
- persons over 60
- carers temporarily looking after children or family members
- lone parents
- 16 and 17 year olds in full time education or work training schemes and not living with their parents.

To determine whether claimants are eligible for IS they are 'means tested', that is their current income is checked to see if it falls below a particular threshold. That income includes:

- most other welfare benefits
- maintenance and child support
- any earnings
- any accumulated capital such as a savings account.

In his highly readable handbook *Welfare Benefits,* Keith Puttick (2000) outlines the main points determining eligibility for Income Support. A claimant must:

- Have under £8000 in capital (which includes that of any partner). Capital between £3000 and £8000 is assumed to generate a certain amount of income on a sliding scale (all amounts pertain to the year 2000).
- Fall within one of the prescribed categories listed above.
- Work no more that 16 hours a week, or have a partner working no more than 24 hours a week. Lone parents have greater flexibility in this respect.

If a person is eligible the amount of IS payable depends on two variables. The first of these is the 'applicable amount', that is the formal 'needs' which the claimant has. The applicable amount is arrived at by combining personal allowances, any housing costs (that is, mortgage commitments but not rent, which is covered by housing benefit) and any premiums for further specific needs. The latter includes a family premium paid to couples with at least one dependent child. Other premiums are available for disability, severe disability, a disabled child, pensioner and carer. The impact of such premiums can be difficult to work out since some can be paid jointly while others cannot.

The second variable is income which, as stated above, includes earnings and other benefits, such as child benefit, and child maintenance. Certain benefits are ignored in this calculating however, such as housing benefit, council tax benefit, attendance allowance and disability living allowance. As mentioned, part-time earnings from work of up to 16 hours a week are permitted for those receiving Income Support but those earnings are still treated as income in calculating benefit. (See Puttick 2000: 166.)

Those who are unemployed and are required to be available for work, but have not previously made sufficient contributions to be eligible for contribution-based

Jobseeker's Allowance, claim may apply for the 'income-based JSA' rather than IS. The 'income' in this case refers to the same sources of income that determine eligibility for IS. Income-based JSA is similar to IS in the form of means testing and in many respects the system is almost identical (Puttick 2000).

For the purposes of means-testing 'a couple' is defined when both partners are over 16, married and living in the same household or are not married but 'living together as husband and wife' in the same household. Gay and lesbian partners do not count as a couple and must claim as single people. The notion of 'household' is also critical but left undefined. Whether two people should be considered as members of the same household depends on (sometimes quite subtle) circumstances. A house can contain a number of separate households – for example a person living in exclusive occupation of separate accommodation, say in a self-contained flat, will be deemed a household. Nor is physical presence always essential: there must be a 'particular kind of tie' between two people together in a domestic establishment such as lodging house or hostel (Wolfe 2000).

There are also a number of non-means-tested benefits which can be placed in two broad categories – contributory and non-contributory benefits. Among the first group are the Jobseeker's Allowance, incapacity benefit, maternity allowance, widow's payment and retirement pension. Contributory benefits are funded by the National Insurance contributions a person pays while at work. Non-contributory benefits are paid out of general taxation and there are no contributory conditions that individuals need to establish in order to receive them. The main non-contributory benefits are: severe disablement allowance, invalid care allowance, disability living allowance, attendance allowance, child benefit and industrial injuries benefit.

Working with users

Since the advent of 'welfare reform' – which broadly means linking some aspects of the benefits system to taking up paid employment – practitioners should have some understanding of the interrelationship between benefits and work. For example 'tax credits' are designed to help people in low-paid work obtain a minimum income. There are two types of tax credits: working families' tax credit and disabled person's tax credit. To receive either of these you have to be in full-time work with your income and any capital sufficiently low to qualify.

It is important to hold on to two objectives in working with any users or families to maximise their income. The first is to be able to look across the whole benefits system so that you can pick up linked entitlements. People can qualify for some non-means-tested benefits and as a result then be eligible for means-tested benefits. For example, if a young mother is under 16 she cannot claim Income Support or an income-based Jobseeker's Allowance but she can claim child benefit as well as exemption from certain health charges such as prescriptions or dental work. If that young mother's parents can include her in their family for their own benefit claims her infant can then also be included (CPAG 2000). The second objective is to help the user look closely at the inter-relationship between benefits and work. For example, if a person is in full-time work with childcare responsibilities she may qualify for working families tax credit but this may raise difficult issues – such as whether to encourage a person to take up employment when they have caring responsibilities which would be undercut by that employment. Intangible matters, such as the social contacts outside the home that a job might bring, have to be weighed against the caring responsibilities.

Recent benefit reforms by government have attempted to enhance the 'employability' of those not in paid work by linking their benefits to training or work itself, through so-called 'active benefits'. There are differing views on the consequences of this policy; many authoritative commentators say that it seems to imply that only by holding a job can a person avoid exclusion. Yet, since the job market is highly unpredictable, it is often itself exclusionary in the way it operates.

As a social worker who may be advising users on whether or not to seek work, you will have to know the direction that these reforms have taken. The core of the active benefits regime is the Jobseeker's Allowance (JSA) for the unemployed which combines benefit payments with job search or training and skills acquisition. All JSA recipients have to demonstrate they are actively seeking work although claimants can assert that for physical or mental reasons, care responsibilities or religious conviction, certain kinds of work are not appropriate for them. To help specific groups that have long had difficulties in entering the labour market such as lone parents or people with disability, a range of 'New Deal' programmes have come onstream. These help to identify skills and build confidence and offer advice and support in the job search and on entitlements after the person has found work.

ACTIVITY 3.2: THE HICKEYS

Mr and Mrs Hickey have three children: Karen, fourteen, Alex, eight, and four-year-old Denise. Mr Hickey is unemployed and Mrs Hickey has a casual part-time job.

The family rent a three-bedroom house which has damp in two of the bedrooms. They have a telephone and a ten-year-old car which is constantly breaking down. Alex, their eight-year-old, is disabled. Mr Hickey is paying off a fine for a conviction for breach of the peace. He keeps a greyhound which he sometimes races. Both Mr and Mrs Hickey smoke.

You are interested – as they are – in maximising their income. What benefits are the Hickeys entitled to? Try to do a check on what amounts the Hickeys might receive by consulting a welfare benefits handbook for up-to-date rates.

Take-up campaigns

Take-up campaigns seek to maximise benefit claims across a whole area through a concerted effort to remind those eligible for particular benefits to claim them. Organising take-up campaigns is generally productive both for the user and local authority social services departments. You should use a variety of methods to contact service users and hold this principle in mind: *a claim for one benefit suggests eligibility for others.* Requests for community care assessments are a logical place to start, ensuring that those approaching a social service department – carers, older people or disabled people – have had the opportunity to review the range of benefits for which they may be eligible.

- Housing benefit records provide another source from which to predict and pursue further claims.
- As young people with physical or learning disability reach the age of 16+ in schools and colleges the nature of previous contact that social workers have had with them changes, but knowledge of their situation may prove instrumental in securing extra resources.
- Publicise widely. Ensure that notices of entitlements and of the campaign itself are placed in locations where people will encounter them – schools, day centres, surgeries, libraries and other public places. Small or infrequent notices simply will not suffice at a time when people are bombarded by all sorts of information and advertisement.

(Randall 2001)

It is always worthwhile for local authority social services departments to invest a maximum effort in take-up campaigns. For every new claim for Income Support the local authority may receive £500 increase in revenue support grant.

STRENGTHENING NETWORKS

A social network is the web of relationships through which people are connected. They may be supportive or not, plentiful or virtually non-existent, close and intense or far-flung and distant. An essential element of social work is promoting the development of dependable social networks that fulfil certain functions for people. When thinking about networks it is important to remember that they exist in relation to individuals, families and neighbourhoods. They also exist in relation to specific groups of people, for example around types of work or shared interests or predicaments. The quality, purpose and functioning of networks of course varies dramatically: in terms of the numbers of people involved, the degree of interconnectedness and frequency of contact, the quality and duration of the relationships and the degree to which they are supportive or undermining (Jack 2000: 328). Networks are not confined to close personal relationships – we have already made the distinction between networks for getting ahead and getting along – two very different types, with social work historically showing even less interest in the former than the latter.

A number of structural factors dramatically affect the kind and quality of networks that a person has; for example income, educational background, age, gender, disability, ethnic origin and employment. Parents with pre-school children at home tend to have smaller, less reliable and more localised networks, particularly if they are lone mothers. People with higher income, in employment and higher education tend to have more extended social networks (Jack and Jack 2000).

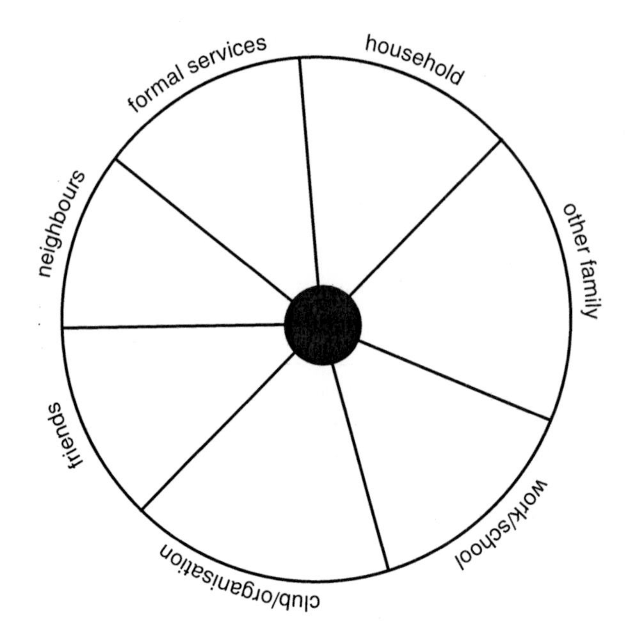

FIGURE 3.1 The social network map
Source: Tracy and Whittaker 1997.

For individuals and families

Networks are crucial to families in their struggle to overcome exclusion. Although social work has long had a person-in-environment focus in theory most of the practice approaches and techniques have been person-centred, with few techniques developed for assessing networks. Taking stock of these networks jointly with family members should be part of a routine assessment.

Social network map

Using a social network map overcomes these difficulties (Figure 3.1). It collects information on the composition of the family's network and also the extent to which the networks are supportive, undermining or conflicted. It helps the family construct an understanding of both the structure and function of its networks (Tracy and Whittaker 1997).

Through the simple method of putting initials or first names of people into the various segments network members are recorded in seven areas:

- household or people you live with
- family or relatives
- friends
- people from work or school
- people from clubs, organisations or religious groups
- neighbours
- agencies and other formal service providers.

Once the network is clear you can ask further questions regarding the nature of the relationships. These cover the types of support available; for example whether they provide information or emotional support, how critical a member of the network might be, the closeness or intensity of the relationship or other features such as frequency of contact and length of relationship. Although any one map is constructed from the point of view of a single family, through use practitioners will become more familiar with the different characteristics of families' networks. These include the size, perceived availability of different types of support through the network, the degree of criticism and attack that networks contain and the extent of reciprocity.

The importance of networks should not lead practitioners to regard the business of putting such a map and grid together in an overly formal way. Remember the aims: drawing on strengths, getting the big picture, encouraging family members to tell their story and reflect their perspective. It provides a basis for both practitioner and family to discuss the specific nature of a family's networks and highlights potentially useful resources.

Your professional network

FOUR TYPES OF NETWORK USERS

Angus McCabe, Vivien Lowndes and Chris Skelcher have categorised network users as four types:

- Enthusiasts who believe that networking has opened up community work because it encourages greater local participation and innovation. Enthusiasts value networking because it overcomes the constraints of bureaucratic systems, organisational boundaries and narrow, institutional policies.
- Activists who view networks as a managerial approach to ensure that strategic goals are met and that initiatives are delivered in an integrated way.
- Pragmatists who see networks as a necessary evil in the sense that they have to be up and running in order to secure financing from government programmes.
- Opponents who are hostile to networks because they can be oppressive and imply that poor neighbourhoods can pull themselves up by their own bootstraps.

ACTIVITY 3.3: YOUR ATTITUDE TO NETWORKS

1 What is your attitude to networks in general? Are you best described as an enthusiast, activist, pragmatist or opponent – or a mixture of these? Think of one or two examples of how your attitude to networks has influenced your recent work.

2 Think of your own professional network and list its key members. Why are they in your network? What contribution do they make in terms of knowledge, contacts or skills? Ask yourself three key questions: Who does each network member represent? To whom are they accountable? What are the mechanisms for that accountability?
3 Map the leadership in your network by listing the key activities it undertakes and make a note of which individual or organisation exercises leadership in each one. What is the means by which they secure their influence – through dominance of their organisation, election by network members, personal commitment and time spent or self-selection? Is leadership formal or informal?.

(adapted from McCabe *et al.* 1997)

Your own professional network is a critical tool that you can use to achieve certain objectives. Partnerships, for example, grow out of networks as trust and confidence in the capacity of your network links deepen. Networks also generate innovative projects and multi-dimensional thinking. You will see that these work-oriented networks are different in nature and purpose from those of users discussed above and the techniques for strenthening them also differ. When thinking about your own networks, keep the following principles in mind:

- Networks are reciprocal: if you ask others for information or help in solving a problem, in what circumstances would you be able to offer the same in return? Think in terms of *proactive networking*, that is, connections you set up yourself that respond to your requirements, as well as *reactive networking* which is generated by the needs of others. Both are interlinked; neither can thrive without the other.
- Personalise your networks. You will have more than one and they have to deliver results. Be explicit with yourself as to who constitutes your network. You will have different networks for different tasks.
- Networks are created through the most basic moves. Shared experience and common interests are a powerful glue to cement relationships. These may arise from your personal life, shared adversity or discrimination or simply from having to knuckle under to the same set of organisational tasks; they may grow out of an exchange of views on job roles, new projects or your hopes for the future. Be sure people know where, how and when to get hold of you.
- But remember the 'strength of weak ties'. Lengthy chat with the same set of colleagues every day, while pleasant and supportive, does not create the kind of network that you need for developing partnerships or collaborative multi-agency initiatives. Whether a social care worker, social worker or social services manager you should be looking across and outside your agency for those productive links that in time may pay off.
- Networks thrive on use. Depending on the nature of your relationship, some form of regular contact is probably desirable.

(Catt and Scudamore 1999)

ACTIVITY 3.4: CHECKLIST FOR NETWORKING

Work through the following checklist to see how effective your own professional network is.

- Reflect on your approachability. Are you responsive and receptive to other people's requests for advice, resources, informal help and guidance?
- Do other people gain by networking with you? Do you put effort into supplying what they need? Can they look to you in the future as someone who shows commitment and provides results?
- Are your work patterns and domestic routines compatible with creating and sustaining networks?
- Communication is all important and there are of course several ways for people to get in touch with you. Have you invested in the range of equipment now required? Do people have the information for getting in touch with you – by email, mobile phone, fax, office and home phone?

BUILDING PARTNERSHIPS

A partner may be defined as 'one who has a share or part with others' implying that there is an overall goal or organisation of which individual partners are aware (Pratt *et al.* 1998). Successive governments have invoked the concept of partnership when proposing ways of overcoming social exclusion. In this context, partnership means involving a number of different organisations in formal or semi-formal arrangements in which goals are agreed upon, some resources are pooled and common strategy planned though each partner may be responsible for implementing a different part of that strategy. Partners frequently linked together in fighting social exclusion include:

- Local authorities, who are often the dominant or leading players in local partnerships. As they have ceased to become sole providers of services, they have developed experience in partnerships for delivering services, particularly with the voluntary sector and also in engaging the private sector in local economic initiatives.
- The range of public service agencies who often contribute heavily in their own right to partnerships combating exclusion – the police, the health service, local schools and social services departments.
- Voluntary sector agencies, whether large and well-known organisations such as Barnardos or Age Concern, or small, local organisations representing specific groups in the community or providing specific services, for example an Asian women's refuge.
- Local community organisations such as tenants' or residents' associations who bring local knowledge and experience to bear on the needs of specific local constituencies and neighbourhoods.

- The private sector, which can embrace a range of employers, job trainers, consultants and other experts.

(Geddes 1997)

EXAMPLES OF PARTNERSHIPS

Increasingly, you will have to become familiar with the new generation of initiatives based on partnership that have arisen to tackle social exclusion. These include:

- Neighbourhood regeneration projects such as New Deal for Communities
- One-off initiatives by local organisations to relieve overcrowding or a project to allow young teenage mums to complete their schooling
- Early years forums
- Health action zones
- Sure Start projects
- Youth offending teams.

Why partnerships are needed

Because the problems associated with social exclusion are deep-rooted and complex a single professional approach or agency cannot resolve them on their own. The objective is to develop integrated programmes at all levels of working, including neighbourhoods and local communities. Partnership makes holistic solutions possible, providing the means by which practitioners to move beyond the specialisms of social work such as care management or protecting children (Scottish Office 1999; P. 6 *et al.* 1999).

Developing local responses to social disadvantage are built from the bottom up by bringing together partnerships between local people, community groups, voluntary and private agencies, religious organisations and statutory services. They are necessary because only by pooling local knowledge and professional expertise can complicated problems be addressed (Taylor 1995).

To understand the importance of partnership for reversing social exclusion it helps to conceive of the major services – health, education, housing, child protection and social services – as 'silos'. You may recognise the image: a silo is a large, tall structure found on farms for storing foodstuffs. They are self-contained and immovable, with no access between them. Our major services are constructed like that: huge, immovable and interested only in what goes on inside themselves. As a result people are often 'dumped' – excluded – outside one or more service silos and hence receive no service at all. The rising exclusions from school of hard-to-teach pupils are a perfect example of dumping. Because of school performance tables, disruptive, hard-to-teach pupils are unwanted by any school and there is no other service in place for them (P. 6 1998: 32). In social work we can point to the shifting back and forth of individuals between hospital care and long-term residential care with neither service wanting to absorb the cost. Professional discretion in decision-making and the growing culture of managerial focus on 'core' responsibilities and competencies has only reinforced the problem of dumping.

MAKING PARTNERSHIP WORK

The staff at the Park Family Centre in Ellesmere Port, a blue-collar industrial town on the edge of the Mersey in Cheshire, believed passionately in providing education for young teenage mothers in the area. These young women wanted to keep their infants, meet the demands of parenthood and still achieve GCSEs but they were not able to go back into school to do that. The staff knew that if mothers under 16 were to have any chance in life – and if their children were to avoid exclusion themselves as they grew up – they would need to finish their education 'to be given currency' as the project's teacher Anne Cunningham puts it.

The partnership that was mobilised around the Teenage Parents' Group at the Park Centre gives an indication of what can be done at ground level through the drive and initiative of a few (networked) individuals. First, they secured space at the family centre itself and then obtained funding from the health authority, local education authority and social services for staffing the project which included teachers, support workers and crèche staff. It was important both to practitioners involved in the project and the mothers themselves that they did not have to leave their babies so that bonding would not be disrupted and parenting skills would continue to develop. To accomplish this a crèche was set up next to the teaching room in the centre so that the young mums could go in and out to meet the needs of their infants. A range of professional advice was also made available at the time of the teaching sessions, from midwife, health visitor, school nurse and social worker. The manager of the Park Centre, Sally Hesketh, worked hard to negotiate the resources and provided supervision for the staff.

The first class of seven young mothers chose subjects from a range of six GCSEs taught at the centre – English, mathematics, art, social studies, science and child development.

The mission of the partnership was realised when all achieved good pass rates.

Difficulties with partnerships

Partnerships do not automatically produce achievement and at times they can be worse than nothing at all; they may exist only on paper simply to provide a smokescreen for capturing resources. The individual organisations in a partnership may have vastly different levels of influence. While centrally imposed conditions for competitive bidding for funding require the formation of partnerships, the time-frame is often extremely short, thus giving considerable advantage to those major agencies with highly specialised workforce and the capacity to do the hours of planning and report writing that are necessary. Local organisations, users and residents usually have no such resource to fall back on (Hastings *et al.* 1996; Mayo 1997; Pierson *et al.* 2000).

Nor do partnerships automatically rise above the discriminations and prejudices of society at large. A survey of partnerships in Scotland revealed that while women make up a majority on partnership boards (53 per cent) it did not automatically mean that women's issues were effectively addressed as a result. There was widespread lack of childcare during meetings and little allowance made for time to read and respond to papers because of home- and care-based responsibilities. In short, the researchers found no evidence whatsoever that the planning and development of partnership activities were based on a systematic gender analysis or strategy. Women's targets were seen as unnecessary or counter-productive. The authors concluded that 'unless they are genuinely based upon shared interest, with agreed mechanisms for negotiating differences, partnership can actually be destructive, either mutually destructive or perhaps more typically destructive for the weaker partners' (Mayo 1997).

Creating successful partnerships

PARTNERSHIPS: SOME LESSONS

- Partnership between organisations is hard to achieve because cultural, departmental and organisational differences are not easily overcome.
- Inter-agency tensions will not go away just because there is money to oil the wheels.
- Creating a truly shared purpose is paramount.
- Success will depend on local autonomy and initiative.
- Local power struggles over steering groups and management boards can become a painful distraction, lasting for many months or years.
- It is relatively easy to mount a collaborative bid and become a trail-blazer; sustaining enthusiasm and commitment over time is altogether different.

(adapted from King's Fund 2000)

In working to create effective partnerships there are a number of things for you to think about:

- Make sure that any issues from past activity are aired among would-be partner organisations. From these discussions you can begin the process of identifying future positive behaviours, redefining roles and changing the language from the politics of agency self-interest to the mutual responsibility of partnership. The biggest gap to be bridged in any partnership involving residents is between the professional and residents' interests.
- Familiarise yourself with the 'turf' and core interests of would-be partners; few partnerships are agreed without some losses as well as gains for all parties.
- Establish a number of joint problem-solving teams to identify solutions. While holistic or joined-up services are the aim, the path is strewn with practical difficulties both small and large. The advantage of smaller problem-solving teams is

that in the more informal atmosphere the 'sacred cows' can be discussed and all parties become involved in the identification of problems and in generating the solutions to overcome them (Anastacio *et al.* 2000).

- Joint problem-solving provides the ability to debate the issue in purposeful ways without resort to traditional blocking-type tactics.
- Action learning – an action team of a dozen people can be useful in exploring complex problems. It may choose to acquire expert assistance and policy specialists or conduct study visits and seminars.
- Partnerships reflect a state of mutual trust and respect that has to be earned. The behaviours, language and spirit of the new relationship emerges and the competence of each participant is tested and established. To create a partnership without strong foundation is merely a declaration of friendship, or a short term measure that will struggle to survive the challenges facing it (Sabel 1993).
- Developing working relations takes time among agencies who may have competing interests. Collaboration is not easy for competitors. The single biggest drawback to the partnerships in government initiatives such as New Deal for Communities is the short time-frame for forming partnerships which must be done before proposals can be submitted.

ACTIVITY 3.5: THE PRISONER'S DILEMMA

This justly famous scenario highlights how difficult it is to create a relationship of co-operation and mutual trust between potentially competing parties with a strong sense of their own self-interest.

Assume that you have committed a serious crime with a partner and that you have both been arrested and are now being questioned separately. The police have very little evidence against you and offer you a deal. The deal is this: (i) if you confess that the two of you committed the crime and your partner denies it, we will let you go free and send him down for five years; (ii) if you both deny the crime, we have enough circumstantial evidence to put both of you away for two years; (iii) if both of you confess to the crime then you both will receive a 4-year sentence. Your dilemma is that they have probably offered the same deal to your partner as well, and if you both testify against the other you will both receive the maximum sentence.

From a 'rational' point of view, and in the absence of co-operation and trust, whatever your partner does you will do best if you testify against your partner. Since this is also your partner's best strategy, the outcome will be that you both testify against each other. You have in fact been set up to compete with each other, to pursue your self-interest over that of your opponent, and so both of you do worse than if you worked together.

With a small group of colleagues work out the different options that each prisoner has and what the results would be. What catalysts for co-operation are there?

ACTIVITY 3.6: PARTNERSHIP – WHO HAS INFLUENCE?

Think of a partnership in which your agency is involved. Write down all the agencies and organisations which make up the partnership and, on a scale of 0 to 5, rate the degree of power that each holds within the partnership (with 5 as the highest). After you have done this reflect on three issues: What are the reasons and what is the basis for the degree of power that each organisation holds? Have the power relationships changed over time and if so why? What are the key characteristics of the power relationships of that particular partnership?

ACTIVITY 3.7: PARTNERSHIPS – A COST–BENEFIT ANALYSIS

Using the same partnership that you chose above assess the costs and benefits involved for your agency in joining for each of the areas listed below:

- funding
- staff time and other non-monetary resources
- aims, goals and missions
- personal values and beliefs
- reputation of your organisation
- local community needs

For each of the above what do you think are the risks that costs will outstrip the benefits? How do you think those risks could be minimised?

(adapted from McCabe *et al.* 1997)

PROMOTING PARTICIPATION

Ensuring the participation of users and citizens in discussing, planning and arranging the very services and programmes that will affect them is the fourth essential element in any practice aimed at reducing exclusion. The notion of participation is broad and varied and is often used in the same context as partnership. It may help to see that participation strives to achieve many of the same objectives as partnership, but focuses on local people: users, residents, citizens.

You may be able to see why the participation of users and local residents is so critical in reducing exclusion. For citizens *not* to be involved is itself exclusionary: not only are users' views not taken into account but their sense of powerlessness is also reinforced. Historically both central and local government have designed top-down service programmes relying on notions of infallible professional expertise and bureaucratic procedures. Their impact only created further stigmatisation and powerlessness.

Social work and its main agencies have recognised this over the course of the last fifteen years or so and have attempted to reverse this deep-seated tendency. Movements for greater voice from different groups of service users began in the late 1970s with learning disability advocates promoting service choices and community participation. Child-care practices in the mid-1980s were found to freeze parents out of the decision-making process when the local authority social service departments were considering taking their child into care. Adults needing some form of social care – whether a place in a residential home or home care – have fought to establish means of giving opinions in decisions affecting them (Braye 2000).

From this low baseline successive important pieces of legislation began to re-shape user participation in the assessment and provision of their own service. The Children Act 1989, the NHS and Community Care Act of 1990 and the Disabled Person's Representation Act in 1996, among others, required local authorities to consult closely with users when they undertake assessments and devise care plans, and in the follow-up reviews of how those plans are actually unfolding. Recent government initiatives such as Quality Protects, New Deal for Communities and the Best Value framework all require citizen participation. In the future it is likely that even higher levels of user participation will be required in service development and evaluating practice through the creation of local service agreements and neighbourhood management teams.

Yet the degree of influence on social work decisions that a user and his or her family will actually have varies quite considerably and depends on the attitudes of the practitioners involved and the policies of their agencies. Genuine dilemmas arise when local authorities have statutory obligations to exercise authority and provide a service which users have little choice but to accept, for example in cases where parents are strongly suspected of child abuse or in instances concerning young offenders.

Social work has developed a number of tools which provide users and their families with a greater voice in key decision-making:

- Assessments that give far greater weight to user opinion.
- Written agreements which incorporate user objectives.
- Task-centred work which is based on the short-term goals defined by users.
- Family group conferences which effectively give the wider family important powers in cases of child protection and youth offending.
- Service planning in which users, user organisations and local citizens help shape services themselves by contributing their views, personal experiences and expertise through a variety of channels such as joint planning meetings, advisory groups, public meetings, membership of task groups or taking part in the inspection and monitoring of a given service.

Advocacy and pressure groups for users have accelerated this process and provide an important recent lesson as to how participation (empowerment) is actually achieved. A new development is that of user-led services which are independent of the local authority and organised by committed advocates with a clear view of how society excludes users of mainstream services. Not only do they provide distinctive forms of support but they offer powerful examples of flexibility, choice and involvement which itself exerts wide influence (Braye 2000).

Arnstein's ladder

Sherry Arnstein developed her ladder (Figure 3.2) as a way of mapping out the different gradations of what 'participation' can mean (Arnstein 1969). Although it has often been adapted it has never been improved upon and is still referred to regularly in discussions on participation. The higher up the ladder you go the more control citizens exert over the initiative or service.

While practitioners may be individually committed to maximum levels of user participation, they will often find that legal obligations, agency policy and user expectations all constrain participation. Each project you engage in should be looked at carefully to determine what level of participation is both desirable and realistic. For example, in working with advocacy groups on developing local mental health services or with community groups in developing a family centre, levels of user participation are likely to be high and encouraged by social work agencies. By contrast, developing appropriate forms of community care for older people in a particular area could well have less intensive user involvement.

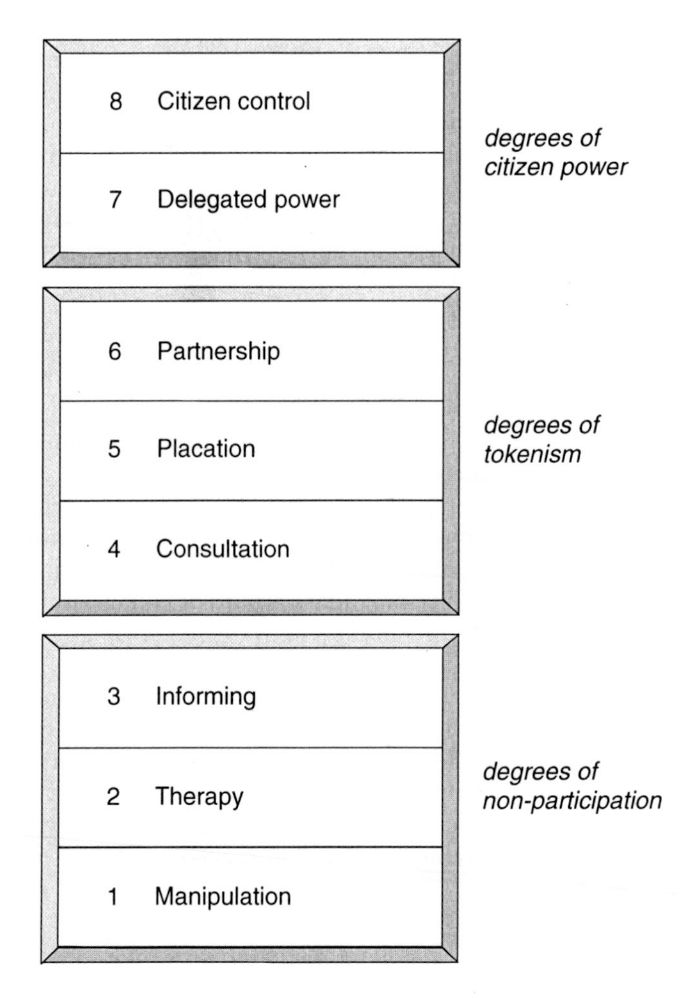

FIGURE 3.2 Arnstein's ladder

Participation: deeper, wider, longer

The nature of social exclusion requires complex programmes with new ways of involving diverse groups of people dealing with difficult and conflicting issues. Thus participation as a concept can no longer be confined to users and to a particular service. Virtually all projects, whether originating with government, community groups or practitioners and their agencies themselves, need to think hard about what kind of participation they seek and what approaches they should use.

Information

Giving information to people is fundamental to effective participation; people need to know the specific details of a project or service that is going to affect them. However, if you are providing information *only*, there are some drawbacks: this is a take-it or leave-it approach which may prompt those affected to wonder whether there really is no alternative to the approach you are putting forward. You may get more vocal feedback than you anticipated. 'Information only' is appropriate if you have no room for manoeuvre and must follow one course of action or if it is the start of wider consultation with the opportunity to participate later (Wilcox 1994).

It is important to know your target audience: what do they know already and what might they expect? Make sure your audience will understand your ideas and language. Be clear from the start about why you are just informing rather than consulting.

Ways of providing information include the following:

- leaflets, newsletters, posters and other printed material
- presentations at meetings
- briefing the media with press releases and conferences
- advertising
- exhibitions
- using a short video.

Consultation

Consultation, in effect, gives people a limited role and choice in devising a project or service outcome. You offer some options, listen to feedback and comment and take these into account before proceeding with your action. You are not looking for involvement in implementation, although you hope it will enjoy the consent of those you have consulted. Social work uses this widely to obtain feedback on services and to win support from users when options are limited and the overall aim is already in place. Consultation is not sufficient when you are seeking to empower local interests or you are not in a position to take up the suggestions put forward.

Make sure you are clear about your own role and who ultimately will take decisions and how this will be done. Offering false choices is worse than offering none at all. Also be clear about how realistic the different options are; if you form a task force, local forum or committee, be sure its terms of reference are clear (ibid.)..

Methods for consulting include:

- carrying out local surveys and questionnaires
- forming consultative committees
- consultation days with presentations, scenarios and feedback built in.

Try to found out in advance what information and other forms of support should be given to those whose opinions are sought so that they can reflect, discuss, learn and deliberate before giving that opinion.

ACTIVITY 3.8: CHECKLIST FOR CONSULTATION

To think in a structured way about the participation of users or local residents in a project you may be working on, run through the following checklist:

- Make sure you clearly define the different interests and groups to be consulted, whether based on gender, income, age, disability or ethnicity. Are they likely to have different perspectives and will you need to consult with each to be certain you have the whole picture?
- Ask yourself if they are likely to be satisfied with consultation.
- Can you present your vision and options for achieving it in a way that people will understand and relate to?
- Have you identified appropriate means for communication for the time available and the likely participants? (It is important to remember the power of visual representation and concrete examples.)
- Have you and your colleagues decided how to handle the feedback? By what means will it be logged or recorded? Have you arranged to report back to those you have consulted?
- Are you really just seeking endorsement of your plans or are you prepared to change your position?

ACTIVITY 3.9: HOW MUCH CONTROL AND INFLUENCE DO LOCAL RESIDENTS HAVE?

Using urban regeneration funding for homelessness, workers from a local voluntary organisation in King's Cross, London, convened a regular focus group on homelessness. The group was able to secure funding to map local housing needs and develop a set of principles for housing strategies in the area. Arising from this work the project obtained further funding for a series of 'Speakouts' in which local homeless people spoke to local government decision-makers from social services and housing departments. These efforts resulted in changes to local authority housing procedures for people in bed and breakfast accommodation (drawn from Anastacio *et al.* 2000).

Consider the project outlined above or think of a project that you and your team have been involved with. Using Arnstein's ladder, what level of participation do you think was achieved in either?

Joint action

Joint action means accepting other people's ideas, working through decisions together, and having the time to engage in lengthier deliberations. Joint action is appropriate when users and residents need to own the solution, when fresh ideas are needed, when you need help in implementing your project or when empowerment and building capacity are themselves the objective. Make sure you plan the process before you start and allow plenty of time for its development. Make sure that roles and responsibilities are clear and that different interests are recognised. Acting together may take you into partnership, as discussed above, but equally you may remain on an informal level using temporary structures such as working parties, steering groups or small teams for overseeing and implementing decisions.

Your methods here are more open-ended and require time for trust to build up between parties. They include:

1. Team-building exercises
2. Working through scenarios
3. Running 'Planning for real' exercises (see Chapter 7)
4. 'Future search' conferences which revolve around four key points:
   - get all parties in the room so that all aspects of the system are represented
   - think globally and act locally
   - focus on common ground and desired futures rather than problems and conflicts
   - allow discussion to be self-managed and take personal responsibility for implementation (Pratt *et al.* 1998).
5. Citizen juries
6. Community visioning.

Winning the trust of the community for joint action is difficult but essential for neighbourhood development work. Low-income urban neighbourhoods have seen service providers periodically gripped with a desire to get 'close to the people': they come, promise the world and then leave when funding runs out. Community trust is not automatic and must be earned too.

Citizen power

At the top end of the ladder – citizen power – the look and feel of work changes significantly. Practitioners should endeavour to act as convenors, catalysts and facilitators. We have to put our knowledge, ideas and categories in second place. Our role is to enable local people to do their own investigations, analysis, presentations, planning and action, to own the outcome, and to teach us, sharing their knowledge. They do the mapping, diagramming, listing, sequencing and analysing (Beresford and Croft 1993; Mayo 1999; PRA 1999). This is discussed at greater length in Chapter 7.

WORKING IN THE NEIGHBOURHOOD

DEFINITION OF NEIGHBOURHOOD

A neighbourhood is a geographic zone or area which is continuous and surrounds some other point, usually home, and is smaller in size than some other recognised spatial entitity, for example a city sector or city. Neighbourhoods can be defined by individuals, groups of individuals or organisations and they may be defined for single functions or the overall set of household activities.

(Maclennan 2000: 11)

'EYES ON THE STREET'

A good example of 'neighbourhood effects' is highlighted by the strength of informal mechanisms by which residents achieve some degree of informal social control. These include the monitoring of spontaneous playgroups among children, a willingness to intervene to prevent acts of intimidation by teenage peer groups and confronting persons who are exploiting or disturbing public space. The capacity of residents to control group-level behaviours is an important dimension to the social environment.

In her classic account *The Life and Death of American Cities*, the sociologist Jane Jacobs coined the phrase 'eyes on the street' to summarise this capacity of informal local control and how it could easily be disrupted by the poor planning of unthinking bureaucrats (Figure 3.3). Older neighbourhoods that had physically developed over time presented far greater opportunities both physically and socially for the public to stay involved in the social life of the neighbourhood.

We have come to know much more about how powerful the social and organisational characteristics of neighbourhoods can be in the lives of people who live there. These 'neighbourhood effects' can be positive by providing resources and strengths that far outstrip anything that professional services could offer. Neighbourhoods with high levels of activity are likely to participate in projects at higher rates with, for example, more representatives on committees or higher levels of volunteering. Neighbourhood effects can also be quite destructive, presenting people with challenges such as high rates of crime, non-existent job opportunities and poor schools that very few individual families could surmount (Wilson 1996; Sampson 1999). Neighbourhoods can also be 'closed' in their affiliations, hostile to diversity, and a seedbed for hate groups

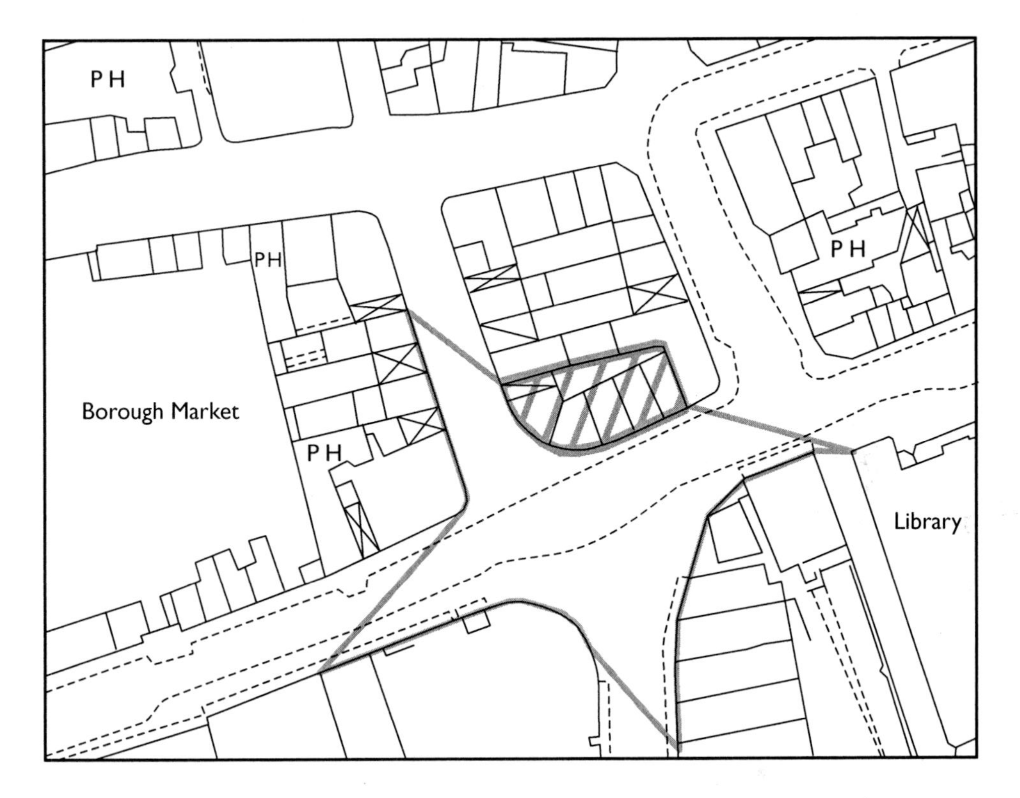

FIGURE 3.3 'Eyes on the street': street map indicates how, in an older, physically diverse neighbourhood, large areas of public space (outlined in grey) were watched over by residents from just a few houses or shops

and physical attacks. But either way the importance of neighbourhoods cannot be ignored. Government has recently come to understand this very fact which is why so many programmes now have an area focus.

Neighbourhoods may have definable features – railway tracks, highways, rivers or a specific type of housing, but although they may have geographical features neighbourhood remains a flexible and diverse concept. If you rely on 'walkable distance' as a criterion, for instance, people with disability could well take a different viewpoint. Political entities such as wards or constituency boundaries can be important but so can attendance for specific churches or mosques. Neighbourhoods may or may not have a common feeling of 'community' in which residents perceive certain common interests that arise because of their relative proximity.

Your practice and that of your agency must come to terms with the importance of the powerful and independent impact that an area or locality has on the lives of its residents.

Here are two elements for you and your team and agency to consider:

- The neighbourhood as the basis for the local delivery of services – this includes moves to decentralise in common with other services, and the concept of the neighbourhood management team.

- Community development – this means working to capitalise on existing strengths and to enhance the capacity of the neighbourhood itself to solve problems and accomplish tasks such as the social control of young people. Community development encourages individual and collective action allowing people to identify their own potential, understand the processes of disadvantage and exclusion and participate in the mainstream of their community, not on the margins.

(Cannan and Warren 1997)

Whether in service plans, in central and local government policy documents or in social workers' own discussions, too often the assumption is that 'the community' exists as a single entity. The consequence can often be practical: a poorly arranged effort at a consultation meeting or a single service plan that assumes the community is a homogenous entity.

ACTIVITY 3.10: IDENTIFYING THE DIFFERENT COMMUNITIES IN YOUR AREA

Consider the different kinds of communities that may be found in your local area. From the list below check which you think are the most important for (1) your work and (2) for the area as a whole.

- Geographical communities – where at least a sense of common boundaries and certain common interests are widely if not universally acknowledged.
- Communities of interest – in which strong affiliations emerge from shared culture or similar social attainments; examples include communities around schools.
- Ethnic and religious communities – around culture and place of worship.
- Communities of identity drawn from shared social identity (gender and disability apply here) or of sexuality, such as gays or lesbians.
- Workplace communities – a large hospital will have an important presence in the locality, as will a large industrial enterprise such as a car factory.
- Service users.
- Age-based groups.

ACTIVITY 3.11: FINDING OUT ABOUT THE LEVEL OF LOCAL ACTIVITY

If you are serious about focusing on at least one neighbourhood in your work it is essential to know the current levels of activity as a baseline. Burns and Taylor (2000: 12) have developed this mapping exercise to establish such a baseline. They suggest several categories to examine, which are listed below. Using these categories map the baseline of activity for the neighbourhood you work or live in.

- individual contributions – for example, keeping gardens tidy, volunteering

- individual involvement in community activities – such as local football teams, lunch clubs
- informal mutual aid – such as childcare, looking after neighbours
- organised mutual aid – credit unions, neighbourhood watch
- participation in local networks and associations – tenants' and residents' groups, community associations.

ACTIVITY 3.12: WHY THE CONTRASTS? THE RIBBLE VALLEY

Form a team of four, either from your training course or from your workplace or point of volunteer activity. Gather as much basic population data, including ethnic make-up and numbers in different age groups (0–5, 6–13 and so on) on the towns of Clitheroe and Blackburn. Also see if you can find information on available services whether public, such as schools (and whether they are selective or not) or private such as banking and financial services. See if you can find any information on levels of deprivation in each town. When you have found a reasonable amount of information set it out in two columns. What comparisons can you make between the two towns? Why do you think the differences exist?

KEY POINTS

The chapter has explored the five building blocks for a practice that aims to combat social exclusion. It covers:

- The importance of focusing on income and of having a broad working knowledge of the benefits system as a whole.
- The contribution that networks make both as a professional tool for yourself and as a source of social support for users.
- Partnerships with other service agencies and local organisations through which holistic, 'joined-up action' is delivered on the ground.
- Some of the benefits and difficulties in building high levels of user and resident participation.
- The importance of 'neighbourhood' and strengthening local capacity through community development.

KEY READING

Henderson, P. and Thomas, D. *Skills in Neighbourhood Work*, 3rd edn. (Routledge, 2001). This manual is full of approaches and tactics for effective neighbourhood development work.

Beresford, P. and Croft, S. *Citizen Involvement: A practical guide for change* (Macmillan, 1993). Although this is written from the citizen's point of view you will find many practical, down-to-earth ways of accelerating citizen involvement in local affairs and projects you may be engaged in.

Wolfe, M. *Debt Advice Handbook*, 4th edn. (Child Poverty Action Group, 1999). Mike Wolfe is an outstanding welfare benefits adviser who runs the Citizens' Advice Bureau in Stoke-on-Trent and campaigns for gay rights. He has also written a superb handbook on money advice and the interrelationship between jobs and benefits.

CHAPTER 4

WORKING WITH SOCIALLY EXCLUDED FAMILIES

OBJECTIVES

By the end of the chapter you should:

- Understand the extent of social exclusion experienced by young children and their families
- Understand the concept of children in need and its overlap with exclusion
- Have thought through issues of income and work in maximising family income
- Have become familiar with family support initiatives such as parent groups, family literacy and breakfast clubs
- Understand the significance of early years work in combating exclusion
- Be able to apply what you have learned to a family scenario.

The previous chapter described the five building blocks for social work practice dedicated to reducing social exclusion. These will underpin your work aimed at reducing the social exclusion of users, their families or local residents and neighbourhoods. The purpose of this chapter is to guide you through what you can do with those building blocks, and how they, together with the skills and perspectives from Chapter 2, can be applied in your work with young children and their families. We suggest a number of approaches and ideas that will help you address some of the components of exclusion as experienced by families with young children: low income, powerlessness and poorly performing social networks. We also pay considerable attention to projects that are innovative and embody joined-up work with other agencies. These should be considered closely as they contain guidance and pointers that serve as a model and inspiration for your own work.

SOCIAL EXCLUSION AND FAMILIES

The number of children in the UK affected by poverty and social exclusion is among the highest in the developed world. A recent study of 25 nations showed that Britain has the third highest proportion of children in poverty over all and the highest of any European country (Piachaud and Sutherland 2000). In 1998–9 a record four and a half million children were living in households with less than half the average national income after housing costs. By this standard one in three children were living in poverty, twice the rate in France or The Netherlands and over five times that in Norway and Sweden.

If the proportion of poor children in the population was the same as the proportion of poor adults, there would be something like a million and quarter *fewer* poor children. While the government has estimated that its new measures over the last three years will lift over a million children out of poverty this will merely bring the number of poor children roughly into proportion with the number of poor adults (NPI 2001: 14). Half of all lone parents do not have paid work and 4 in 10 were on incomes below 40 per cent of the national average in 1999 (Rahman *et al.* 2000). The realisation that poverty in childhood increases the likelihood of exclusion in later adult life only further underscores the costs of childhood exclusion.

INDICATORS FOR CHILDREN IN POVERTY AND SOCIAL EXCLUSION

- Number of children living in workless households – indicating the extent of polarisation between families with and without work.
- Children living in households with below half-average income – a standard threshold for determining relative poverty.
- Low birth-weight babies – reveals the persistent inequalities in health.
- Low attainment in GCSE results – educational attainment is strongly associated with social deprivation or affluence.
- Number of permanent school exclusions.
- Children whose parents divorce – a number of adverse outcomes are associated with divorce and separation.
- Number of births to girls under the age of 16.

(adapted from Rahman *et al.* 2000)

Rahman and colleagues have developed several indicators for estimating the number of children living in poverty and social exclusion. They are useful to practitioners who can use them in their own area to form a profile. You may wish to consult the information which they have compiled in their annual monitoring of social exclusion; it provides an extremely accurate picture of the contemporary extent of social exclusion among children.

ACTIVITY 4.1: A CHILD IS ILL

Charlene, a lone parent, lives with her children in a high-rise block of flats which she rents from the local authority. She has no phone and does not work. She has three children: eleven months, three years and six years.

Susan is also a lone parent. She lives in a three-bedroom house privately owned. She works during the day and has full-day childcare starting at 8 a.m. and finishing at 5.15 p.m. Her children are also eleven months, three years and six years.

Both families wake up one morning to find that their toddler is running a very high temperature and they need to see a doctor. What different experiences will they have in getting to see a doctor? Think about these differences along the following points: calling the doctor; arranging childcare; getting to the surgery; talking to the doctor; caring for the sick child and administering any prescribed medicine.

(Anti-Poverty Alliance 2001)

ASSESSING SOCIAL EXCLUSION

Children in need

The concept of 'children in need' has been fundamental to social work with families since the implementation of the Children Act 1989. It also overlaps with the notion of children who are socially excluded with which it bears some similarities. Understanding how these two basic concepts relate to each other makes a good starting point in developing particular approaches to practice.

Broadly determining whether a child is in need relies on a socially established norm, that is a 'reasonable standard of health or development'. Should the child fall sufficiently below this norm, in either health or in developmental progress, or if the child's development is impaired to the point as to require services, that child is then deemed as 'in need' in contrast to children who attain a reasonable standard of health and development. Thus established, the concept of 'in need' provides the basis on which the local authority social service department decides whether a child and its family should be supported in some way.

There are clear similarities between the concept of 'in need' and the social exclusion of children. For instance both concepts draw attention to the wider environmental and ecological dimensions in which the child is being raised, particularly now that the Department of Health has expanded the number of factors that social workers should

DEFINITION OF CHILDREN IN NEED IN THE CHILDREN ACT 1989

Section 17(10) of the Children Act defines 'children in need' as follows:

(a) he is unlikely to achieve or maintain, or to have the opportunity of achieving or maintaining, a reasonable standard of health or development without the provision for him of services by local authority under this Part;
(b) his health or development is likely to be significantly impaired, or further impaired, without the provision for him of such services; or
(c) he is disabled.

(It must be stressed that in the Act where the child is referred to only as 'he' we are to read 'he or she'.)

consider in assessing need (see below). Both concepts also focus on the barriers and obstacles that parents have to contend with such as unemployment, and both highlight the importance of the levels of family income, the quality of family networks and informal sources of family support.

There are also some differences between the two, particularly in the way local authorities have used the concept of in need. For example, assessment has tended to focus on deficits and weaknesses in families, especially in the parents' capacities to look after children, and not on strengths or resilience. Equally family poverty, worklessness and exclusion from information or social networks have not been central to that assessment process. The high priority given to child protection also has sucked resources away from preventative work and neighbourhood development, despite well-argued reports which urged a reversal of those priorities (Audit Commission 1994; DoH 1995).

Assessment of 'in need'

A major reconstruction of practice in relation to children in need is now under way: recent government initiatives are gradually harmonising services for children in need with those for vulnerable children suffering social exclusion. This is clear, for example, from the priorities set out in the White Papers *Modernising Social Services* (DoH 1998) and *Social Services – Building for the Future* (DoH 1999). These identify some of the challenges facing social workers including:

- The need to better protect children by using a wider range of services and methods of reducing risk rather than just statutory child protection systems.
- The fact that too many children are in need because they are from poor families struggling to cope on their own.

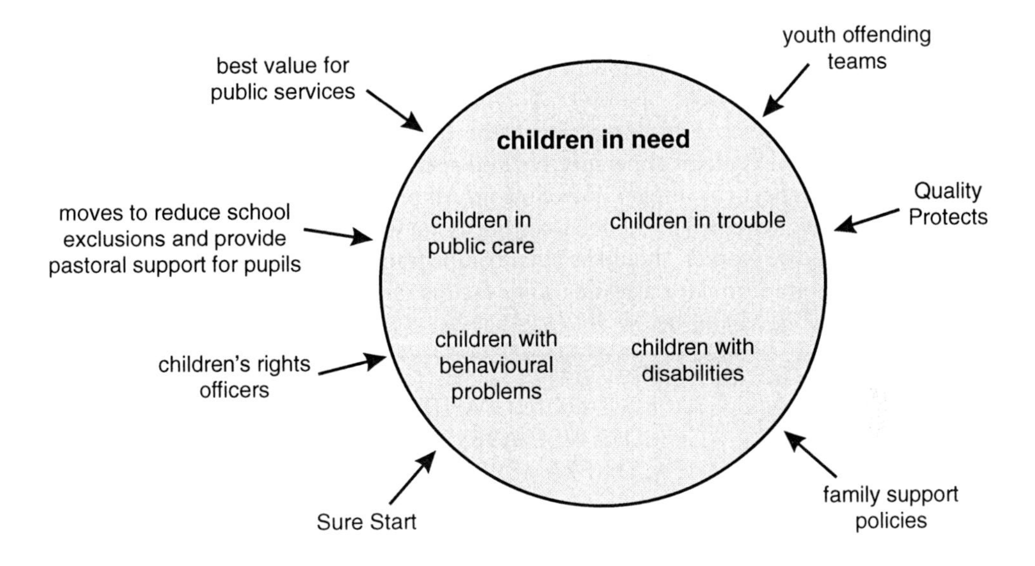

FIGURE 4.1 Initiatives for excluded children and children in need

Source: Adapted from *Getting the Best from Children's Services*, Audit Commission 1999: 4.

- Too many children leave school without any qualifications or cannot go to school at all because they have been excluded.
- Too many children who leave public care do not get work, a home of their own or play a full part in society.

(Audit Commission 1999)

Putting all the various pieces of the jigsaw together in developing services for socially excluded children and children in need is a considerable challenge.

This strategy is also evident in *Quality Protects* (in Wales, *Children First*) announced in 1998, which brings similar objectives together in a single structure. *Quality Protects* outlines the following eight objectives.

- A stable attachment to carers should be nurtured.
- Children should be protected from significant harm.
- Maximum life chances for children in need.
- Maximum life chances for children who are looked after.
- Social and economic inclusion for young people leaving care.
- Strategies should meet the assessed social needs of children with a disability.
- Effective referral, assessment and delivery services need to be in place.
- Service delivery should ensure best value with responses appropriate to individual need and choice.

(Department of Health 1998)

The emphasis now is on re-focusing services away from crisis intervention in order to ensure that services are provided for children in need without families having to go through a child protection investigation first. The Quality Protects objectives are broad and relate directly to exclusionary barriers. For example, ensuring 'maximum life chances' for children in need means helping them to gain the benefits of education by achieving better results in their SATs and GCSE examinations (Audit Commission 1999: 14).

In its new *Framework for Assessment*, the Department of Health (DoH 2000a) explicitly adopts an ecological perspective and specifies more clearly components of assessment that reflect the impact of exclusion. All practitioners who work with children and families, whether in the local authority or voluntary sector, whether social worker or social care worker, should be aware of the framework. In effect the framework becomes an important tool for assessing *some* factors underpinning social exclusion.

ACTIVITY 4.2 SAFEGUARDING AND PROMOTING THE CHILD'S WELFARE: THE DEPARTMENT OF HEALTH FRAMEWORK

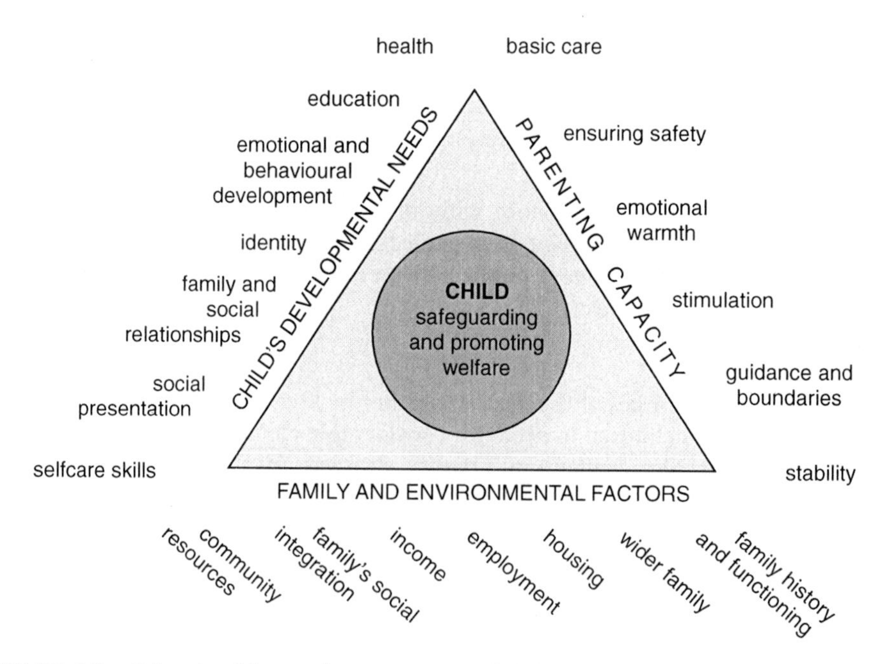

FIGURE 4.2 Triangle of factors for assessment of children in need

The diagram above is taken from the DoH's *Framework for Assessment of Children in Need*. It indicates the three key domains that are fundamental to any assessment of children in need. Before you read any further consider the different dimensions on each side of the triangle. Which of these would be most affected by the the process of social exclusion? How many of these dimensions rely on social resources that are ultimately found outside the family?

DEPARTMENT OF HEALTH CHECKLIST ON FAMILY AND ENVIRONMENTAL FACTORS

- Family history and functioning – members of the household, significant recent changes, nature of relationships to siblings, parental strengths and difficulties including those of an absent parent.
- Housing: does the accommodation have basic amenities and facilities appropriate to the age and development of the child?
- Employment: who is working in the household, their pattern of work and the impact this has on the child.
- Income: income available over a sustained period of time – is the family receiving all of its entitlements? The way resources are used and sufficiency of income for the child's needs.
- Family's social integration: exploration of the wider context of the local neighbourhood and community and its impact on child and parents, including the degree of any social isolation.
- Community resources: the facilities and services available in the neighbourhood – health, day care, schools, places of worship, transport and leisure.

(DoH 2000a: 23)

Strengths perspective: assessing risk and resilience

Family strengths are crucial to identify since building on specific individual or family capacities is often the first step in that family's mastery over their social environment. Increasingly childcare professionals are looking at the concept of 'resilience' (Fraser *et al.* 1999). Although resilience – that is survival in the face of significant threats to development – can be seen as an individual response of the child or family, it is shaped by both individual and environmental factors (ibid.: 138). Thus the search for factors that promote resilience must include family, school, neighbourhood and other wider influences.

In your work it is always helpful to remember the inherent resilience of most children and families. Children grow up in several contexts besides families, such as schools, peer groups, shared interest groups or clubs and other institutions such as church, temple or mosque. Each is a source of risk and development. There is a 'self-righting drive for development' when combined with actions of adults and nurturing a child's assets can overcome the effects of exclusion (Gilligan 2000). The Department of Health's framework provides a 'family pack' of tools for doing just that including a 'Strengths and Difficulties' questionnaire to be completed by parents. This pack goes a long way toward correcting some of the 'deficits only' tradition in local authority assessment. Other scales provided by the department allow parents to report their own sense of hassle or level of family activities (DoH 2000a).

In practice assessment of strengths is not always easy: notions of resilience and psychological strength are particularly hard to pin down and may draw more on your

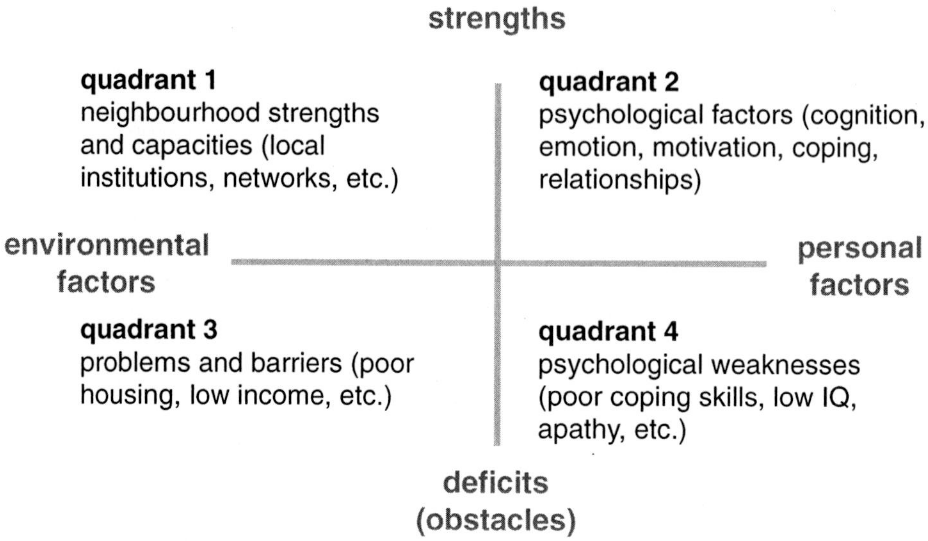

strengths

quadrant 1
neighbourhood strengths and capacities (local institutions, networks, etc.)

quadrant 2
psychological factors (cognition, emotion, motivation, coping, relationships)

environmental factors

personal factors

quadrant 3
problems and barriers (poor housing, low income, etc.)

quadrant 4
psychological weaknesses (poor coping skills, low IQ, apathy, etc.)

deficits (obstacles)

FIGURE 4.3 Strengths: a framework
Source: Saleeby 1992.

own views than you might at first think. The parents who argue vociferously with a social worker may be seen as 'difficult' and 'obstructionist' by one worker or as 'feisty' and 'standing up for themselves' by another. And for families approaching social work agencies the balance between resilience and vulnerability may have shifted to the latter so that neither the social worker nor family members may be able to see their own strengths.

Yet building on existing strengths increases that family's sense of influence within a social environment. A strengths assessment focuses on the following areas:

- Cognitive and appraisal skills – family members' ability to perceive, analyse and comprehend the challenges and barriers confronting them, including their own capacities and possible alternative strategies for surmounting them.
- Coping mechanisms to deal with sources of stress.
- Temperamental and dispositional factors – characteristic ways of seeing the social world.
- Interpersonal skills and supports – the ability to develop and maintain intimate and supportive social networks.
- External and social factors – support from social institutions, sources of advice and effective social networks.

(McQuaide and Ehrenreich 1997)

One of the main proponents of the strengths perspective, Dennis Saleeby (1992), encourages practitioners to think of setting out a joint appraisal of the users' situation on a quadrant that focuses on obstacles and the capacities for overcoming them. The quadrant (Figure 4.3) relies on an ecological approach. Used informally it encourages users to identify those specific sources of strengths that they can draw on as well as pinpoint certain weaknesses or deficits that affect their lives.

MAXIMISING INCOME

Paying attention to sources of income whether from benefits or work is part of your job in addressing issues of social exclusion. For families this can be a complex task, particularly as a consequence of 'welfare-to-work' policies and other innovations that make the interrelationship between benefits and employment more problematic. As stated earlier, while you are not expected to have specialist knowledge you should be familiar with the major benefits that impact on parents and their children with access to more detailed information should you need to call on it.

Income Support

We have seen that this is calculated on the basis that the 'applicable amount' or formal 'needs' of a claimant exceed their income. The 'applicable amount' is made up of

- Personal allowances of the claimant, partner (if there is one) and dependants (if there are any); these vary according to circumstances and age.
- A family premium which is paid to couples or lone parents with a dependent child; the separate and higher family premium for lone parents was abolished from 6 April 1998 but is still available for those lone parents who began claiming before that date it as long as they remain lone parents and are entitled to Income Support.
- Housing costs may be included within the calculation for those claimants responsible for mortgages while help with rent or costs to cover a hotel, hostel or bed and breakfast are usually met through housing benefit from the local authority. The latter is often claimed at the same time as Income Support.

As for any income received, claimants may keep part-time earnings from up to 16 hours a week. For lone parents £25 can be disregarded from any earned income for the purposes of calculating housing benefit or council tax benefit and £15 can be disregarded for Income Support or Jobseeker's Allowance.

Working Families' Tax Credit

The Working Families' Tax Credit (WFTC) is an offset in taxation rather than a benefit as such, directly paid to most claimants by the Inland Revenue but through the claimant's employers. As a result, the take-up of WFTC is substantially higher than that of the old Family Credit for low-income working families which it replaces. This is principally because of greater publicity and the fact that employers have to pay the credits once a claim is decided and notifications ('start notices') have been sent to the employer (Puttick 2000a). Proponents claim a number of advantages for WFTC:

- it reinforces the distinction between work and remaining on welfare
- it provides greater incentives to take up work
- it overcomes the 'poverty trap' previously experienced by low-paid workers who lost benefits as they begin to earn

- it provides improved assistance for childcare costs through a further 'credit' within WFTC which complements other policies for lone parents especially.

(ibid.: 181)

WFTC can be paid to people who have responsibility for a child or children and who work for 16 hours a week or more in low-paid work. It is usually paid across a six-month period and does not usually change even if family circumstances do. It may be however that some parents would be worse off, at least in terms of income, working and claiming WFTC rather than receiving Income Support or income-based Jobseeker's Allowance. Lone parents who work over 16 hours a week can receive an additional tax credit covering 70 per cent of the cost of a registered child-minder, school scheme or other specified play group. In the year 2000 this applies up to a maximum of £100 in costs for one child (that is £70 in care tax credit) or up to £150 for two or more children (£105 in care tax credit). Childcare costs can also be disregarded from their earnings when calculating their housing benefit and community tax benefit.

In addition to Income Support and WFTC you should also be familiar with other important benefits that relate to families. For example eligibility for child benefit, which has a higher rate for the first child of an eligible lone parent, should already be well established in your working knowledge. So should free school meals, and grants for school uniform and grants under section 17 Children Act 1989 (Puttick 2000a).

Lone parents

Lone-parent families have repeatedly been shown to be materially worse off than the poorest categories of two-parent families (Bryson *et al.* 1997). Any practice determined to reduce the exclusion of young families must focus on the particular predicaments of lone parents, with whom a large percentage of children in poverty live. Again, an overview of where lone parents stand in relation to benefits is essential. In addition to the points established above this should include:

- Entitlement to the higher rate of child benefit for lone parents if the person had already been receiving it before 6 July 1998.
- The rate of personal allowance for determining 'the applicable amount' for a lone parent 18 or over is the same as a single claimant aged 25 or over and thus substantially higher than for a single claimant aged 18–24.
- Eligibility to claim Income Support for lone parents under 18; lone parents are also eligible for Income Support when on parental leave from work to look after their children provided that during that period they are not getting payment of any kind from their employer *and* would be entitled to WFTC at the point that parental leave began.

There is now some flexibility in the benefits system to help with the transition to work. The old notion of the 'poverty trap' – in which the security of benefits, low as they were, were deemed preferable by lone parents to the risk of poorly paid work – does not necessarily now hold.

- Lone parents starting work may be entitled to up to two weeks of Income Support when they start and up to four weeks extended payments of housing benefit and council tax benefit.
- They may also be eligible for single payments when starting work as a kind of 'back to work' bonus. If a lone parent begins to earn part time and receives less in benefit as a result he or she can receive up to half the amount of that reduction as a lump sum when commencing work full-time.

For a lone parent with young children whether to work or not, and if so for how many hours a week, presents a huge dilemma. Income support levels, according to central government, provide sufficient income to remain out of poverty; but there is wide agreement that such levels are too low to achieve this purpose. Because of this, recent government policy has strongly encouraged, even pressured, lone parents to either find work or prepare for work through training or education.

For the parent coming off benefit and going into work there can be gains in income, improved networks and wider social contacts. But such gains vary greatly from individual to individual and depend on their earning capacity. Bryson *et al.* (1997) have established that to secure these gains investing in 'human capital' – that is qualifications, job-related training, and accumulated work experience – is crucial to lone mothers in securing higher wages. Other barriers to work may also arise such as cultural or social values that restrict the search for potential jobs or lack of suitable kinds or work in the local area, the prejudice of employers or the costs of transport or childcare (Gardiner 1997).

For a parent on her own with care for under fives, work can present many difficulties. It is important not to exaggerate the benefits of work. For those with low levels of skill or educational attainments and for those who, because of care commitments, can only work part time the work that is available is often low paid, temporary and unsatisfying.

The New Deal for lone parents, part of the government's general welfare to work initiative, crystallises this dilemma. It is a voluntary programme for those lone parents receiving Income Support and whose youngest child is over five years and three months old. If a person is in the target group she does not have to respond to the invitation for an interview, nor can Income Support be stopped or suspended for refusing to take part. The New Deal is also available for those with children under five although they are not invited to take part (CPAG 2000). The New Deal package includes advice and help on job applications, help with CVs and rehearsals for interviews.

ACTIVITY 4.3: LONE PARENTS AND WELFARE TO WORK

Abby is a 19-year-old mother with a nine-month-old daughter. Her former partner and father of the child has thus far evaded paying any child support although on occasion he stays at her flat and they do talk about living together at some point in the future. She has now been called for an interview to assess her prospects for working. As her community support worker you have offered her a range of family support services, including childcare, since she herself left care at the age of 18. To how much Income Support is she approximately entitled? What other benefit-related issues do you think might arise?

She is uncertain as to whether to try and find work and she turns to you for advice. What kind of guidance would you offer? Write down the gains and losses for her and her child as you would imagine doing in collaboration with her. If she decides to seek work what services do you think would need to be provided?

(adapted from Puttick, 2000)

FAMILY SUPPORT SERVICES

The concept of family support covers a broad spectrum of practitioner activity and service provision, the aim of which is to help families contend with difficulties and overcome specific obstacles they face when bringing up children. Under the Children Act local authorities have a positive duty to provide a wide range of support services for families with children in need (DoH 1991). The act recognised that parenting is a difficult and at times onerous job and sought to persuade practitioners that requests for help were not an expression of parental inadequacies deserving a paternalistic, grudging provision of service but a natural element of parenting. The support services mentioned in the Children Act include day nurseries and child minding, holiday activities and help with travel, Section 17 cash payments to cover financial emergencies and short-term local authority backed accomodation for children (ibid. 1991).

Much of this activity has focused on family relationships, particularly in relation to child abuse. The National Research Council in the US (1993) extensively reviewed evidence on prevention and summarised three pathways along which prevention is achieved:

- Parent support programmes such as those available in family centres (see below).
- Community-based programmes which operate through local institutions and in particular schools.
- Programmes to foster change in cultural and social values, for example in prevailing attitudes to children.

The review underscored the benefits to abused children of social service interventions that focused on changing parenting practice *in the context of better income support.* Such work is particularly successful when provided from the family's local community (Little and Mount 1999: 65). Relatively few local authorities in the UK have responded to the Department of Health's important review of research on the effectiveness of child protection programmes which makes similar points to the US study. It found that family support services should be seen as a way of protecting children and not as an option once child protection issues are out of the way (DoH 1995).

Many family support initiatives now explicitly counter the exclusion of families with an emphasis on holistic provision. Our understanding of the effectiveness of how strands of family support and early intervention reinforce each other has also increased greatly since the act was first implemented, in particular how environments interact with children. 'A community that is caring and supportive,' Little and Mount declare, 'that has high expectations of its members and encourages all to participate in communal activity will be healthy and produce few casualties' (1999: 56).

SIX MAJOR AIMS OF FAMILY SUPPORT

This list of aims is hard to improve upon when thinking about the long-term objectives of your work, your team or your agency. It provides a checklist to see whether the projects that you initiate or the activity that you undertake are moving in the right direction.

- Enhancing a sense of community
- Mobilising resources and supports
- Sharing responsibility and collaboration
- Protecting family integrity
- Strengthening family functioning
- Developing proactive human service practices.

(adapted from Dunst *et al.* 1994)

In providing family support it is important to think of the family in its widest sense. For a child in need, suffering neglect, or coping with high levels of stress relationships with brothers and sisters or grandparents and other family relations become important sources of support (Family Rights Group 1986). Identifying where those links are and nurturing them within the wider family is an essential first step. Should a child need to live away from her or his parents a placement within the extended family is a first option to consider. The Children Act embodies this understanding by requiring social workers to consult within the family before such placement decisions are made.

Other forms of support may draw on ties that extend beyond family and these may or may not be neighbourhood based. Friends who live outside the neighbourhood or acquaintances and contacts made through schools, churches or mosques and community groups such as a tenants' association can also provide support for children and their parents at critical points (Gilligan 2000). Using the social network map as explained in Chapter 3 is one such tool for helping practitioners uncover what these connections might be for any one family.

Gilligan (ibid.) suggests that a key objective for family support practitioners is to enhance the number of identities available to parents who face elements of social exclusion or constrained opportunities. Providing opportunities for adult education, or for job placement and training, as well as good childcare all have a part to play in family support. Through these, parents can develop their roles and social connections which enhance their morale and self-esteem, and develop their parenting capacities.

While the benefits of family support are not fully understood there is accumulating evidence to show that it is critical to forestalling difficulties in school, anti-social behaviour in children and improving the experience of family life. One of the first studies to document this was Jane Gibbons and colleagues (1990). They found that one of the areas they examined, where family centres had developed out of partnerships between health, education, social services and voluntary agencies, and where social workers had moved out of central offices into such centres, had a far more effective record of keeping families together compared with other areas with more traditional service organisations. Since then, further evidence has accumulated that newer initiatives such as parent support groups and breakfast clubs also provide the kinds of support that parents are looking for (Donovan and Street 1999; Herbert and Napper 2000).

In thinking about what families want it is important to remember that social work theory and agency language tend to express objectives to do with 'partnership' and 'empowerment' in abstract terms, while parents from disadvantaged neighbourhoods tend to focus on the immediate and concrete issues facing them. Smith's study showed that when they talk about their family lives they give voice to:

- anxieties over dangerous environments and the lack of safe places to play
- lack of money to buy shoes for their children, curtains for the house or a holiday
- worry about their children's health before their own
- the particular difficulties of bringing up children as a lone parent
- the lack of day care
- the importance of support from family and friends.

(Smith 1996)

The breadth of family support has expanded considerably in the ten years since the Children Act was implemented. It now includes projects that strengthen the social network supports, for example parent support groups or multi-agency projects such as family literacy programmes and breakfast clubs. In supporting families with young children you may well find yourself working with or within one of the several projects discussed below. Indeed if you are committing yourself to a practice dedicated to reducing the effects of poverty and exclusion you may deliberately choose such work. Each of the approaches explained below have strong empirical evidence behind them that establishes their effectiveness in tackling exclusion. It is timely to recall that this is a period of unprecedented flux because new thinking, solid evidence and some targeted extra resources are coming together at the same time. This provides scope for you to be imaginative yourself and to engage in 'social entrepreneurial' activity. The range of possible projects for tackling exclusion are numerous but it often takes a small circle of like-minded practitioners to get them off the ground in any one area.

Homestart and NewPin

These are both well-known programmes in England and Wales that use parents to support one another. Homestart aims to help mothers restore control over their lives so that they can establish a positive environment for rearing their child. NewPin is similar in that it aims to relieve emotional stress, increase self-esteem, reduce depression and help create better parent–child relationships. Both schemes train women to provide emotional and practical support to new mothers who need it – whether in budgeting, cooking or coping with a crisis. Although referrals mainly come from health visitors social workers may also refer. The lessons from NewPin and Homestart are important: the programmes work with mothers on low incomes, living in poor housing, many of whom have suffered from domestic violence; some two-fifths have been lone parents and are socially isolated. Both programmes have received close evaluation indicating that even high-risk mothers felt greater levels of confidence and satisfaction and were better able to use other available supports (Little and Mount 1999: 63).

Parent-support groups

Parenting is a difficult task at the best of times; under exclusionary pressures, whether these are high neighbourhood crime rates, local racist activity, low income, overcrowding or poor housing, that task becomes highly stressful. Whatever their circumstances parents often want to learn more about parenting and to share their experiences. Perhaps they want to break the patterns set by their own parents when they were young or to gain the support of other parents locally or to learn techniques that would improve their own parenting skills. One way you can help parents to achieve more confidence and mastery is through a parents' support group.

Parent-support groups vary widely in what they cover. The focus may be on helping parents change the behaviour of their children or on the self-esteem and social networks of the parents themselves. What a group covers is related to who comes and why, and this may well depend on what organisation you work for, for example, parents may have to attend as part of a plan for having their children back from the care of the local authority.

A FATHER SPEAKS

'For me, in the early days, professionals appeared relatively infrequently and encounters with them were more easily containable. But as time wore on and the situation had become complex, the professionals came to feel present psychologically in our home, as if a camera were perpetually trained on us. Our life became the proverbial open book. Everything felt open to scrutiny, everything potentially to be justified. Our actions and our characters were dissected and discussed by others whom we did not know, whom we had not invited into our home, yet who would have an immense influence on our lives.'

(Paul Tosey, 'Making sense of interventions: Stranger in a strange land' in Wheal 2000)

Parenting is often carried out in isolation and can be emotionally draining since family relationships are close and often intense. Before establishing any group it is essential to find out what parents want. Make sure you have drawn on a range of contacts and consultative methods whether one-to-one interviews, focus groups, flip charts at meetings or questionnaires. The importance of this groundwork is crucial and parents must be involved from the start. Joint ownership and mutually agreed aims help underpin motivation and commitment to personal change. Above all involve parents in setting up and negotiating the programme. This is critical in making sure you have reached an agreed list of parenting issues. Often these may be around control, how to communicate more assertively, or wanting information on behaviour disorders such as attention deficit; you may want to think about how your group can respond to these.

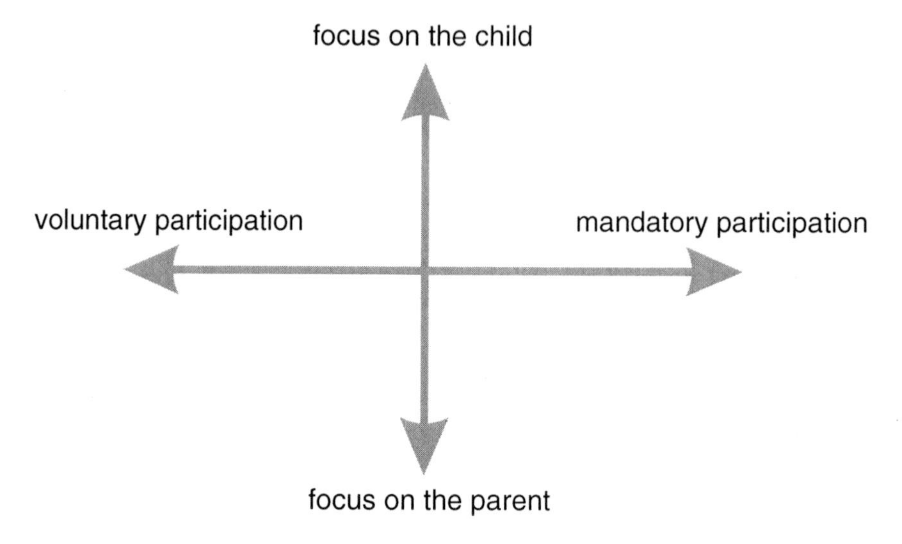

FIGURE 4.4 Types of parent education
Source: Adapted from Herbert and Napper 2000.

Grimshaw and Maguire (2000) interviewed a number of parents involved in parent groups (including those who decided not to attend). They found that:

- over half wanted to have access to a programme before the child reached the age of three
- a quarter were interested in children's behaviour, another quarter wanted information about child development and under 10 per cent were interested in educational issues
- most mentioned childcare as a basic requirement before they could attend
- there was strong preference for a 'leader' to be a parent or a professional *and* a parent.

ACTIVITY 4.4: RUNNING A PARENTS' GROUP

Prepare yourself for running a group by asking these questions:

- Values: why am I doing this? why do I think this is a good idea?
- Goals: what is my vision? what do I want to see happen in the long term and short term?
- Parents: what do I know about parents and their issues? what do I need to find out?
- Allies: who can I talk it over with? who has needed resources (able to free the time, provide seed money)? who will be encouraging but realistic?
- What do I need to equip myself to do it – training, materials, money?

In planning what your group will do and techniques in running such groups you can receive powerful assistance from publications such as *We Can Work it Out: Parenting with confidence* from Save the Children or *Tips: Tried and tested ideas for parent education and support* by Herbert and Napper. (Save the Children also run effective courses for would-be organisers.)

The important thing to remember is that you do not have to be a master of small-group work to start a group. Nor do you have to be an expert on parenting yourself. The qualities parents look for in a group leader are nearly all to do with being a good counsellor – the ability to communicate and listen, and to have patience, openness and compassion. You are first and foremost the facilitator of something extremely important to parents that will help them to regain a sense of control over their lives. As long as you have done the right groundwork with high levels of involvement the 'content' and the running of the group will emerge from that.

Neighbourhood family centres

One of the most flexible and effective ways of providing family support has proven to be family centres. They emerged in the early 1980s from existing children's nursery and day-care facilities to engage families in a number of different ways other than simply providing care for their child. Usually with a neighbourhood focus, they began to combine play facilities with a meeting space for parents, sometimes offering sophisticated interventions such as counselling, and leisure or educational activities for neighbourhood residents. There was from the start a flexibility of service and staff roles, the use of volunteers, an emphasis on participation and consultation, and a focus on the whole family rather than just the child. The range of services and participatory

TYPES OF FAMILY CENTRE

There are broadly four types of family centre.

1 Those with a client focus, which usually work only with families referred by the local authority because they are concerned about the neglect or abuse of the child.
2 Those with a community development approach. They are run by local organisations but encourage local residents to identify issues and offer indirect help as catalyst and enabler to community groups rather than providing services directly.
3 Those with a neighbourhood focus, which serve the immediate locality with a range of services.
4 Those making adult education provision and providing skills training, which overlap with the neighbourhood and community development types.

The latter significantly enhanced the self-esteem of users by equipping them with recognised skills for the job market and showed higher levels of participation and commitment.

(Holman 1988; Cannan 1992; Smith 1996)

approach offered a strong contrast with the risk-oriented proceduralism of local authority social services departments (Smith 1996).

THE PARK FAMILY CENTRE

The Centre is one of two run by Cheshire Social Services Department in the Chester and Ellesmere Port area. Its core purpose is to keep families together by promoting the upbringing of children in need by their families. At the Park fieldwork, outreach and sessional day-care service for families with children under 11 years of age are all integrated. Among its key tasks the Centre:

- offers support and guidance to parents where child protection concerns have been raised
- develops parenting skills to promote health, development and wellbeing of their children by running parent support groups
- provides support for looked-after children and foster parents through structured play sessions and summer scheme activities.

What is distinctive is the way the Park Family Centre has energetically responded to social exclusion. It has researched and been responsive to community needs by mounting adult literacy and family education groups. One of its notable projects is the education it provides for teenage mothers in the area, a joint project between social services, health and education.

The Centre has taken on partnerships enthusiastically. Staff are involved in the early years forum, are helping to initiate a local Sure Start and contribute to the Education Action Zone programme around school exclusions. It has strong links with the Cheshire Society for the Deaf and runs a support group for deaf parents and parents of deaf children. It also provides a range of community development activities – after-school clubs, adult basic skills programme and a family education scheme.

And this is essential: staff right through to management no longer view such work as residual, compensatory or optional but as vital to tackling exclusion in this industrial town on the eastern end of the Mersey. It has explicitly adopted the conclusions from *Messages from Research* (DoH 1995) and the concept of Best Value and made them central to the mission.

Family literacy schemes

Low achievement in education increases the probability of poverty and disadvantage later in adult life. But performing well in school is no longer regarded as the outcome only of the child–teacher relationship. Parental involvement in their child's education has been demonstrated to vastly enhance the attainments of that child.

One way of encouraging this is through family literacy schemes. These involve family members in suppporting the development of their child's reading, writing and talking. But they achieve more than that. They increase parental confidence and break a cycle of overly disciplinary styles of parenting through increased parental control and improved self-esteem. They also have been shown to break the cycle of disadvantage by removing some of the risk factors that may pre-dispose young males toward crime as they grow older (Crime Concern 1999a).

There is a positive correlation between levels of parental education and a child's proficiency in school. There is voluminous evidence to suggest that the involvement of parents in their child's education fosters that child's achievement. Yet children from poor and excluded backgrounds are less likely to have the advantages of living with highly educated adults and tend to perform less well on measures of reading comprehension (Handel 1999: 15). Literacy influence in families begins at the most basic level with children learning speech as their caretakers talk and interact spontaneously with them; later they watch their parents' and siblings' literacy behaviours and may use them as a model for their own (ibid.: 16).

Establishing family literacy schemes emphatically requires a partnership approach. Youth offending teams, social service agencies and local voluntary and community groups will all have an interest in the benefits of such a scheme. Those schemes that take place within primary schools (as opposed to nurseries, playgroups or local colleges) have been judged most effective principally because of the involvement of the head who drives the project forward. While teaching staff may play a prominent part in selecting children, if the scheme is collaborative selection should be a joint process (Crime Concern 1999a).

Families that are most likely to benefit from a family literacy scheme are those with:

- Children between 7 and 9 who show signs of school failure, particularly in literacy
- Children who demonstrate emotional and behavioural problems
- Parents who have low educational attainment themselves and may need help with literacy
- Parents who are reluctant to become involved in school activity but do seem to value education
- Parents who may benefit from advice on positive parenting.

(Crime Concern 1999a)

In most family literacy projects, parents will play an active part by reading or learning to read themselves alongside their children, carrying out library visits and writing shopping lists and notes. Families can build up a fund of expectations and attitudes toward literacy in which family routines and resources of information are put into place. Of course practitioners will have to be extremely sensitive as to what is at stake for the parents themselves. It is easy for an initiative to slip into paternalist habits. Parents may associate school with failure and feel inadequate; you do not want them to repeat the experience. The use of volunteers, whether retired or from a different social or ethnic background, may lead to transactions that are perceived as condescending, while attempts to develop charts and targets could be misunderstood and resented as not adult-oriented.

Breakfast clubs

Breakfast clubs are another initiative with strong evidence supporting their effectiveness. Children may be coming to school tired or hungry and unable to absorb the ideas or marshal the concentration for learning no matter how good the teaching at school. Breakfast clubs meet a number of important objectives simultaneously:

- They help to overcome 'food poverty' for families by providing a balanced meal at the beginning of the day.
- They ensure that children start the school day on time, feeling well nourished and settled.
- They enable parents to reconcile family and work life through the provision of a safe, supervised environment before school start, forming part of the network of out of school childcare which is a vital support for families with school-age children.
- They overcome educational difficulties arising from erratic attendance and poor concentration and behaviour, especially in the first years of primary school.

(Donovan and Street 1999)

Breakfast clubs usually run from 7.30 or 8.00 a.m. until school begins. Children may attend one, two or more days a week depending on the working patterns of their parents or carers. They can take place in schools or community centres and usually combine the opportunity to eat with other activities such as free play, arts or homework, depending on the age of the children. They may be organised by the local authority, voluntary agency, local businesses or by schools themselves.

The process of setting up an effective breakfast club

- Assess parental demand beforehand either through questionnaires to parents or informal meetings; follow these up with newsletters and feedback forms so that the extent of parental interest and commitment is always known.
- Encourage parents to use the club – it is important to build up general support for it.
- Check what the children like and vary what is offered to keep the club fun; involve children in collecting money and choosing the menu; have 'special days' and packs to reward good attendance.
- Open access for all minimises stigma and encourages maximum uptake.
- Community clubs need good links with their schools; schools actively encourage children to attend and reinforce the importance of breakfast, nutrition and health through teaching.
- Keep it simple in terms of staffing, funding and activities; many clubs draw on existing school staff such as dinner personnel and teaching assistants but volunteers (with police checks) are also important.

Participation and family support

In all family support projects that invoke parental involvement there is the risk that participation will be tokenistic. This may be because the *process* of setting them up may be participatory but the *objectives* may be pre-set and have wholly to do with various benchmarks or targets for attainments by the users – parents and children – who have had little say in the overall framework. Smith notes two different ideas of power embedded in notions of participation in work with children and families (1996: 183):

1 Parents' learning to parent or cope with their children's behaviour from role models in places like family centres depends on high levels of participation – requiring their active presence day after day – yet power rests with the staff and associated professionals throughout. This will apply to referred clients within a context of child protection objectives.
2 People's rights to make decisions that affect their lives, which does not demand so much day to day involvement but does assume high levels of user influence. In practice, however, power still rests with practitioners because that is how the situation is set up in the first place. Tellingly she writes that 'staff may be more or less "empowering" only once [this] basic fact is recognised.'

(ibid.: 183)

Getting the balance right, and finding the right ways to ascertain parents' views and to utilise their contributions, is an important skill. One way is to draw on participatory techniques more associated with community development. Since many family support initiatives have a neighbourhood dimension such techniques become increasingly helpful. One such is participatory appraisal (PA), a methodology that creates a cycle of information gathering, reflection and learning. In PA groups of participants move through these stages looking at their perceptions of their present situation, identifying blocks or gaps that prevent them from obtaining what they want or need and then proposing solutions or areas for change. Normally sessions are undertaken by groups of peers with people choosing to participate at their own level (New Economics Foundation n.d.) The merit of PA is that it can be used with large or small groups, and in homes or small relational meetings for a range of diverse purposes. It is also highly visual – relying on diagrams, rankings of priorities, timelines, mapping. (For this and other ideas the New Economics Foundation's guide *Participation Works!* provides a helpful source with further contacts listed.)

EARLY YEARS WORK

Our understanding of the importance of a child's pre-school experience has greatly expanded from the time the Children Act was passed in 1989. Indeed overcoming the effects of deprivation and exclusion through concerted initiatives for children age 0–4 has matured, and a number of recent studies point to several important conclusions:

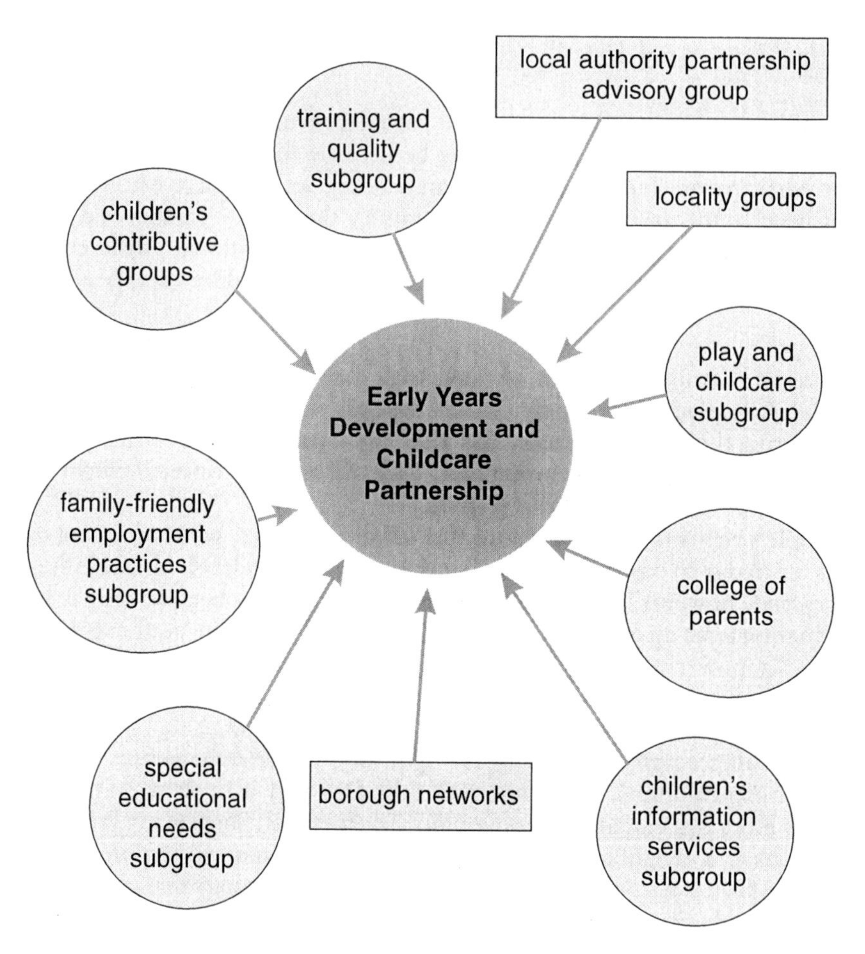

FIGURE 4.5 Sefton's early years partnership model

Source: Adapted from NCB 2000.

- The need for a variety of learning experiences which are active, relevant and enjoyable
- Integration of education and care in a well-planned, stimulating and healthy environment
- An appropriate curriculum encouraging active learning and 'purposeful play'
- Partnership between parents and educators.

Despite the positive underpinning given family support initiatives in the Children Act most local authorities were wedded in the mid-1990s to a deficit model of services giving highest priority in terms of resources to child protection. By the late 1990s the convergence of evidence and a number of voices from the Confederation of British Industry to the Labour Party were urging the benefits of an integrated early years service as a way of moving beyond this. Persuasive data from the US demonstrated that for every dollar invested there was a long-term net return of at least seven times that amount (Jamieson and Owen 2000: 13). With the election of a Labour government in 1997 each area was asked to develop early-years partnerships, including local authority departments, in an attempt to try and establish service integration for the 0–5-year-olds at ground level.

Local partnership plans should:

- Enhance the care, play and educational experience of young children.
- Be directed by the diverse needs and aspiration of children, and of their parents.
- Pay attention to the support of families.
- Build active partnerships that can bring together enough members to ensure coverage of all relevant local initiatives.

Children with disability

With the arrival of a disabled child the family is suddenly exposed to the exclusion experienced by many disabled people: parents of disabled children report that the family is frequently marginalised and isolated by friends, relatives and customary social networks. They become used to being stared at in public and the topic of other people's conversations (Dobson *et al.* 2001). Their family no longer evokes positive feelings and warmth but becomes the object of pity. As Dobson and her colleagues write, 'By being treated as a "matter of regret" they [are] stripped of their family status and denied the same emotional and social worth as "normal" families' (Dobson *et al.* 2001).

Economic hardship for the family also often ensues since the costs of raising a child with a disability are more than twice those for a non-disabled child, with heavier expenditure on medical items and toiletries, such as nappies, creams and clothes, as well as items to amuse, occupy and stimulate. Parents' earning power is also more constrained as a result of diminished employment opportunities from having to provide greater amounts of direct care even for older children, while benefit levels do not meet the extra costs or loss of earning power. Of the families with disabled children that Dobson *et al.* surveyed parents were able to spend only half of what they felt was required to ensure a reasonable standard of living for their child; this particularly applied to children up to the age of five.

For social work the dominance of an individual rather than social model has prevented practitioners from recognising as clearly as they should these exclusionary barriers. The Children Act 1989 requires local authorities to provide services in their area designed to minimise the effect of disability on disabled children and to give disabled children the opportunity to lead as 'normal' lives as is possible (see Schedule 2, section 6). But services have not necessarily succeeded in this objective. Part of the difficulty has been professional detachment from the concerns and objectives that families with young disabled children have. Too often services for disabled children have been located with a risk and protection perspective thus marginalising services to promote inclusion (Oliver and Sapey, 1999: 85).

The framework for assessment should help practitioners to focus more intently the exclusionary social factors that thwart full development. As a consequence, since April 2001 social workers are required to adopt a child-focused model of assessment that will do away with the split between safeguarding the child and promoting her or his development (Wonnacott and Kennedy 2001).

Jack (2000) shows how an ecological approach addresses many of the multiple barriers experienced by families with disabled children because it encourages the practitioner to look at areas such as material disadvantage and local discriminatory attitudes within services. According to Jack families with disabled children require:

- information on services and how to access them, particularly practical services such as child care, short breaks and help in the home
- changing local social awareness around discrimination in transport, recreation and leisure facilities
- focus on the strengths or weaknesses of social networks
- income maximisation.

To obtain these social workers should use their organisational roles to develop procedures, allocate resources and shape public attitudes that challenge the exclusion and discrimination disabled children face by explicitly adopting community-building strategies (Jack 2000).

Providing information is the essential starting point. Parents of disabled children advance strikingly similar criteria for good-quality information irrespective of the child's disability:

- The way in which information is presented and delivered and how it is organised is crucial
- Information on the roles of *all* the different agencies involved in providing services for families with disabled children is needed
- Books, leaflets and videos are not enough by themselves; all such formats need to be supplemented with personal contact and guidance from those giving the information.

(Mitchell and Sloper 2000)

Thus parents tell us there are three dimensions to useful information: i. brief leaflets outlining services and benefits; ii. longer booklets for more detailed understanding; iii. a person with whom to interact.The role of a professional variously called 'key worker' 'link person' or 'facilitator' to guide parents through the maze of service provision is important here (Mitchell and Sloper 2000; Braye 2001). Braye suggests that there is potential for such a key worker to under take holistic assessment of need and to co-ordinate any specialist health or medical involvement within the framework of the social model. To make the role work well for the family, family members have to be engaged from the start with the role negotiated and spelled out clearly. Set up in this manner the key worker can become effective in promoting inclusion (Braye 2001).

Addressing the exclusion of disabled children requires the acknowledgement that institutional discrimination of disability is inherent in the systems that surround the child in ways similar to institutional racism. The need to develop materials, procedures and practices to enable non-verbal disabled children and those with complex health needs to participate in assessment and careplanning is pressing. Equally pressing is the need to adapt services to meet the perspectives of distinct ethnic communities. Some initiatives now underway – a Bangladeshi social worker in one London borough working with families, using local voluntary organisations to provide befrienders and advocates or an Asian Disability Training Team to influence the design and delivery of services in Bradford – offer useful examples of what might be done.

Short breaks

Short breaks for parents with disabled children are a crucial service for supporting those families within the community and expanding family networks (SSI 1998). The Quality Protects programme also specifically mentions expanding short-break provision for families with disabled children as does Children First in Wales. According to the SSI some 10,000 children use short-break services to have time away from home in new environments and the chance to develop new relationships and try new activities.

Short-break carers until recently have provided overnight services but are now expanding to include day care, sitting and befriending, and in home support for families (Prewett 2000). In her survey, Prewett found that most carers within short-break schemes had experience with disabled children, either through personally knowing a child who needed a short break or through working with disabled people professionally or as volunteers. Carers themselves reported finding a range of rewards and satisfactions for themselves in the work with developed commitment to the individual children they cared for (ibid.).

CASE STUDY 4: SHORT BREAKS

A seve- year-old boy, with autism, moderate learning difficulties and behaviour problems was one of five children. His parents were wary of the way social services arranged 'respite care' and chose not to use it. Their chief objection lay in the fact that they had no voice in the selection of any proposed carer. The organiser of a local parent support group, however, found a couple specifically interested in befriending a child with special needs. The social worker, in touch with that support group, encouraged the boy's parents and the boy to meet this couple at the local Saturday club that he attended with other children with special needs. They all met at the club and the beginnings of a relationship was formed which had the parents' confidence. The boy subsequently began short visits to the couple's home and these eventually extended into overnight stays.

(Jack 2000)

While the gains of short breaks for disabled children are clearly established and address some exclusionary barriers, the biggest problem for social workers is having enough carers in local schemes to meet need. Prewett has summarised effective practice in boosting recruitment of carers for local schemes (2000):

- Use professional quality advertising with positive disability images
- Highlight the enjoyment, satisfaction and rewards for short-break carers
- Highlight the skills and experiences gained which are useful in other careers
- Involve current short-break carers and users in raising awareness
- Emphasise the quality training in preparation and the ongoing training and support that follows

- Adopt a community-wide strategy:
  - give talks to community groups
  - ensure that specific groups – young people, black carers, lone parents, for example – are welcome
  - employ scheme managers and workers from minority ethnic backgrounds.

The way breaks are arranged is also important. The service-based model for respite care is usually triggered when a family makes a request for short-term care and a project worker identifies a suitable carer. But in what has come to be called a 'resource model' the social worker works with parents to identify and extend existing child care networks – whether babysitters, playgroups, childminders and family centres – and finds sources for short-term breaks within them and with the family's active collaboration (Jack 2000).

Sure Start

The aim of Sure Start schemes is to provide concentrated help for low-income families with young children under four, in the form of multi-agency attention to early cognitive development, parent education and health of the entire family. Local programmes are neighbourhood based and generally include between 500 and 1000 children under four. While all children in a designated area are eligible the programme focuses primarily on disadvantaged children. The aim is to work with parents of children aged three years and younger to promote the physical, intellectual and social development of their offspring so that they thrive when they do get to school (Glass 1999). Sure Start objectives include:

- Improving social and emotional development by helping families to function more effectively.
- Improving the ability of children to learn by encouraging stimulating play and so improving language skills.
- Strengthening families and communities by enhancing involvement in the community and improving the sensitivity of existing family support services.

Sure Start is evidence-based, so that research such as that concerning HighScope becomes extremely relevant to individual projects. All programmes are required to involve parents, so that they can solve their own problems, and together with children's services decide those approaches most effective for them. Cowley has concisely brought together evidence from across the various domains of early educational and social intervention, community development and health visiting (Cowley 1999).

The HighScope 'curriculum', which originated in the US, has had a significant impact in the UK, both on the direction that partnerships should take and their day-to-day work. It is based on the following principles:

- Certain key experiences are central to young children's development and these can be grouped under various headings: social relations and initiative, creative representation, music and movement, language and literacy, classification, numbering, sequencing, space and time. These key experiences happen most

MAKING A SURE START APPLICATION

1. Don't wait for other agencies to take the initiative: in conjunction with your agency set the ball rolling yourself.
2. Make sure you know your target area well:
   - health needs: take up of ante-natal care, perinatal illness and mortality
   - demographic profile
   - degree of deprivation (family needs indicators), overcrowding, rate of unemployment, children in poverty
3. Engage with parents to the fullest extent possible. This means plenty of meetings, one-to-one sessions, small house meetings, approaches to community centres and other places where parents gather. All the time keep in mind that you are trying to find out what parent and family needs for under-fours are in the area – you are not there to sell your service.
4. Draw on existing service partnerships between agencies; make sure you communicate what you learn fully and swiftly to other interested parties. Primary care groups, early years' development and child-care partnerships are obvious places to begin. Discuss findings on need and what they signify.
5. Demonstrate the effectiveness of your work. Talk about it and write about it. Always give credit to the families – which in truth *is* theirs. A good community organiser remains in the background supporting and facilitating the work of local residents.
6. Secure evaluation and forms of monitoring. All projects must achieve certain targets; for example 75 per cent of families reporting experience of improved services for family support and a reduction of 10 per cent of children on the child protection register.

(Bidmead 1999; DfEE website 1999)

often when children are actively learning through handling materials, talking about what happened, experimenting and exploring for themselves.

- Adults should take an interactive role by observing, supporting and extending the children's interests, knowledge, skills and understanding.
- The environment should be arranged in a logical way, allowing children to help themselves to what they need; thus rooms are carefully arranged with different items labelled.
- Work with parents as part of the team.

(O'Flaherty 1995)

HighScope uses a well-defined pattern. At the beginning is 'circle time', when each child is greeted and acknowledged. Then in 'plan–do–review' sessions the main sequences of activity are planned out for the day. These are child-led, with less emphasis on keeping tidy and more on 'doing' and 'exploring'. During the day the child's experiences are linked immediately to learning:

- using language and literacy: reading signs, symbols and their own writing
- classifying, comparing and arranging things in a series or in patterns
- numeracy
- initiative and social relations: taking care of their own needs, expressing feelings, becoming sensitised to the feelings of others and to group routines
- tidying up; recall and review afterwards
- lunch: rest and recreation.

The gains in such an approach are well established: language deficits are addressed, while behaviour, through adherence to the daily routine of plan–do–recall, improves concentration. The 'child-choice' philosophy gives a sense of control over the child's life (O'Flaherty 1995).

ACTIVITY 4.5: MS RICE, RICKY AND ROBERT

Ms Rice is 23 years old and the mother of two boys, Ricky aged six, and Robert aged three. Three weeks ago she left her male partner one evening, fleeing their home with both children before he returned from the pub. He had assaulted her twice in the month prior to her leaving, both times after drinking heavily. There were no violent incidents prior to this. They lived on a housing estate on the edge of the city that mixed some owner-occupied homes with homes owned by a housing association.

After she left she went first to a women's refuge elsewhere in the city, then briefly to her own mother's home near where she had previously lived. She has now been re-housed on a social housing estate on the city edge by the local authority. She can't help but notice that there is a high percentage of lone mothers also bringing up children in the neighbourhood.

Ms Rice is white and has two South-east Asian women friends whom she met when living with her husband. Both are devout Muslims. She misses their company and found their conversation about spiritual matters the first really interesting discussions she had had for a long time. On alternate Saturday afternoons she observes a group of six men with football scarves parading out of the estate toward the local football ground. She knows that there are racist comments and hate-chanting in the stands when visiting teams with black players play, because it has been reported in the press.

Ms Rice intended to find work, perhaps two or three days a week, before her husband assaulted her; now she is not sure she can. She has no GCSEs and left school at 16 with a record of truancy. Her older son Ricky began school near their previous home; he was extremely restless in class, and unable to sit down for more than a few moments. Much individual teaching time was devoted to him and the school suggested it was possible that attention deficit disorder and hyperactivity were getting in the way of his learning. When the family were re-housed he had to attend the primary school on the new estate. Although bright and cheerful inside, the school is dilapidated on the outside. It is also the target for regular vandalism and has grates on some of the windows. Ricky's behaviour has become much worse since he started there and in that short time Ms Rice has been called in several times for discussions about him with the head teacher. She has no idea how to settle him down.

Review the initiatives and perspectives outlined in this chapter so far. With a colleague brainstorm those which you think might help Ms Rice and her children. Then decide which of those you would raise with Ms Rice first. What are your reasons for such a priority? Ask yourselves how practical such approaches would be in your area. What could you do to make facilitate their implementation? As for income, what benefits is Ms Rice entitled to? What are the strengths and weaknesses in her social networks?

COMMUNITY DEVELOPMENT AND THE IMPORTANCE OF NEIGHBOURHOOD

Many studies have linked local conditions of poverty and deprivation to a high proportion of children in need and incidence of child abuse.

Garbarino and Gilliam (1980) have argued that child abuse is strongly linked to three conditions in the social ecology of the neighbourhoods:

1. A cultural context that condones domestic violence in general and violence toward children in particular.
2. Families that experience stress in their life circumstances combined with isolation from important support systems that might protect them.
3. Consensual values concerning family autonomy and parental 'ownership' of children.

In the UK the Rowntree Foundation *Inquiry into Income and Wealth* described a cycle of 'poor parenting' on the poorest urban social housing estates in which poverty is the context for other factors such as high rates of family break-up, inability to provide for the needs of children, social isolation and high rates of unemployment among young people who may at the same time already be parents (Hills 1995). Five times the number of children were placed on child protection registers from such estates than from other areas in the same city(ibid.: 35).

We have already underscored the importance of locality in understanding social exclusion. For families with low income experiencing high levels of stress and with vulnerable children, the neighbourhood within which they live underpins much of their predicament. Thompson (1995) summarises how deprived neighbourhoods reinforce the exclusion of families. In what he calls 'transitional neighbourhoods' there is a shift from collective to individualistic strategies of family management. Parents are willing to delegate authority to formal institutions that have lost their credibility and command of external resources. Informal networks become weak as kin and close friends move out and are replaced by new residents who are regarded as outsiders. The family grows distant from formal and informal structures that reinforce parental standards. Other adults in the community are no longer relied on to supervise and sponsor children (Thompson 1995).

The attention to 'neighbourhood effects' on families generally focuses on social isolation, feeble networks and poor quality services that parents experience. For example, Garbarino (1983), in his careful research in the US, concluded that the difference between high-risk and low-risk neighbourhoods lay primarily in mothers' perception of the nature of *neighbourhood exchanges*. Mothers in high-risk neighbourhoods (in those localities where children were significantly more at risk of abuse) were more likely *not* to ask for assistance from neighbours. In high-risk neighbourhoods there was a limited reciprocity of assistance, although their perception of sources of help on which they could draw – family, co-workers, friends and neighbours – was the same. Thus within similar neighbourhoods the perception of and reliance on networks were powerful considerations.

This evidence does not establish individually low-income parents are more abusive because they are poor, but it does point to the necessity of incorporating a neighbourhood-oriented, community development dimension to work with children and families. Lloyd argues that community development methods combat social disadvantage by targeting the first level of prevention on Hardiker's framework (see Chapter 2) for local populations and vulnerable communities. Community development enables 'people living in poor communities to participate in projects and to increas[e] the strengths of such communities by enhancing the capabilities of individuals to enter into reciprocal exchanges – the basis of a social network' (1997: 144 citing Canaan 1992).

In a similar vein Henderson suggests that we reconstruct community development so that we can work more strategically and skilfully with excluded children. To do this he says that we have to undertake two paradigmatic shifts:

1 Move away from a narrow social work interpretation of the phrase 'working with children'. By this he means social work's preoccupation with 'direct work with children', gearing its services primarily to detecting child abuse, and with therapeutic models of family intervention that have encumbered wider engagement with neighbourhood and local institutions.
2 Move towards integration with economic and regeneration programmes. This is to play a full and important part in the many joined-up programmes around neighbourhood renewal which are focusing as much on the social fabric and social capital of a locality as on economic regeneration.

(Henderson 1997: 28)

Community development involves working on issues that affect children and families – drugs, prostitution, homelessness, problems with school – or helping to establish a credit union, women's refuge or adult education classes. This emphasis assumes that resources and individual behaviour are influenced by both neighbourhood attitudes and by services operating in a neighbourhood. To mobilise stakeholders in an area requires community development skills of enabling and liaison (Smith 1996: 179).

Both relational skills and community development skills need to be deployed and we explore these in Chapter 7. For now, to see how the one set of skills can reinforce the other it is important to listen to parents and what they need, and to read widely in the accumulated research of what parents want. Users say that learning about children's development and coping with their own children is their most important aim. Parents approach projects wanting somewhere for their children to play and to have a

CASE STUDY 5: BARNARDOS ANTI-POVERTY STRATEGY

Barnardos launched its anti-poverty strategy in 1995, with pilot schemes in eight different disadvantaged communities across the four nations of the UK. Among them are Tullycarnet in Belfast, Ley Hill in Birmingham, Hollinwood in Oldham, Possilpark in Glasgow and Tonyrefail in the Rhondda. It is an experimental initiative designed to highlight what works; as such it is being extensively evaluated from the beginning using the 'theory of change' approach (see Chapter 7).

The strategy has adopted a number of principles:

- Participation through the involvement of local citizens and community groups in the planning, implementing and reviewing of activities. These include community campaigning and representation on multi-agency forums. The active participation of children is particularly important and is being systematically developed.
- Partnership with local voluntary and community groups, the public sector and some private sector interests. Pilot staff are increasingly acting as a catalyst and conduit for strengthening local groups to work with each other and other agencies.
- Multi-dimensionality, in that a third of the initiatives within the schemes are adult oriented, including skills training, confidence and capacity building, supporting local community groups and campaigning. Improving the environment and making a safe place to live and play is a main focus for six out of the eight projects. In Oldham, for example, there are schemes to bulk-buy nappies, safety equipment and nearly-new clothes, and a credit union has been established.
- Child focus is found in activities such as arts, crafts, drama and play. Children and young people are involved in planning and reviewing each project with concerted efforts now under way to broaden the channels for their having a say about their communities

(see Traynor and Davidson 2000 for a comprehensive evaluation of the strategy)

local baby clinic. They want to go to nearby adult education classes in numeracy and English, sewing or sociology. They want to be able to meet friends, to obtain day care for older relatives and to be able to ask staff or other professionals for advice; that is what they want projects for (Smith 1996).

In devising community development approaches that tackle the exclusion of families with young children the large voluntary organisations have generated important models and ideas. Among others, Barnardos and Save the Children have set up multi-city projects that combine family support services, such as family centres with neighbourhood work in the form of co-ops, credit unions and family literacy schemes. This work, under way for the better part of a decade, is now being extensively evaluated and offers a fund of ideas and experiences (see Hughes and Traynor 2000; Lloyd 1997; Traynor and Davidson 2000).

ACTIVITIES IN OLDHAM

The Barnardos project in Oldham has initiated or become involved in numerous community-building activities which are broadening the local capacity of families and neighbourhood. These include:

- Library Arts and Crafts providing structured activities for children after school with local parents and teenage volunteers helping to organise and run it.
- Holiday activities offering provision during school holidays, again using local volunteers.
- A homework club at a primary school which has established study support groups for pupils of local schools, with parents and adult volunteers helping to run the club.
- Limeside Learning Centre, providing facilities for homework and study as well as opportunities for further learning.
- Baby bulk-buy, providing low-cost nappies to parents in the Limeside area and training volunteers to run this as a community activity.
- A parenting skills group which provides a course aimed at local parents, with a crèche run by local volunteers.
- A Job Shop, providing information and assistance for people seeking work.
- A Credit Union, which provides a simple way for people to save and borrow money. Training has been provided to enable local people to become officers and committee members. The long-term view is that this should become a community-controlled bank.
- 'Redlining', an awareness programme showing how credit applications are being refused by city financial institutions on the grounds of postcode.
- Providing community work training for local people who are, or who want to be, involved in community work.

(from Traynor and Davidson 2000: 59)

SOUTH BIRMINGHAM FAMILY SERVICE UNIT

In one of the pioneering efforts to combine casework with community development South Birmingham FSU made major investment in a deprived housing estate throughout the 1980s. It:

- persuaded all major services to conduct regular surgeries on the estate. As a result of this the take-up of claims increased and the scheme gave local residents a greater understanding of how service systems work.
- offered a greatly expanded advice service with major outreach, including door-step encounters for whole streets to find out how much need was going unmet.

- a major campaign to fit insulated windows and doors and other insulation in dwellings that were hard to heat because of their construction.
- organised clean-up campaigns to clear unwanted rubbish while getting the departmental health departments to review the positioning of rubbish chutes and providing skips so that large items of refuse could be discarded;
- began income maximisation efforts focused on additional benefits for those with incontinent children and adults in the family
- inaugurated a drop-in service for parents. This became the mainspring for more formal groupwork which focused on literacy and numeracy, confidence raising, self-defence and parent education.
- started a nursery for pre-schoolers, where previously there had been no child-care facilities on the estate, and introduced holiday schemes for school-aged children.

(Thomas 2001)

ACTIVITY 4.6: MS RICE AGAIN

Assume you are a community support worker for a large voluntary agency that works with children and families and that you have been asked to work with Ms Rice and her children (see p. 94). The health visitor attached to the refuge had 'concerns' for the children's health and is worried that the level of domestic violence they have perhaps witnessed has been destructive. Ms Rice's former partner is full of remorse and has written her a letter saying how much he wants her back. He has not however made any financial contribution thus far. On your first visit to the estate you notice that there are no child-care facilities, that there are significant amounts of rubbish lying unattended, and that there are no sources of advice for parents on their children's behaviour.

What neighbourhood-based initiatives do you think would be helpful to Ms Rice and others in a similar position? What practicalities would you have to contend with to put these initiatives in place?

KEY POINTS

- ❑ The relationship between children in need and social exclusion has been explained and the importance of the Department of Health's assessment framework for both has been underlined.
- ❑ Some of the building blocks for tackling exclusion have been applied to working with low-income families with young children, focusing on income, networks and joining in partnerships to create new multi-agency initiatives.
- ❑ Pathways for creating parent-support groups, breakfast clubs and family literacy schemes have been laid down.

- ❑ The critical nature of early years' work in tearing down exclusionary barriers for families has been underscored, and two projects (Sure Start and anti-bias programmes for very young children) have been explained.
- ❑ Practitioners were offered a family scenario through which they could explore and apply some of the approaches discussed.

KEY READING

Michael Little and Kevin Mount, *Prevention and Early Intervention with Children in Need* (Ashgate, 1999). This is a wonderful text that draws together the evidence on the effectiveness of many different programmes and approaches to working with children and young people in need. It is concise – only 112 pages long – and its format is so engaging that its teaching is both profound and easy to digest.

Department of Health, *Framework for the Assessment of Children in Need and their Families* (The Stationery Office, 2000). This is required reading, certainly for all social workers with direct or indirect statutory responsibilities for children in need. The framework gives greater weight to factors responsible for social exclusion and is a collaborative effort between the Department of Health, the Home Office and the Department for Education and Employment.

Crescy Cannan and Chris Warren (eds) *Social Action with Children and Families. A community development approach to child and family welfare* (Routledge, 1997). This volume has a number of important contributions on family centres, family support services, children's rights and community development.

CHAPTER 5

REVERSING THE EXCLUSION OF YOUNG PEOPLE

OBJECTIVES

By the end of the chapter you should understand:

- How exclusion undermines the transition to adulthood
- The tasks and responsibilities that social workers have for young people leaving care or accommodation.
- Approaches to working with excluded young people such as truants, teenage mothers, young offenders and young rough sleepers
- The importance of links with schools
- How to strengthen young people's networks through mentoring schemes.

We have explained that social exclusion as a process is grounded in poverty and disadvantage but works across several dimensions of social life, with lack of access to education and work, weakened social networks and loss both of self-esteem and influence over events. As a process social exclusion has a disproportionate impact on young people. This chapter explains why this is so and lays out a number of approaches that social workers may adopt, either on their own or in partnership with other agencies and local organisations.

SOCIAL WORK AND YOUNG PEOPLE

Today's social workers undertake many different tasks in relation to young people. These may include: diverting young people from offending by working as part of a local authority youth-offending team, helping to tackle youth homelessness by working with a voluntary agency, looking after adolescents who are subject to care orders in a residential home, or supporting 17- or 18-year-olds in learning to live independently. Social workers may act as family support workers with young mothers, or as education social workers (also known as education welfare officers or social inclusion officers) helping to resolve problems around school attendance or exclusion from school.

A social worker in the early 1980s would not have difficulty in recognising these roles and indeed might have undertaken them all within a varied caseload. But that same social worker would be surprised at how much of this work is now closely enmeshed in that of other professionals. He or she would be even more surprised at the range of new posts that require social work skills, for example New Deal counsellors, Gateway advisers and personal advisers with the Connexions scheme.

To understand this new joined-up approach to working with socially excluded young people you need to know something about the immense changes affecting the transition from youth to adulthood. In Chapter 1 we emphasised certain key economic changes that have made life choices more competitive, uncertain and skill-dependent than twenty or thirty years ago. The impact of these changes has widened the inequality between groups of young people. For example, at a time of near full employment for the population as a whole there has been a substantial rise in youth unemployment. In 1998 some 18 per cent of 16- and 17-year-olds were unemployed as were 11 per cent of 18–24-year-olds (Howarth *et al.* 2000). While it is true that periods of unemployment are relatively short, the number of *recurring* applications for Jobseekers' Allowance within these age ranges is also high. Thus precisely at that time in life when family relationships and leaving home already make a transition to adulthood difficult, the casual, temporary nature of available work adds a further burden, especially for those with few skills.

For nearly 10 per cent of those aged between 16 and 18 the high-skill economy leaves them poorly equipped to become independent. These are the so-called 'off register' youth – those not in education, employment or training, mothers under 16 years old and the hidden unemployed among them. Their passage to adulthood is encumbered with personal or family problems, poverty and other kinds of social exclusion so that clear steps to independence are missing and their goals and transition points are

GOVERNMENT INITIATIVES FOR YOUNG ADULTS

- Effective outreach for marginalised young people
- Advice and guidance services for young people (Connexions)
- Community-based organisations' contributions
- Smoothing the transition from learning to workplace.

(adapted from Howarth *et al.* 2000)

confused. When leaving home is triggered by problems such as pregnancy, unemployment or family conflict it is even more fraught (DSS 1999).

Listening and participating in decisions

Before we look at specific kinds of work that practitioners undertake it is helpful for you to think about what young people want who face exclusionary barriers. There is no substitute for hard listening to the young people you work with but in the meantime you can do important preparatory work here by reading several publications that convey what young people themselves are saying such as *The Real Deal* and *Listening to Young People*, or *All*

YOUNG PEOPLE SPEAK ABOUT 'COMMUNITY'

Tim, a young black Londoner of 24, says:

> 'No, I don't [feel part of a community]. No, I fought it at home to make it in this world. You have got to make it for yourself. There is no community willing to help you or are helping you at the moment – not that they can't, there are the resources there to help you if [they] want to but they don't'

Stacey, a white Londoner of 18, says:

> 'It depends, community is lots of different things, you want a community when you're living in a hostel atmosphere like a group of people who are in the – like – the same situation as yourself and things like that. I mean community could be anything, like in Liverpool where I'm from, the community could be something like the little house where I come from'

Young white people say:

> 'This is a bad estate. It's well known to the police and I'm well known to the police. I always feel vulnerable and I'm always being picked up just because my face is known. I would like to be able to move and make a fresh start but I can't.'

> 'A lot of getting into trouble is about where you live. The estate is a bad place. The people are all right but the houses and everything are bad. It's all run down. No one else seems to care about us so we get that way that we don't care either.'

> 'There are gangs of kids all around the estate. There's nothing else for them to do round here so they are on the street all the time. I don't like it and there's always the possibility of trouble there's nothing else for them to do, do you know what I mean?'

(Bentley and Oakley 1999; Goldson 2000)

Together Now. There you will encounter a sense of the aloneness and distrust in some of the very sources of support that we might presume to be effective, but you will also be briefed on how a diverse range of young people perceive community, adults and issues of identity. You will also discover that young people regularly return to the same issues: drugs, decisions about education, training and employment, bullying and harassment, lack of money and debt, contraception and pregnancy and problems with the law.

From these conversations you get a different notion of 'community' – sometimes something that is limiting and intrusive, sometimes referring to anyone who helps out or listens (as among homeless people). What comes through is the importance of self-reliance, the wish to escape rules and feelings of isolation and exclusion, particularly by older people.

What young people want for themselves in the end differs little from what people in general want, but their perceptions about how to obtain these wants and what supports there are along the way differs significantly from what an older generation of practitioners might have experienced. Young people want:

- respect and understanding
- to be consulted and taken seriously
- accessible and affordable places to meet
- to share the aspirations of the rest of us: to have a job, a home and significant relationships
- to share concerns over environment and matters like personal safety, transport and leisure.

(Save the Children 1998)

Young people of all backgrounds have a strong interest in the environment and many ideas as to how their local area should develop. Along with this they have expertise and solutions to the problems that they uniquely face. So it is important to develop initiatives that involve them not only in decisions that affect them individually or on specific services but also in forums and decisions that shape their communities collectively. Ensuring that the diverse voices of young people – across gender, cultures and age groups – are heard in ways that have impact is extremely important.

Encouraging young people to express their views in relation to the kinds of services they want and to contribute to decisions about specific initiatives requires new structures. Many of the regeneration projects that we refer to in Chapter 7 mandate high levels of participation and often young people are involved formally in this process. There are also young persons' parish councils and other citizenship-building projects. More general youth councils are now emerging, drawing on specific constituencies such as school, to discuss a youth agenda and to take decisions to raise the concerns of young people with local government.

Young people have had a longer tradition of giving voice on services that affect them. The National Association for Young People in Care and now organisations led by young people, such as Who Cares? (Scotland), play a vital role in shaping services and at the same time offer practical support for young individuals (Save the Children 1998).

Gender differences

Differences in the behaviour and outlook of young people persist although there are perceptible changes in attitudes to some areas of social life (Williamson 1995). Boys

BOLTON YOUNG PEOPLE'S ADVICE AND SUPPORT SERVICE (BYPASS)

BYPASS provides advice, support and information for young people aged 16–25 years. User involvement is the cornerstone of its operation which is run from an advice and drop-in centre. It offers advice on welfare rights and housing, counselling and sexual health; it supports young people in care and runs a supported accommodation for homeless young people.

The casual, friendly welcome has been wholly arranged by young people themselves. Half the volunteers are former users of the centre who have had peer education training and then become friends and counsellors. The system of volunteering creates a dynamic sense of community through which young people change their own lives and contribute to the wellbeing of others.

(adapted from Save the Children 1998)

are more likely than girls to perform delinquent acts, engage in bullying, play truant, become permanently excluded from school or commit suicide. They are more likely to engage in anti-social behaviour and abuse drugs. There is also evidence that boys are less likely to seek help or to talk about their problems with others.

Girls are more prone to eating disorders, engage in more acts of deliberate self-harm and have a greater likelihood of becoming young carers. They may also have greater problems with self-confidence (Madge *et al.* 2000). It is easy to develop stereotypes around such gender differences and to miss the fact that each set of behaviours can create a basis on which the young person is excluded from work and community, whether through poor educational attainment, anti-social behaviour or early pregnancy. But the differences in behaviour and in the ways that help is sought and used are sufficient to raise the question of whether different approaches to working with boys and girls is required (ibid.).

Relationship building

Building relationships with many marginalised young people is not straightforward because of negative past experiences and perhaps constricted opportunities for personal and social development. Sometimes unresponsive in conversation, erratic in time planning, acting on impulse – these are common habits among adolescents (Coleman and Hendry 1999). But it is important always to remember: despite the difficulties and your feelings of not getting anywhere, the young person's interaction with parents, teachers, friends, mentors and you is the crucial catalyst for marginalised young people overcoming those barriers and securing what they want.

Much of your work will be directly or indirectly involved in creating and strengthening such bonds. Nick Luxmoore (2000) is as good as any interpreter of the inner preoccupations of young people concerning identity, anxiety and their future. His open, experience-laced volume explains ways of developing lines of communication that are responsive to their concerns. For a practitioner working with young people helping them to sort out their feelings is an important objective. What they value above all is their relationship with the counsellor, social worker or youth worker who is attentive and available. 'For some', he writes, 'an experience of safety, consistency, trust and acceptance may be their first experience of these qualities. It may be a revelation. "I'd never been taken seriously before! He didn't seem fazed! I felt like he was bothered!"' (ibid.: 74). This goes some way towards balancing previously hurtful, unsafe experiences with adults and gives the young person a broader emotional understanding for dealing with the dilemmas they face.

One of the hardest things for a young person to learn is to distinguish between 'what's me' and 'what's not me' (ibid.: 75). The practitioner's skill in 'reflecting back' – which means listening to what the young person has to say and then repeating it so that he or she can clarify what they actually feel – is an important tool. Luxmoore cautions against a practitioner giving dollops of praise and admiration. A social worker or counsellor should be warm but remain non-judgemental so that young people can begin to discover their own sense of good and bad. He suggests, when talking to a young person who feels particularly helpless, asking 'who would understand how you're feeling?' or 'who could speak up for you in this situation?'. He thinks that most young people have another person, somewhere in their life, who is an ally: a friend, relative or adult. What matters is that they consider the character 'good'.

Service brokerage

Another element in working with young people is brokerage. We have spoken of the 'service silos': large public agencies with limited, pre-set functions and responsibilities with no links in between them. Brokers have the task of connecting individual needs with a broader chain of supports and resources and *of sustaining this role over time* even as the circumstances of individual young people change and pass through different stages of development. The brokerage role may be located in a voluntary agency or in a single practitioner but is characterised by becoming 'trusted, flexible intermediaries [who] play a vital role in negotiating the fault lines between different services, institutions and opportunities' (Bentley and Gurumurthy 1999: 84). You need the capacity to build trust and operate in informal and semi-formal environments – not a skill always acknowledged in social work but one that is of crucial importance. Effective brokerage can deliver high dividends, reducing crime and drug use, raising skill levels and forestalling unemployment, raising a sense of security and providing jobs.

A SOCIAL ACTION FRAMEWORK

A social action framework for working with young people can be helpful. Social action with aims to move away from 'deficit' models in which professionals step in at the outset to define the problems and to embark immediately on what young people themselves regard as the remedies. Social action emphasises young people's empowerment and participation in process, drawing in part on Mullender and Ward's approaches to group work (Mullender and Ward 1991). It is also more *reflective* and

DEFINITION OF SOCIAL ACTION

'The objective of social action – and good youth work practice more generally – is, *through* individual support and informal education ... to enable young people to understand those aspects of their lives about which, given motivation and encouragement as well as information and ancillary and professional support, they may be able to effect some change.'

(Williamson 1995: 8)

This approach underscores the collective situation of young people. It seeks to explore what common experiences they share and what stories they have to tell, whether of separated parents, racial harassment, leaving care or experiences of entry into the job market, as well as the usefulness (or otherwise) of specific networks and channels of information.

THE SOCIAL ACTION PROCESS

- What are the important issues? (identification)
- Why are they important issues? (explanation or understanding)
- How can these issues be addressed? (strategy or plan)
- Action (carrying through with the plan of action)
- Does the plan need changing in the light of experience?
- Reflection and review: participation and empowerment or fade-out and disillusionment?

(Williamson 1995: 13)

resists the temptation to leap swiftly from an agreement (with young people participating in that process) around *what* the problem is to a solution – or *how* those problems should be defined. The approach spends much time probing *why* certain problems are being experienced by groups of young people. This is crucial. 'Only through injecting the "why" question did the *structural* explanations for the predicaments of young people become more apparent to them, thereby sidelining the tendencies towards individualistic explanations and blame' (Williamson 1995: 5).

The social action approach bears strong resemblance to the process of neighbourhood capacity building explained in Chapter 7. It requires patience, with an emphasis on hearing experiences and telling stories, and lending yourself as a resource (writing reports, helping with applications for funding and negotiating with officials). With young people that role is modified and adjusted, perhaps along a sliding scale while they acquire the skills and the learning to address complex social tasks for themselves. The objective is for young people to acquire the confidence, standing and recognition

CASE STUDY 6: FARE

The Family Action in Rogerfield and Easterhouse (Glasgow), or FARE as it is known, began in 1989 with the aim of promoting the welfare of the local residents. It runs largely on voluntary donations and is overseen by committee members who are elected locally. Its premises are five hard-to-let flats. It runs a number of youth activities:

- youth clubs in two schools at lunchtimes and evenings with 300 children participating each week
- outings for bowling, swimming and skating in the group's minibus
- summer holidays have been arranged for 150 young people.

FARE members are also involved in the community helping to set up a credit union (see Chapter 7) and providing help for families in filling in social security applications, accompanying families to meetings with social workers or negotiating with housing officials. Relationships – what Bob Holman, one of the catalysts for the project, calls 'resourceful friendship' – play an important role. The regular availability of an adult drawn from the local community for listening, providing advice and acting as a role model over a long period of time is instrumental in enabling local young people to develop self-respect to the point where they can contribute capacity to the local community themselves.

(Holman 1998: 68)

to achieve a variety of ends that are transferrable across time. No doubt you will also need other skills if groups are to survive: to act as fundraiser with knowledge of funding sources, to use management and administrative skills to keep accounts and oversee volunteers and, on top of that, to be effective in inter-agency working.

We now look at the specific kinds of approach available for work with young people excluded through difficult transitions to adulthood, leaving local authority care and through having poor educational qualifications.

KEEPING YOUNG PEOPLE IN SCHOOL

Truancy and school exclusions together form one of the most visible indications of excluded or 'disaffected youth'. The numbers of pupils out of school without authorised absence is large: some 1 million are truant (both short and long term) while the number of permanent exclusions has trebled since 1997 (Howarth *et al.* 2000). Such numbers of 'out-of-school' pupils constitute a significant source of pressure on others to abandon education as well as constituting a kind of reserve army of unskilled young people who will face exclusion right into adulthood.

Schools as a resource and partner in tackling exclusion

It is important to recognise that schools are local institutions through which an increasingly wide range of resources are released, and in which joined-up programmes are based. The notion of the 'full service' school, available for use by the community as a whole with community libraries, community sports hall and the like is increasingly widespread and has many implications for facilitating parental involvement in their offspring's education. And, 'school-plus' programmes build out community development initiatives on the back of the connections between school and locality.

Your attitude toward school in general is important because it will govern how you perceive and develop relations with individual schools. Generally, social workers do not see schools as experts in problem children and believe that family support for children in need lies outside of education (Vernon and Sinclair 1999; Witney 2001). Social work training may sometimes inadvertently plant the idea that schools are overly authoritarian and social workers may come to identify with pupils' lack of influence in that environment. The professionally acquired values of empowerment may also only encourage this perception. Head teachers, for their part, sometimes distance themselves from social workers who may be perceived as too 'anti-authoritarian' (Witney 2001). In itself this clash of perspectives is not wrong; how it is handled is however crucial.

ACTIVITY 5.1: YOUR FEELINGS ABOUT SCHOOL

To work in partnership with schools, pupils and parents it is important to be honest about your own perceptions. On your own jot down on a piece of paper ten words that capture the essence of what schooling means for you. (They may well reflect your own personal experiences at school.) Do you see schools as authoritarian environments? Broadly, do you see schools as having the capacity to change, to respond to pupils' individual needs or to build relationships with parents? Would you feel able to share your list of words with a teacher or a young person attending school?

ACTIVITY 5.2: YOUR KNOWLEDGE OF LOCAL COMPREHENSIVE SCHOOLS

With two or three colleagues pool your knowledge about the comprehensive school in your area. Run through the following checklist:

- Do you know the head and others in the school management team?
- Do you know any of the teachers individually, for example heads of departments, form tutors or heads of year?
- What is the ethos of the school?
- What are its strengths and weaknesses?

- Are you familiar with basic school data such as GCSE results, GNVQ attainments, A-level and AS-level results?
- Do you know the attendance levels and the number of temporary and permanent exclusions?
- What is the school's disciplinary policy? What are the grounds for temporary and permanent exclusions?
- Do you know the incidence of bullying in the school and the school policy on it?
- How effective is the pastoral support programme in the school?
- What learning support is available for pupils in mainstream classes?
- How are the average attainments of children looked after by the local authority?

Truancy and school exclusions

Pupils who under-perform or fail at school are more likely to lose out in the job market and to face exclusion in adult life. Reducing poor attendance, school exclusion and disruptive behaviour also reduces the risk of a young person becoming delinquent. Social workers make their contribution in relation to vulnerable children, mediating between schools and the child's family and in relation to non-academic aspects of curriculum (Penrose 2001b).

There has been much recent focus on the link between boys' behaviour and their later involvement in crime. The pattern links lack of parental control and low

CHILDREN AND YOUNG PEOPLE MOST AT RISK FROM SCHOOL EXCLUSION

Children and young people most likely to be exluded from school fall into the following categories:

- those with special educational needs
- those in the care of local authorities
- children from an ethnic minority
- travellers
- young carers
- young people from families under stress
- pregnant schoolgirls and teenage mothers.

They are also more likely to be participants in bullying and anti-social activities.

(DfEE 1999)

educational achievement at a relatively young age with a later tendency toward 'anti-social behaviour' and truancy around the ages of 12–14 with outright offending later in adolescence. In this field there are a number of competing points of view: from the proponents of moral discourse comes the argument that boys reared by lone mothers are lacking a male 'father' figure and are able to evade parental control; this is only reinforced by primary schools where the great majority of teachers are female.

Feminists argue that it is certainly not the mother's fault but point to received messages on masculinity embedded in peer-group opinions, media imagery and corporate marketing techniques (Harris 1995). Somewhere in between is an emerging third view – that in school (and the world of work) young unskilled males are increasingly ill-equipped to cope. They point to the fact that boys now experience more difficulties in school, reflected in tests at all age levels. Boys are also more likely to be diagnosed as having attention deficit disorder, dyslexia or other learning impediments with attendant disruption of learning and disaffection with the world of education (Coleman and Hendry 1999). The reason often advanced is girls' relatively greater capacity to focus on non-physical tasks, the intensive nature of literacy and numeracy hours and parental pressure on schools for academic achievement that do not allow boys to do as much physical education or sports (Borrie Commission 1994; Power and Tunstall 1997).

ACTIVITY 5.3: SCHOOL DISAFFECTION

Rose is in Year 10 at her local comprehensive school. She is the youngest of six children and both parents are now in their sixties. She is reluctant to attend school and both parents are busy looking after various grandchildren during the day. They never place any pressure on her to attend school and will often write notes verifying the various excuses that Rose puts forward to the school for not attending.

Mark is in Year 10. He has a son aged six months and is living with his girlfriend aged 16 with whom he shares the childcare. Recently he took a week off to look after the baby when his girlfriend was ill.

Carly is in Year 10 although she is of Year 11 age. She is the second eldest of five girls. Of her sisters, one is 18 and pregnant, one is in Year 6, another in Year 2 and the youngest is pre-school and attends a playgroup. She has been statemented by the local authority: that is, formally assessed and considered to have special educational needs. She hates school, feeling isolated from her peers. She is on work experience two days a week which, although not exciting for her, she prefers to school.

What do you think is going on in each young person's mind as she or he prepares for school each day? How does this affect his or her ability to learn once they are in school? What do you think you might do to facilitate their learning? As a social worker what approaches and strategies do you think would improve matters for each pupil?

(Adapted from Penrose 2000a)

In managing school difficulties or exclusion itself parents are almost always overlooked and yet their involvement is crucial to resolving the difficulties. Penrose (2000a) found that there were very different accounts – from parents, school and pupil – of the events that trigger exclusion. For parents of the excluded child the event was particularly shocking and caused anger and disappointment with both their child and with the school. In all cases it brought disruption and extreme inconvenience because of prior work commitments. For some the exclusion was devastating and resulted in alienation from the school and loss of trust in it as an institution.

Few parents thought that the investigation had been sufficiently thorough or that they were given adequate information. They often believed that they had inadequate information about their own rights, felt powerless and unable to influence professional decisions. Often parents added their own punishment in addition to the exclusion, such as additional domestic duties, keeping in at night or loss of TV (Penrose 2000a: 6–7). Enhancing parental control and parent self-esteem, together with support activities such as homework clubs and after-school clubs, helped secure parental engagement.

Pastoral support programmes (PSPs)

Pastoral support is a school-based intervention to help individual pupils better manage their behaviour. The objective, spelt out in a government circular (DfEE 2000a) is to set up realistic behavioural objectives for the pupil that she or he can work towards with support. The involvement and agreement of the parents is the first vital step in setting up a PSP. While a school-based staff member is usually nominated to oversee an individual programme its effectiveness relies on the close involvement of other agencies such as social service departments, housing departments, voluntary and statutory youth services agencies, careers services and local community groups.

Social service involvement in PSPs is critical for pupils who are being looked after by the local authority, on the child protection register or who are young carers looking after another sibling or parent. For children that are looked after by the local authority pastoral support should form an integral part of the care plan so that the targets and

CASE STUDY 7: WHALLEY RANGE HIGH SCHOOL

Whalley Range comprehensive school in Manchester introduced peer counselling in the mid-1990s as one of several initiatives to counteract high levels of truancy. The scheme involves young people providing a listening service for fellow students who want to talk in confidence about a matter that bothers them. While peer counselling is not the only factor in reducing truancy and exclusions from school, it has helped set a new, positive atmosphere in the school which promotes education of the whole self and gives students an active part in shaping the life of the school. As such it provided the beginning for more peer-led actions.

(Crime Concern 1999b)

outcomes are known to the young person's social worker. A pastoral support plan should review any difficulties with learning, especially in literacy skills. It should also make suggestions as to any supplementary or remedial activity such as attendance at homework clubs, whether parts of the National Curriculum should not apply to that particular pupil and whether he or she should be offered specialist support in dealing with matters such as bereavement or drug addiction.

Neighbourhood programmes

Outside of the work with individual pupils there are a number of other preventive initiatives which include:

- schemes to help a young person to get a new start in a different school
- school support schemes specifically targeted at children looked after by the local authority, a high proportion of whom are not in school
- mentoring initiatives linking individual volunteers with excluded young people for longer periods of time.

(Sinclair 1998:9)

Social workers are involved in a range of projects for disaffected youth and are involved as partners in a range of projects to do with community safety, education welfare, youth service, local education and training. Any partnership focusing on neighbourhoods with high crime rates will see the gains in investing in services for excluded or truanting children. A specialist worker funded jointly by education welfare, youth justice and the youth service could make a signficant difference at the neighbourhood level by organising daytime programmes and mentoring schemes. Promising approaches include:

- training older teenagers to befriend or mentor persistent truants
- support for parents through meetings, leaflets, parent groups
- truancy watch schemes involving education welfare and police
- targeting the younger child in secondary school (and primary and pre-school)
- exploring the potential for furthering school liaison once the project is under way.

(Crime Concern 1999b; Sinclair 1998)

SALFORD TRUANCY PROJECT

The project brings together many partners in a wide range of measures to address poor attendance. The approaches include a pupil mentoring scheme to help with the transition from primary to secondary school, a Truancy Watch scheme which involves Greater Manchester Police, and multi-agency working to agree strategies for individual pupils.

(Crime Concern 1999b)

ACTIVITY 5.4: SCHOOL EXCLUSION

You are the local authority social worker for three brothers, currently being looked after by the local authority for a pre-planned four weeks. During these four weeks they have been permanently excluded from school for fighting. Their mother is white British and their father is black Nigerian. One of the brothers is in Year 11 and, with learning support, is doing two GCSEs; he has been statemented. The two other brothers are in Year 10; one has mild brain damage and he has also been statemented. The head teacher ordered their permanent exclusion by invoking the school policy against serious fighting, a decision which the governors have upheld. The teachers have threatened action if any of the brothers return to school. The school is rural without nearby alternatives; there is no counselling programme at the school.

What kinds of support do you think the three brothers and the school would need to have in place in order for the brothers to be re-integrated successfully back into school?

MOVING INTO ADULTHOOD

The major services have become 'impossibly fragmented and incoherent' (Bentley and Gurumurthy 1999: 50) and are widely regarded as failing young people as they move into adulthood (Howarth *et al.* 2000). Managing this transition period in their lives requires negotiating a path through several complex systems: moving into higher or further education, finding employment, arranging benefits or grants system, and finding a place in the health and housing systems. For excluded youth – those who come from deprived neighbourhoods, have dropped out of school or committed an offence, or who have left home and have no family to support them – fragmented services present even greater difficulties. The Social Exclusion Unit itself has readily admitted as much by noting three main shortcomings in services for young people moving into adulthood:

1. Gaps in individual services: not enough emphasis on prevention, not delivered in ways which recognise the specific needs of disadvantaged young people and are not provided where they are needed.
2. Allocation of resources: evidence that the state spends on average 14 per cent *less* on young people in the most deprived areas than on the average young person.
3. Fragmentation of policy thinking and service delivery: the absence of someone to pull together services nationally, locally, individually. Instead at least four local authority services – social services, employment, education and housing work directly with young people.

(Social Exclusion Unit 2000)

Connexions

The government's Connexions strategy now dominates efforts to co-ordinate support services for young people as they move from school to work and from family to independence.

Connexions works with several objectives that particularly assist excluded young people. First is the notion of a flexible school curriculum that engages young people with diverse interests and abilities and leads to the relevant, sought-after qualifications. This includes the flexibility for young people within school to opt out of elements of the GCSE curriculum to spend more time on work-related learning. All pupils, regardless of their curriculum path, receive a Graduation Certificate by the age of nineteen that certifies the young person's accomplishments including the development of key interpersonal skills. Second, alongside the more diverse curriculum is a new system of apprenticeships offered through sixth forms and colleges of further education that combine trade skills with further learning. Third, there is targeted financial support both to reward participation in learning and to reduce the financial barriers to further education. Finally Connexions has put in place a network of personal advisers to work with young people recognised as at risk from 'disaffection' (DfEE 1999b).

The personal advisers are key to overcoming the fragmentation of services. They are drawn from a range of agencies including the youth service, youth offending teams and social workers and will be seconded to a variety of locations such as schools and FE colleges. Their role is to befriend and support individual young people while identifying what their particular needs are, and to increase their employability. They will:

- ensure school attendance up to the age of 16
- provide information regarding future learning and work opportunities
- conduct basic skill assessments
- provide support in gaining access to education and training
- broker work placements.

Social services departments and youth offending teams (see p. 130) have a particularly important role within the Connexions scheme in relation to looked-after children and care leavers, work with parents and carers, and achieving *Quality Protects* education targets (DfEE 2001). In this 'joined-up' attack on exclusion across education, employment service and social services such involvement poses a dilemma for practitioners whose values, training and professional perspective lead them to object to the 'new paternalism' in Connexions. The prospect of preparing young people for a job in the labour market, dominated as it is by telephone call-centres, fast food outlets and low-level retail, will trouble many practitioners. They will ask where in the scheme is support for acknowledging the deeper purposes in life or for sustaining the young person coming to understand their identity? Each practitioner will have to work through this dilemma, perhaps in collaboration with colleagues. Built in to the scheme is a greater emphasis on citizenship with its obligations and responsibilities, so that is one important contribution to a richer life. In the end practitioners have to compare it with what exists at the moment; in relation to the appalling legacy of neglect that confronts care leavers, for example, Connexions is a step forward.

ACTIVITY 5.5: EXAMINE A GOVERNMENT PRONOUNCEMENT

The summer after compulsory education is a key transition point, when many young people are vulnerable and at risk of dropping out of learning, and so excluding themselves from future opportunities. We are developing proposals for post-examination summer activities for all 16-year-olds, before they take up post-16 education, traineeships or work with training. All young people can benefit from the experience of positive activity, which could be a summer camp, aimed at developing team work, interpersonal skills and leadership, as well as building the confidence and self-esteem of the individual. We expect Millennium Volunteers to be included in the summer activities, developing their personal skills as well as benefiting other young people in the community.

(www.connexions.gov.uk/)

What do you consider are the strengths and weaknesses in government policy as revealed in this passage from the Connexions web page? Thinking back to the different ways of interpreting social exclusion in Chapter 1 which strands do you see evidence of here? Do you feel there is too much compulsion behind the pronouncement?

ACTIVITY 5.6: STRENGTHS AND WEAKNESSES OF THE CONNEXIONS SCHEME

Browse through the documents on the Connexions website (www.connexions.gov.uk/) including the one entitled 'Strategy'. If you are able to, download two or three that you consider to be the most important; be careful though – some of the documents are quite lengthy so choosing a chapter or two makes more sense when downloading. After you have read several draw up a list of the pros and cons of the Connexions scheme; highlight those areas where you think your social work role might support or conflict with the intentions of the scheme.

Adolescent support teams

Adolescent support teams have developed rapidly since the early 1990s. In general they aim to divert young people from the care system and provide short-term, intensive preventive service that helps families forestall problems in relationships that might otherwise lead to homelessness. Most of the families that such teams work with have high degrees of conflict, parental mental health problems and domestic violence. Such problems are frequently interlinked with behaviour problems of the young people themselves. In one survey of their work over half the young people had suffered abuse, neglect, placement in care or social services involvement (Biehal *et al.* 2000).

The practice of adolescent support teams is preventive and based on intensive, time-limited, task-centred work. The approach starts to work on the problems identified by the young person themselves, setting out aims to be worked toward in order to over come those problems. Those aims are achieved through working on small steps or 'tasks' which both young person and worker review on at least a weekly basis. Much of the team's work involves negotiation and mediation between young people and parents.

IMPROVING NETWORKS: MENTORING SCHEMES

Mentor means 'a trusted counsellor or guide'. Mentoring mixes an informal educative role with personal support and encouragement, together with the roles of change agent and advocate. Broadly any mentoring project will 'aim to connect two people in a one to one voluntary relationship, with one person being more experienced than the other and with the expectation that their skills and knowledge will be transferred' (Alexander 2000: 2).

Big demands are now being placed on the concept of mentoring and these appear across the board in work with young people, whether over difficulties in schools, engaging in post-16 education, in youth work or in work with young offenders. Mentoring provides a young person with both a role model – that is, a successful example to follow in terms of a career path, personal conduct or in studying – and a source of instruction and guidance. Such is the widespread reliance on mentoring and mentor projects that practitioners, depending on their role, will either act as a mentor or be responsible for initiating mentoring projects for young people in their area (Benioff 1997).

While all of us use the term informally ('she was my mentor' meaning someone you turned to, either colleague or peer, when you were learning the ropes at school or work) what is asked of mentors for young people is substantially more. There are three key features of a mentoring relationship:

1. It is a voluntary arrangement as required by the person being mentored and can be ended by either party at any time;
2. Mentors are equipped with the necessary interpersonal skills to manage and monitor the relationship;
3. Both those mentored and mentors understand the boundaries and purpose of the relationship.

(Crime Concern 1998)

There are many areas of work where a mentor scheme will assist – work with young offenders or those at risk of offending, with poor school achievers, homeless young people, to name a few. In setting up a mentoring scheme you need to think about:

- Who the scheme is for: will it be for all pupils with a substantial record of unexplained absences, those aged 16 plus who are looking for work, for care leavers in the area or for those cautioned by the police? The group for whom a scheme is intended may be large or small, focused or general – but from the beginning, thinking about who the scheme is for is closely linked to your intended purpose and the aims of the scheme. Be sure to collect data on how many young people are likely to be interested.

- Establish aims and objectives: the project needs to think through what its prime purpose is, what it is trying to accomplish, and what kind of achievement it wants to be known for. Its objectives are the more specific steps outlined to achieve those aims.
- Careful thinking around gender: will the scheme be for girls or young women only, for example? What will be the gender balance in the likely supply of mentors?
- Careful thinking around ethnicity: are shared cultural or religious norms between those being mentored and likely volunteer mentors important?
- Overlap: make an audit of existing voluntary and statutory services to ensure that what you want to achieve is not already being done in your area. Decide where the project will be placed within that map of current services.

The best guide to setting up a mentoring scheme is Alison Alexander's handbook (Alexander 2000). She describes the importance of recruitment and selection for all schemes, stressing the importance of creating a recruitment pack with full and accurate information. She also lays out what interviewers should look for in prospective recruits:

Perception of self: do they feel comfortable in front of others? Do they have the capacity to speak about their feelings and are they open about themselves and their experiences? Are they aware of their own prejudices and personal limitations? Do they have a sense of worth?

Warmth and the perception of others: do they believe that people are responsible for their own destiny and that individuals can cope with difficulties when supported? Do they think all people are worthy of help? Are they easily threatened by others and can they challenge others when needed?

Perception of purpose and task: do they believe that an individual's difficulties can be affected by both personal and environmental factors? Can they imagine themselves in others' shoes and perceive the mentor's role as enabling and not controlling? Do they respect difference and value freedom of choice?

Alexander's manual will also provide you with a wealth of detail to do with matching mentors with young people, providing supervision for mentors and logging what happens when mentor and young person meet.

ACTIVITY 5.7: RAYMOND

Raymond is 19 years old and is currently living in temporary bed and breakfast accommodation. He appears unkempt, wears low slung trousers with leg cuffs which scuff the pavement and catch along under his feet; he has rings in his ears and eyebrows and studs in his lip and tongue. He is currently unemployed but is a talented musician and has recently joined a band. In the past he has been known to have misused drugs and alcohol. He completed a rehab programme for drug use six months ago. Now he arrives late for his session and alcohol can be smelt on his breath. He states that he has fallen out with a member of the band.

How should a mentor work with Raymond in this session? What strategies might the mentor find helpful in guiding him?

(adapted from Alexander 2000)

CHILDREN IN PUBLIC CARE: CARE LEAVERS

In general parents act as their children's best advocates from birth, knowing that certain choices, decisions and milestones will affect their children's life chances. In the main parents take their children's needs vigorously into account, pushing schools to respond to those needs, advising their child as he or she gets older, watching out over any special needs or health problems. Parents are particularly involved in their child's education: selecting schools, supporting – and if necessary enforcing – their child's attendance, helping to choose subject option, assisting and reminding on homework, getting in touch with teachers if there are difficulties and advising on work experience.

When a child enters public care, that is, 'looked after' by a local authority, the situation changes dramatically. The child, whether accommodated with the agreement of her or his parents or subject to a care order, rarely has an advocate equal to his or her parents or other family relations. Local authorities have a poor record when acting as the parent for children they look after. Young people in public care are well below average in educational attainment, acquiring basic skills, health or social relationships, and yet their ability ranges match national averages (Jackson and Martin 1998). As a consequence care leavers rank high in all groups of marginalised youth. The under-achievement at school goes hand-in-hand with much higher rates of truancy and exclusions. The effect of this experience takes its toll in later life: a higher than average level of looked-after children are unemployed and homeless and engage in criminal and abusive behaviour (DfEE 1999; Jackson 1998). Among homeless young people, young offenders and the prison population the proportion of those in care is extremely high: roughly some 30–40 per cent of each population.

THE ORPHAN TRAIN

For a powerful metaphor of a young person being left behind by public authorities think of the 'orphan train'. These were trains filled with children and young people whose parents had either died or had abandoned them. As the trains made their way from east to west they would stop at each town along the way. When they did the children and young people would be made to get out and line up outside where the townsfolk who needed servants or an extra pair of hands could take home those they liked the look of. Those not chosen had to get back on the train and ride on to the next town and next inspection. Some were never chosen. None ever saw their families again.

It would be good if the orphan train were only a metaphor for being left behind in public care. Unfortunately it is not: orphan trains ran from the east coast of the United States to the midwest in the late nineteenth and early twentieth centuries (often with European children on board). Outrageous? Without doubt – but in what way is it different to setting up 16- year-olds on their own, in a little room, on benefit, with no skills for looking after themselves, no GCSEs and no visible lines of human support?

In assisting the transition to adulthood the practitioner has to contend with a number of complex factors including accommodation, life skills, education, career paths, social networks and relationships, identity and offending.

Accommodation may involve initial moves to transitional forms of housing such as hostels, lodgings or staying with friends which are often followed up by moves to independent tenancies in the public, voluntary or private sectors. Stein *et al.* (1997) found that over half of the care leavers studied had moved two or more times in their first two years out of care. About one-sixth made five or more moves while one-fifth became homeless at some stage.

Life skills include budgeting, negotiating with officials, landlords, employers, practical skills such as self care, and domestic skills such as cooking, laundry and cleaning.

Social networks, relationships and identity are another facet of leaving care that both the young person and practitioner have to come to grips with. As Biehal *et al.* (1995) have said, the point of leaving care is a time when young people are trying to make sense of their past – to trace missing parents, to find continuity in their lives and a sense of belonging. 'They needed a "story" of their lives that made sense, reduced their confusion about both how and why events had happened as they did and to provide a more secure platform for their futures in the adult world' (Stein 1997: 39). Even if family links had not been positive, retaining them was important and lent symbolic certainty to their lives. Those that did not have even this lacked self-esteem, and were less confident and assertive. Marsh and Peel (1999) noted particularly that awareness of who was in the young person's family was severely limited and that notions of partnership and efforts at family involvement with the care leaver were not really take seriously.

Ensuring success in education

The record of local authority social services departments overseeing the education of children they look after is particularly bad. Practice has to begin with a recognition of this: poor back-up of young people while studying for GCSEs or doing homework, living conditions not conducive to study (particularly in residential childcare), little contact with schools, no interest or recognition of educational success. A full 70 per cent of looked-after children have *no qualification on leaving schoo*l (Biehal *et al.* 1995). In the year 1999–2000 of the 6800 young people leaving care only 30 per cent had one or more GCSE or GNVQ equivalent (DoH 2000). If we look at useful qualifications, that is GCSEs grade A – C, the picture is more disturbing: only three in a hundred care leavers obtain five or more GCSEs at Grade C or above (Jackson 1998: 1) compared with 60 per cent of pupils as a whole.

Part of the problem has been the low expectations held by social workers, whether in the field or residential care. It is imperative not to perpetuate this stereotype: looked-after children fall within the same intelligence range as average children. Whether managing the case, providing advice or providing care you need to have the same aspirations for the young people you are responsible for as parents would have for their children (Jackson and Martin 1998). There is assistance for you. The guidance on family placements (foster care) and residential care already recognises the extreme disadvantage experienced by most looked after children. The *Looking After Children Assessment and Action Records* (Ward 1995; DoH 1998)

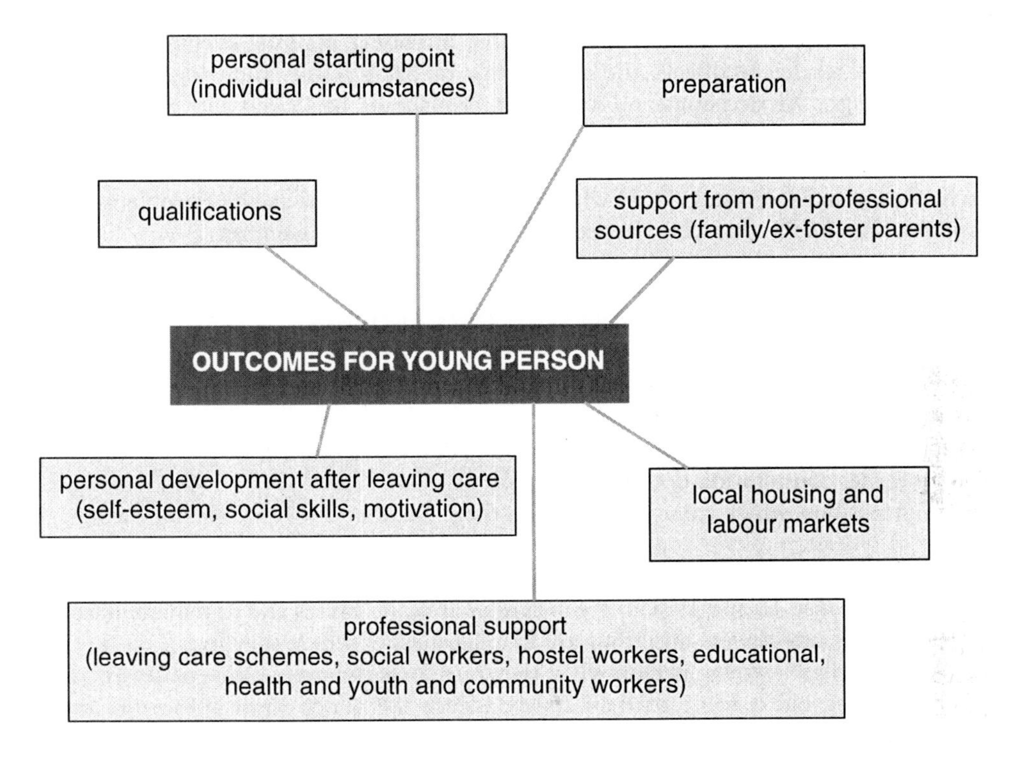

FIGURE 5.1 Factors affecting care leavers

Source: Adapted from Stein 1997.

used by most local authorities indicate the specific questions that need to be asked to ensure a child's education is supported and promoted. But beyond this the full range of educational visits, school trips and spare-time activities need to be supported. Motivation needs to be encouraged and nurtured. To achieve this, organisational culture has to change. Jackson observed in particular that 'residential care provided a positively anti-intellectual environment – no study facilities, reference books or understanding of the sustained effort and concentration required for serious academic work' (Jackson 1998: 52).

HIGH-ACHIEVING CARE LEAVERS SPEAK

We asked all our high-achieving care leavers: 'What part did your social worker play in your school progress and planning for higher education?'

Sadly, 92 per cent replied 'none'.

(Jackson 1998: 52)

For the great majority of young people the parents should be as closely involved in their child's education as possible, including attending parents' evening, receiving reports and teacher feedback, and information on SATs results and progress through the Key Stages. All decisions and documentation should be shared with parents first, either directly from the school or through a small network of natural parents, foster carers or a key worker in a residential home, and social worker. It is important that schools and social services clarify who is to be contacted in the event of problems or to support the child's education, for example attending parent evenings.

Good practice in working with care leavers

Based on research evidence by Jackson and Martin (1998) and Biehal *et al.* (1995) a major new piece of legislation has been introduced to overcome the legacy of poor practice. The Children (Leaving Care) Act 2000 contains a number of new duties based on an earlier consultation document *Me, Survive Out There?* (DoH 1999) Among its main provisions, which came into force on the 1 October 2001, are the following:

- Local authorities have a new duty to assess and meet the needs of eligible young people aged 16 and 17 who are in care or are care leavers and to remain in touch with all care leavers until they are 21 regardless of where they live.
- Every eligible young person when they turn 16 is to have a clear 'pathway' plan mapping out a route to their independence for which local authorities must provide the personal and practical support.
- Each care leaver is to have an adviser who will co-ordinate provision of support, with particular emphasis on education, training and employment.
- The introduction of new more straightforward financial arrangements which offer comprehensive support, especially with education and employment up through the age 21 and beyond if necessary.

Pathway plan

The objective of the Act is to achieve what has been so elusive for local authorities: effective 'corporate parenting' in which the local authority and all professionals involved with a young person leaving care can act as an advocate in the areas of life that really matter. The Pathway plan for each care leaver should be based on the extensive involvement of the young person and should look ahead at least to his or her twenty-first birthday. It should pick up and extend the dimensions covered in the *Framework for the Assessment of Children in Need.* Thus for example the health needs, future education, supporting family relationships all form part of such a plan. Accommodation needs should be carefully looked at before young people leave care and arrangements made for joint-assessment between social services and housing authorities. Sources of income and avenues to employment (Draft Regulations 2000) must also be considered. The new Connexions Service, introduced in April 2001, also plays an important part here.

TEENAGE PREGNANCY

Britain has one of the highest rates of teenage pregnancy in Europe with some 90 000 young women conceiving every year, and with a well-established link between those young women under 16 who become pregnant and social exclusion. A third of pregnancies among 16- to19-year-olds are terminated, with adverse effects on physical and mental health. Some 8.5 per cent of these young mothers are under 16 when they conceive. These rates are three times that of France and six times that of Holland. Over two-thirds of children living in families where the mother is aged 16–24 are in the poorest 30 percent of the population. Some 10 per cent of 18- to 24-year-olds are on means-tested benefits (NPI 2000; SEU 1999a).

As a social worker, whether working in the field, in youth work or as a carer, you may well be helping a young woman who has become pregnant unexpectedly to decide whether or not keep her baby. In their careful research Corlyon and McGuire (1999) found that being in care places extra pressure on young people to embark on a sexual relationship at an early age. Many of the young women in their study, who then become pregnant, feel that they needed more support in making decisions whether to keep the baby, place for adoption or have an abortion. They also said they needed more preparation for parenthood when they have decided to keep the baby (NCB 1999).

ACTIVITY 5.8: SORTING OUT YOUR OWN VIEWS FIRST

Teenage pregnancy involves sensitive issues for us all and will raise difficult problems for you both professionally and personally. You will want to examine your beliefs and values in this first and come to an understanding as to how these might affect your work with a young person. Ask yourself the following:

- What are your views about underage sex?
- What are your views on abortion? Would you advise very strongly that a fifteen-year-old girl have an abortion or would you be neutral and support her whatever her decision is?
- What are your views about young males who engage in under-age sex and who cause a woman in her mid-teens to become pregnant? Should they share in any decision to keep the child?
- What are your feelings about religious strictures on sexual relationships outside of marriage, or on abortion?

The guide from the National Children's Bureau called *Time to decide* (NCB 1999) is aimed at young women and is designed for them to work through on their own if need be. It answers many questions about abortion, changes in pregnancy, antenatal classes and what having the responsibility of a baby entails. It is a superb resource that you should have on hand to help any young woman you are working with in this most difficult decision.

Prostitution

Young people in care turn to prostitution for a variety of reasons. It may be a way of redeeming their low self-esteem, as a result of poor family experiences, or as a way of making 'quick' money. As in so many other areas of youth behaviour the government has announced a set of guidelines to steer local work (DoH 2000). For the first time young people under 18 who prostitute themselves are deemed to be treated by local services as victims of child abuse.

The guidelines suggest that:

- Residential care staff should be alert to any regular contact with older adults or to any individuals loitering outside the home with a view to making contact. Each group home should establish clear procedures for reporting such incidents.
- Area child protection committees should develop local guidelines relevant to their areas.
- Multi-agency response should be developed for dealing with a child involved in prostitution, with social services and police looking at his or her network for gaps.
- If at all possible the young person should be diverted from prostitution without involving the criminal justice system; however the police may, after consultation with others, take criminal action if the young person persistently and voluntarily solicits in a public place.

(DoH 2000)

HOUSING AND ROUGH SLEEPERS

Youth homelessness is one of the indicators pointing to how difficult the transition to adulthood has become, and how these difficulties lead to exclusion. Homeless young people as a group have a number of interlinked problems – alcohol and drug abuse, no qualifications, family conflict, mental health problems (Bentley and Gurumurthy 1999). One-third of homeless young people have been looked after by the local authority which has pinpointed the failure of local authorities social services to assist appropriately the transitions for those young people in their care.

Rough sleepers, that is those without any shelter, are by definition the most marginalised and vulnerable of the homeless, often requiring multiple forms of support in addition to shelter. The government's rough sleepers' initiative offers block grant payments to agencies dealing with homeless people to target explicitly street sleepers and to offer them accommodation in shelters and to work toward their resettlement (Edgar *et al.* 1999; SEU 1998).

As a result of the rough sleepers' initiative there are smaller numbers of homeless young people than in the late 1980s and early 1990s, but those that remain homeless are more vulnerable and great numbers of young people continue to experience homelessness if only for a short period of time (SEU 1998). For example a high proportion of homeless young people who approach Centrepoint, an organisation that offers services to homeless young people, each year are particularly vulnerable: 44 per cent are women (many under 18); 41 per cent are 16 and 17 years of age with no automatic right to benefits; 40 per cent have no income at all; 43 per cent are young black or

CASE STUDY 8: NEVILLE HOUSE

Neville House provides temporary winter accommodation for rough sleepers with multiple problems such as alcohol and drug abuse. It aims explicitly to make a visible impact on a specific area of London and to provide a gateway to more permanent support services. It takes a holistic view of the needs of residents and as a result adopts a multi-disciplinary approach that recognises residents as having multiple skills and interests. It offers health and psychiatric care with other services such as counselling and a drinks crisis centre. Residents can also gain from vocational guidance and various creative activities including screen printing and computer use (Edgar *et al.* 1999).

SAFE IN THE CITY

Safe in the City has been set up in eight London boroughs to provide targeted support for young people at risk of homelessness. It has three aims:

- to help young people stay safely at home
- to find alternative options for young people who cannot remain safely at home
- to develop life skills and employability.

To achieve these aims it combines detached youth work, family mediation, peer education and personal skills programmes.

(Smith *et al.* 1998)

mixed origins and 25 per cent have been in local authority care. Most homeless young people who arrive at Centrepoint, 68 per cent, are looking for work or training.

Family breakdown and abuse are the leading causes of youth homelessness. But there is a background factor at work also: the changing nature of the family and the limits it places on childhood. Many parents see 16 as an acceptable age for children to leave home in cases of conflict but at this age young people are not entitled to benefits except in cases of extreme hardship (Howarth *et al.* 2000).

The principal barriers to finding accommodation thus include lack of financial assistance, lack of any legal right to social housing and lack of adequate support services to make housing arrangements sustainable over time. But there is a geographical dimension to this: disproportionately, homeless young people come from highly deprived neighbourhoods. Hardship payments are one means by which 16- and 17-year-olds can obtain a state benefit with no strings attached. Interviews for hardship payments may be intimidating particularly when pressing for 'evidence' of abuse or traumatic cause for separation from parents. Many young people do not get as far as interview or fail to handle it well (Havell 1998).

Foyers

DEFINITION OF FOYER

At its simplest level the Foyer concept is a form of transitional accommodation for young people linked to training/employment and social support. At a more complex level it provides a tool for integrating alienated youth into mainstream society.

(Foyer Federation 1993: 3)

The concept of foyers came from France through which young workers were provided with protected accommodation, assistance in securing training and monitoring employment. The intention was that where work was plentiful but housing scarce foyers would provide the means through which mobile young workers could be connected to jobs. As such foyers had the backing of French planners, politicians and industrialists, an influential coalition that bears striking resemblance to those supporting foyers in the UK today (Gilchrist and Jeffs 2000).

Foyers embrace a range of activities and rationales. The provisions and services offered through foyers can also vary dramatically from purpose-built buildings with good leisure facilities such as café, information shop and gym to modified older buildings with little more than a residents' lounge, laundry, game machines and communal kitchen: 'Common to all – [is] the offer of a single room in a facility that also has some staff to provide help with personal problems and advice about work, searching for jobs, finding training courses.' They are different from hostels in that residence is conditional on involvement in a training scheme or jobs club (Gilchrist and Jeffs 2000).

ANTI-SOCIAL BEHAVIOUR AND YOUTH OFFENDING

Programmes that reduce youth crime and 'anti-social behaviour' (which generally embraces numerous specific activities such as hanging out in gangs in public places, shouting and verbal intimidation of others, fighting, public drunkenness, vandalism and graffiti) are proliferating. These in turn have generated numerous evaluation studies from which to draw important conclusions about how to forestall youth offending. Much of this evidence is reported and assessed in Rutter *et al.*'s recent volume, *Antisocial Behaviour by Young People* (1998). The Audit Commission's influential review *Misspent Youth* (1996), also contains important messages for social workers in particular. For example, it concluded that general counselling, casework, family therapy and psychodynamic approaches that emphasised 'insight' did not work. Similarly, unstructured groupwork did not seem effective. Punishment-based programmes in detention centres with heavy labour ('boot camps') have not proven effective, nor has close surveillance ('tagging').

But the report also highlights a number of promising approaches:

- behavioural and cognitive behavioural methods
- community-based work that uses local resources and nearness to the offender's home to effect real-life learning
- matching the level of risk of offending posed by a given individual with the level of intervention
- role play and modelling focusing on skill acquisition, problem solving and social interaction
- employment-based programmes through which offenders can progress to real jobs.

(Audit Commission 1996)

Politicians, the electorate and the public in general have become preoccupied with crime, often with good reason, but as Little and Mount have observed in the past social workers and youth justice practitioners have shown little interest in evaluating different types of intervention. Instead they seem to have preferred to stand against the broad trends unfolding in the criminal justice world (Little and Mount 1999: 73). Youth crime is a multi-dimensional problem and demands a multi-dimensional solution, especially when tackling problems such as family stress and youth alienation which are no one agency's primary responsibility (Bright 1996). To give an idea of the complexity of the causes of anti-social behaviour Little and Mount's vector analysis (Figure 5.2) shows how the difficulties in one phase of a child's life can feed into later constraints and low achievement. Preventative practice is the essential ingredient and social work practitioners have a clear role to play here. In an influential paper, Bright

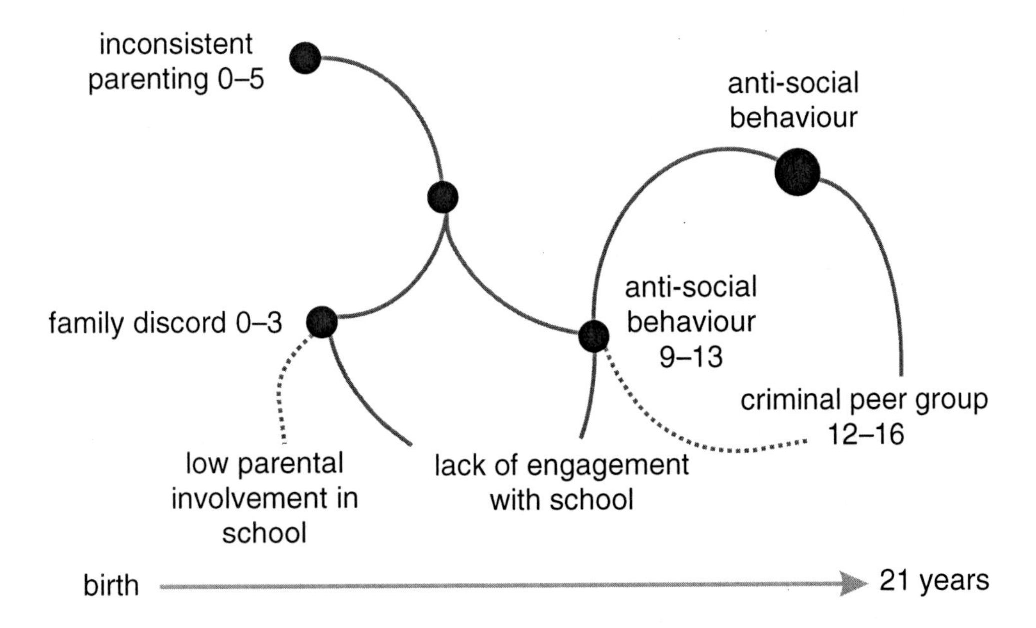

FIGURE 5.2 Vector linking school performance and parental control with later offending

Source: Adapted from Little and Mount 1999.

(ibid.) outlined the main points of a preventative strategy, the aim of which was to strengthen three of the main influences on young people: their family, their school and their community.

Dealing with young offenders and the anti-social behaviour of young people presents certain contradictions for the practitioner, especially for those grounded in the values of empathy, empowerment and participation. These contradictions arise from government policy because young people from disadvantaged housing estates are seen as both excluded *and* a force for excluding others through anti-social and intimidating behaviour. The Labour government has brought in programmes and policies that respond to both sides of this equation, with perhaps the law and order motifs within the Crime and Disorder Act of 1998 being the most prominent.

Such policies have to be set in context:

- 25 per cent of 'known offenders' are indeed under the age of 18
- the public at large, and older people in particular, do fear young people when they hang around in groups
- the main victims of crime are those living in highly disadvantaged areas, lone parents and the unemployed.

(Home Office in Goldson 2000: 262)

THE CRIME AND DISORDER ACT 1998

The key points of the Crime and Disorder Act are:

1. It establishes local youth offending teams, each made up of practitioners from different agencies: police, social services, education, health and probation service.
2. It changes the ethos of youth justice
   - from welfare to punishment and correction: the youth offending teams replace the youth justice teams under social services, underscoring the move away from statutory childcare duties
   - to a more corporate organisational structure: the teams report to the chief executive of the local authority and not the director of social services, and nationally answer to the Youth Justice Board
   - to create a 'culture of shame' around punishment.
3. It creates a child safety order, the aim of which is to reduce the risk of a child under the age of 10 years slipping into offending. The order allows local authorities to apply to magistrates' courts for an order for a named child if one or more of the following conditions exist:
   - the child committed an act which, if she or he was over 10, would be an offence
   - the order is necessary to prevent such an act occurring
   - the child acted in a way that caused harassment, alarm or distress.

The order normally lasts three months and places the child under the supervision of a 'responsible officer', either a social worker or a member of the youth offending team, who can specify what action is necessary to support the child and prevent being drawn into offending.

4 It creates a new Parenting Order which requires parents to take action to help change the behaviour of named children aged 10–17 and especially to prevent repetition of anti-social acts or offending.

- the order can be made if the young person is convicted of an offence, is already subject to another order under the Act or if the parent is convicted for failing to ensure their child attends school
- the order may require the parent to comply with various arrangements such as accompanying the child to school for up to 12 months, or attending counselling and guidance sessions once a week.

5 It introduces a new anti-social behaviour order the grounds for which are:

- if the person acts in a manner that causes harassment, alarm or distress to one or more people not in the household
- the order is necessary to protect persons in the area subject to that harassment.

6 Local authorities have the power to set up local child curfew schemes for up to 90 days if they believe a curfew is necessary to maintain order. Such a scheme bans children under 10 from public places between 9 p.m. and 6 a.m. unless controlled by a responsible person over 18.

This presents the practitioner with a genuine conflict: between providing a diversionary practice which keeps young people engaging in anti-social behaviour from offending, and wanting to reclaim a sense of community safety for local citizens. It is difficult to know where to draw the line between the social policing that practitioners have to engage in and making those that feel they are most likely to be victims of crime, older people and young children, feel secure. Both are legitimate goals for practice. As a practitioner you will need a fine balance to achieve both.

The Crime and Disorder Act 1998 introduced a new framework for youth justice not least in its creation of integrated youth justice teams comprising practitioners from different service agencies but also for its spectrum of new powers to tackle street-level behaviour which can create an intimidating local atmosphere. The Act places a statutory duty on the police and local authorities to work together to reduce crime and disorder in each locality. To this end they must review the levels and patterns of crime in their area, including domestic violence and racist attacks, prepare an analysis of the results and work out a plan to lower crime rates with specific targets.

Practitioners are thus pulled in two directions. On the one hand they are involved with families who have parenting orders, curfew orders and anti-social behaviour orders on family members; on the other they have obligations to provide services for 'children in need' which, under the Children Act, includes:

- children at risk of abuse and neglect
- children who are delinquent or at risk of becoming so
- children with serious family problems or whose home conditions are unsatisfactory
- children in poverty
- children leaving care.

ACTIVITY 5.9: ANTI-SOCIAL BEHAVIOUR IN CHILDREN

Five children, aged between 10 and 14, have been regularly causing damage, stealing, intimidating, threatening and swearing at shopkeepers and passers-by. They spit and scream abuse but know that they cannot be charged with specific offences. Now the magistrates have made them subject to anti-social behaviour orders, banning them from city centre shops. If they break the orders they could face up to five years' custodial sentence. Their father said: 'I couldn't care less. The court case means nothing and there's no need for me to say anything to defend my kids.'

Do you think it is a good idea for the magistrates to impose the order? If the children breach the order should they be placed in custodial facilities as the magistrate threatened?

What would your first steps be if this family landed as a case on your desk?

Note: The anti-social behaviour orders involve civil proceedings with a civil evidence test. This means that courts make their decision on the 'balance of probabilities' as opposed to the criminal evidence test of 'beyond reasonable doubt'. This is a low legal threshold and, providing the relevant incidents are witnessed, the evidence of those witnesses should suffice. Also as it is a civil trial, previous convictions can be taken into account and it is not necessary to hear evidence from the victim.

Youth offending teams

The principal aim of the youth justice system established by the Crime and Disorder Act 1998 is to prevent offending by young people. Youth offending teams play a key role in this. YOTs consist of one or more police officers, probation officers, social workers and representatives of the health and education services. Traditionally, only social services and probation have been involved in the post-sentence supervision of young offenders, but the intention now is to:

> tackle the issues – from poor parental supervision and domestic violence or abuse to peer group pressure, from truancy and school exclusion to substance misuse or mental health problems – which can place young people at risk of becoming involved in crime.
>
> (Home Office 1999)

The origins of the YOTs lay in *Misspent Youth*, which identified a number of difficulties in the local delivery of youth justice (Audit Commission 1996). These included the small proportion of time spent by youth justice workers in the direct supervision of, or even contact with, young offenders; the length of time taken between arrest and sentence; and disproportionately high expenditure on processing the prosecution of young offenders as opposed to preventing youth crime.

ST HELENS YOUTH OFFENDING TEAM

St Helens Youth Offending Team has made integration with the health service the nucleus for its activities. Health staff on the team include a part-time health visitor and a full-time drug and alcohol worker. The health visitor plays a key role in handling parenting orders made to the team, in offering voluntary support to parents and offering health screening interviews and advice. The drug and alcohol worker undertakes assessments, provides advice to families and drugs education in schools.

(Crime Concern 1999)

Much of the effectiveness of youth offending teams will rest on their success in *diversion*. Diversion is the process by which offenders are dealt with through a variety of informal arrangements that in effect shunt them out of the formal processing of the criminal justice system. Generally this is associated with diversion from prosecution based on evidence that has shown young men in particular are susceptible to 'crime careers' with entry into the criminal justice system provoking further and more serious rounds of offence and punishment (Muncie 1998). Diversion usually takes the form of systems of police cautioning, reparation and restorative justice (see below) and family group conferencing.

Final warnings are a crucial link in the chain of interventions designed to stop offending at an early stage. The scheme is designed to:

- end the repetitive cautioning of young offenders
- back up final warnings with effective interventions
- ensure that young people who do re-offend after a warning are dealt with quickly through the courts
- encourage the young offenders to participate in a restorative process.

The key to the final warning scheme lies in the effective interventions organised by the youth offending team in support. This involves the YOT in an assessment of the young person to explore his or her receptivity to a rehabilitation programme and whether or not they would participate in a restorative justice conference (Youth Justice Board National Standards 2000).

ACTIVITY 5.10: THE STRENGTHS AND WEAKNESSES OF SOCIAL ACTION AND THE YOUTH OFFENDING TEAMS

Read through this brief case scenario: Tom is aged 14 and displays a great deal of aggression in school. He is from a large and very poor family; he has already been excluded and then expelled from his local secondary school for fighting. His mother says she cannot control him and is afraid that he will fall prey to local drug users' networks.

With a couple of colleagues read back through the earlier part of this chapter on the social action approach to working with young people and then compare it with the approach of a youth offending team. How might each of these approaches respond to Tom and his mother? If you have chance to do some further reading – the chapter by Bob Holman and the book by Howard Williamson for example, cited at the end of this volume – this will help but is not necessary. Think about what your objectives might be from the point of view of each perspective, what resources you would call on and how you would handle the actual work with Tom. Having listed these what do you consider to be the respective strengths and weaknesses of each approach?

It is important not to see the responsibilities of the youth offending team purely as instrument instruments of social control. As street-level practitioners much depends on how you decide to interpret and implement law. It is surprising what can be achieved within formally constrictive legislation to reconcile value conflicts and indeed to move your practice in a distinctly rehabilitative direction. Bailey and Williams, in their survey of youth justice team practice, have shown that practitioners have succeeded in shaping their work in the direction of prevention and diversion (Bailey and Williams 2000).

Restorative justice

Restorative justice complements legal justice and in this sense offers a more holistic, integrated approach in which the needs of the young offender and of the victim and community are responded to. It recognises that crime impacts on the victim and community and involves them in its process as well as the offender: crime is seen in its social context. Restorative justice adopts a problem-solving methodology, flexible enough to look for solutions to the social and personal needs of all those damaged by crime. To do so it draws on the pooled practical experience of criminal justice and statutory agencies like social services and the probation service as well as on the views and experiences of family members. It is a practical, inclusive and personal way of dealing with crime rather than the adversarial, legalistic and technical approach of court proceedings.

Where guilt is not an issue a restorative conference is called to draw up a sentencing plan. Such a conference includes the victim, young offender, families, friends and perhaps a community representative with a trained facilitator. A restorative conference seeks:

- Condemnation of the offence while recognising the offender's worth and strengths
- Holding offenders personally and directly accountable; direct, individual reparation is achieved by any of the following:
  - by apology or other expressions of remorse
  - financial compensation
  - work to make good any damage
  - work for charity or community activity
- To prevent re-offending by re-integrating the offender into local networks and other social connections.

(Pollard 2000)

Beyond restorative measures are other kinds of engagement with the young offender to which social workers will also contribute heavily. These include short-term counselling or group work to bring about behaviour change in relation to drug or alcohol misuse and anger management, attention to mental health problems, improving attendance at school, and preparation for independence with budgeting skills.

Family group conferences

The family group conference has proven effective in both reaching child protection decisions and in working out restorative outcomes in youth crime (Marsh and Peel 1998). At the same time it is highly participative, giving families, victim and offender considerable influence in negotiating and deciding outcomes. Essentially the conference gathers significant members of the family together with a co-ordinator and police representatives who then sit down together to arrive at a workable, plausible response to the offence. The conference has several important dimensions:

FAMILY GROUP CONFERENCE

Marsh and Peel offer a 'best practice guide' in setting up family group conferences (1998: Chapter 3). They emphasise that the role of the co-ordinator is critical particularly in the personal skills required for engaging the family of the offender while at the same time ensuring that the victim is not again victimised or disempowered by the proceedings.

Stage 1 Full and jargon-free information is given to the family concerning the problems as seen by the professionals; this prompts discussion and evaluation.

Stage 2 Private family time, without professionals, to consider the information and what should be done together with determining the support that the family might offer or services required.

Stage 3 Discussion of the decisions and an attempt to outline a clear plan which will respond to the needs of the victim.

(Marsh and Peel 1998: 44)

KEY POINTS

- Addressing the difficulties that young people face in the transition to adulthood is central to tackling social exclusion.
- Good practice means having to take action that is integrated with other agencies such as schools and the employment service.
- Social workers have to familiarise themselves and find their role within the new initiatives such as the Connexions service which emphasises 'pathway planning'.
- Work with young offenders under the Crime and Disorder Act presents the practitioner with dilemmas between social policing and diversionary and rehabilitative work; the latter is available under the act but has to be thought through carefully in the context of popular opinion and recent trends in restorative justice.

KEY READING

Tom Bentley and Ravi Gurumurthy *Destination Unknown: engaging with the problems of marginalised youth* (Demos 1999) provides perceptive analysis of how the predicaments facing young people combine to cause dislocation and difficult transitions to adulthood.

Audit Commission *Misspent Youth* (Audit Commission Publications, 1996) is an indispensable, readable review of what works with young offenders.

Howard Williamson (ed.) *Social Action for Young People* (Russell House, 1995) provides an overall approach to work with young people that contains many promising leads.

Social Exclusion Unit *Bridging the Gap: New opportunities for 16–18-year-olds not in education, employment or training* (The Stationery Office, 1999). It may not make the most riveting reading but it is the current government's strategy in a single volume.

Sonia Jackson and Pearl Y. Martin, 'Surviving the care system: education and resilience', *Journal of Adolescence*, vol. 21, pp. 569–583. Sonia Jackson has done as much as any single individual to call attention to the inadequate way in which local authorities carry out parental responsibilities. Here she and her colleague urge social workers to look much more closely at the education of children looked after by the local authority.

Nick Luxmoore, *Listening to Young People in School, Youth Work and Counselling* (Jessica Kingsley, 2000) reflects the author's experiences in working with young people in several capacities. It is story based on lots of case studies and provides a fine orientation to what young people are thinking and feeling and how to help them sort out their dilemmas.

Peter Marsh and Mark Peel *Leaving Care in Partnership: Family involvement with care leavers* (The Stationery Office, 1999). Most of Peter Marsh's impressive body of work is aimed at improving the participation of families and children in decisions that affect them. Here he and his colleague have conducted research into the process of leaving care and offer many pointers to involving families more effectively.

CHAPTER 6

WORKING WITH SOCIALLY EXCLUDED ADULTS

OBJECTIVES

At the end of this chapter you should be able to understand:

- How care management with vulnerable adults restricts in scope the efforts of social workers to address exclusionary barriers
- That in tackling the social exclusion of adult users social workers need to combine their more familiar community care practice with community development work
- How to maximise opportunities for user participation within mainstream community care practice
- How to reduce exclusion with specific groups of service users.

Social workers working with adults may wonder what the concept of social exclusion really adds to their work. After all the people they work with – those with disability, mental health problems, learning difficulties, in old age – are already widely recognised as socially isolated, discriminated against, often impoverished and cut off from effective services. What further light, they will ask, can the new vogue of social exclusion cast on their work? They will echo a recent poignant letter to the editor of *Welfare Benefits*:

> 'What does [social exclusion] mean? My granddad, Jes, who is 90 and gets a bit confused, has recently left hospital. They wrote to him saying that if he gets lonely or starts to feel *excluded* he should ring the help-line ... '
>
> (Puttick 2000b: 2)

For practitioners it is vital to remember that while the concept of social exclusion does not identify new groups of people to work with, it does lay out *new ways of working*. What is crucial is the emergent practice that fuses attention to social networks, citizen participation, and improving income, within specific localities and developing integrated, holistic service responses through partnership.

In thinking about how the different elements of the process of exclusion function in relation to adults we can discern three broad components that shift in importance depending on which group of users we are talking about. These are:

- Dominant and dominating ideas in the public mind about the lack of capacity and usefulness to society at large, especially in relation to the labour market.
- An enforced poverty because of exclusion from the labour market resulting in unemployment or low-waged work.
- The professional perception that the various groups need to be protected and sheltered from responsibility because they are not equipped for it.
- Violence and harassment, often from young men, stemming from hatred, fear or physical vulnerability.

In working out a response in social work practice, however, it is important not see those in any excluded group only as social victims who require a strong professional agency to batter down exclusionary barriers. Neither is social exclusion a simple matter, but a complex process of loss of opportunities and social connections (Christie 1999).

Social exclusion affects vulnerable adults in particular ways. It may result in exclusion from their own care planning through lack of influence and awareness of rights or from low income whether through insufficient benefits or poor access to the labour market. Because of ill health or disability they may experience social isolation and loneliness through a combination of discrimination based on widespread social attitudes or the views of just a few individuals. Or they may be isolated simply through poorly performing or non-existent networks or other features of the environment such as poor housing or a menacing atmosphere in public places. Equally their exclusion may arise from the structural impact of inequality in health care for illness and disability or the lack of integrated services, for example in health and social care.

For older people alone there is telling data that highlights the extent of their social exclusion. For example some 1.4 million pensioners have only state benefits to live on and are the largest single group on means-tested benefits in Britain. For this group overall the level of expenditure on essentials did not rise during the 1990s. Meanwhile the number of deaths in winter remains between 20 000 and 45 000, demonstrating the close link between ill health and sub-standard housing for older people (Rahman *et al.* 2000).

On another plane the proportion of older people feeling unsafe out alone after dark remains extremely high: women aged 60 or over are more than twice as likely to feel unsafe out at night than men. Most tellingly the proportion of those aged 75 and over who receive help from social services to live at home *declined dramatically throughout the 1990s*, with some 30 per cent fewer pensioner households getting no help from their local authority to live independently at home (Rahman *et al.* 2000). This in spite of a decade of community care practice from social service departments.

CARE IN THE COMMUNITY

At first sight the approach to working with vulnerable adults brought in by the NHS and Community Care Act in the early 1990s would seem to have much in common with tackling exclusion. The report by Roy Griffith (1988) and the White Paper *Caring for People* (DoH 1989) seemed to promise certain key changes in the practice of social care and social work for adults who needed it. Among their key points were:

- Diversification of care services by stimulating through market-like mechanisms a range of service providers so that local authorities would cease to be the only providers of 'care' through their day centres and residential homes.
- It was envisaged that this would produce increasing choice for would-be service users their and families.
- While assessment of individual's care needs remained with the local authority, the assessment decisions would be 'needs-led'; that is, reflect the individual needs of the person being assessed and not be 'service-led', in which assessment outcomes were pre-determined by the basic services that the local authority provided.

In the event these hopes were not realised. This was in part due to the preoccupation of government with closing large psychiatric hospitals and limiting public spending on nursing care. Equally social service managers and practitioners failed to make the conceptual leap from an essentially institutional model of care to a practice which places individual need in the context of community networks and resources (Barr, Drysdale and Henderson 1997). As a result community care became synonymous with 'care at home' and in practice relied on informal care from families to look after those in need.

Despite many articulate voices linking community care with *community capacity* social workers spent little time or energy on this dimension. In his writings Gerald Smale, who was both prescient and somewhat ignored in his time by mainstream practice, urged bolstering carers through local neighbourhood work and strengthening networks. Concepts such as negotiation and partnership, collaboration with community groups and the value of local knowledge all figure prominently in his thinking so that his work is still fresh and relevant today (Smale 1994). He and his like-minded colleagues noted the conflicting responsibilities of local authority social workers between gatekeeping resources and letting service users make decisions, and between professional assessment and user choice. Such dilemmas leave the practitioner with the conundrum: how to conduct practice so that people are not made more powerless and actually rendered more excluded by the assessment process?

Care in the community: dependent on women?

When community care practice relies on informal carers from within the family, women shoulder the main burden and responsibility for providing that care. The argument made by feminists is that caring is essentially a gendered activity and that community care policies rely on this fact but do not acknowledge it. To refer only to 'carers', without also specifying the fact that the preponderance of caring is carried out by women, hides the exploitation on which the policy is based and without which it could not succeed. Ungendered references to 'carers' suggest that *who* carries out caring tasks is not important and at the same time underwrites the assumption that women will take up these tasks as a matter of course. This has the effect of perpetuating the general subordination of women in what dominant social conventions consider to be an informal set of chores that carries little or no value in the labour market. This exploitation, it can be argued, extends also to those who carry out care tasks within the public services such as home carers, lower ranking nurses and residential care workers. Because caring carries so little public recognition or standing those that perform it may undervalue their own work and lose self-esteem.

Thus 'community care' can mask the vastly different sets of interests among men and women and much needs to be clarified before embracing the concept of 'community care'. If it is little more than another ideological device to extract unpaid, low-prestige labour out of women then it is an oppressive concept in its own right (Langan 1992).

Assessment and care planning

Smale (1993) has pointed out the illogical nature of the care management system which became embedded in local authority practice. He was particularly scathing over the local authorities' transformation of the user into a 'customer' to convey a sense of consumer control; this type of participation could only go so far without its limits becoming obvious and pointed out its absurdities when applied to shopping in a supermarket.

CASE MANAGEMENT IN THE SUPERMARKET

Imagine turning up at the supermarket to be met by an 'assessor' or 'gatekeeper' of resources, perhaps called a 'shopping manager'. On entering the shop to acquire your goods, this person explains that their job is to work with you to identify what you need and to form an opinion of what kind of package of goods you need. The shopping manager also explains that this particular supermarket no longer provides many 'goods' themselves but the manager will contract with a supplier who does. Perhaps the shopping manager visits you because somebody has told them you need some groceries but cannot go out.

(adapted from Smale 1993)

If in this process choices are falsely presented and people do not receive the services they need then their powerlessness and sense of exclusion increase. Many of the approaches to needs assessment used by local authorities are dominated by procedural rationale establishing whether a person is eligible for services and to what degree they may have to be charged for that service. Unmet need, criteria for eligibility and limited budgets put care managers in a difficult position. Tanner (1998: 453) notes: 'Practitioners are required to behave in a disempowering way but to believe that they are in the business of empowering those who are oppressed'.

Inadequate resources combined with targeting and a poor relationship between services and carers have made inequalities worse (McLeod and Bywaters 2000). Practice has often been counter-productive and accelerated exclusion rather than diminished it. For example there has been a 50 per cent rise in the number of hospital admissions since the care in community 'revolution' was introduced (Sheldon and Chilvers 2001). Meanwhile local authorities have steadily cut back on the services such as home care that help support people in their own home – leaving carers and users even more isolated (Rahman *et al.* 2000).

There is a sharp contrast between the rhetoric of service user empowerment in professional training, especially for social workers, and the dis-empowering realities that arise in practice largely as a result of inherent contradictions of care management as policy. Tanner argues (1998) that care management practice with its increased administrative and managerial responsibility given to care managers has significantly diminished professional autonomy and discretion to the detriment of users. The only real hope for empowerment that she detects lies in the encouragement and support of user-led initiatives in service planning, evaluation and provision.

Part of the difficulty lies in the definition of need in guidance which is highly normative. Here need equates with the 'requirements of individuals to enable them to achieve, maintain or restore an acceptable level of social independence or quality of life, as defined by the particular care agency or authority' (SSI 1991: 12). Thus user need is defined by what the local authority says it is and moreover is prescribed by bureau-professionals in a manner that is 'individualised and divorced from its social context' (Tanner 1998: 450). This blurring boundary between assessment of need and eligibility for services renders meaningless the disctinction between service-led and needs-led assessment. The prospects for any kind of preventive, or in Smale's term 'developmental', intervention has all but vanished since only those in extreme need are defined as eligible. To obtain any kind of resource for users, social workers as care managers have to play up problems to establish a user's eligibility thus creating assessment procedures dominated by pathology and deficit rather than strengths and capacities.

An authority such as Tanner asserts that there is some limited scope for increasing service users' control over decisions, for example in local authority assessment procedures, but when it comes to challenging the social sources of oppression users exert negligible influence. Her admonition to practitioners is that at least they ground their practice on a realistic understanding of the limitations imposed on them while continuing to search for and the opportunities offered by their role (Tanner 1998).

Notwithstanding these difficulties the practitioner can begin to shift his or her community care practice towards anti-exclusionary objectives by:

- expanding the channels for user participation
- beginning to develop some elements of community social work around care management tasks.

Participation in assessment

Essentially the formulation of a problem is an endeavour undertaken between the people involved and the social worker. For users especially the different stages of social work – assessment, intervention and service provision – are the same activity. To incorporate this notion of dialogue as establishing the nature of a social problem that families are contending with Smale *et al.* (2000) have developed two models of assessment.

In the Questioning Model of assessment (see Figure 6.1) the practitioner gathers information from the 'client' and others such as carers and family members before reaching a judgement or 'assessment' on what their needs or problems are and the solution to them.

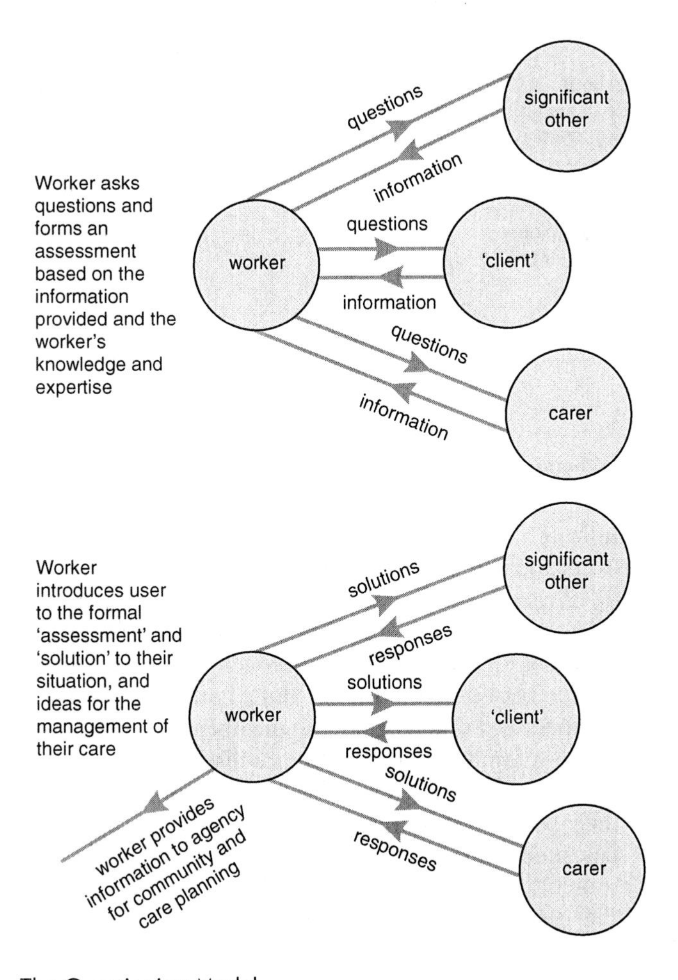

FIGURE 6.1 The Questioning Model

Source: Smale *et al.* 2000.

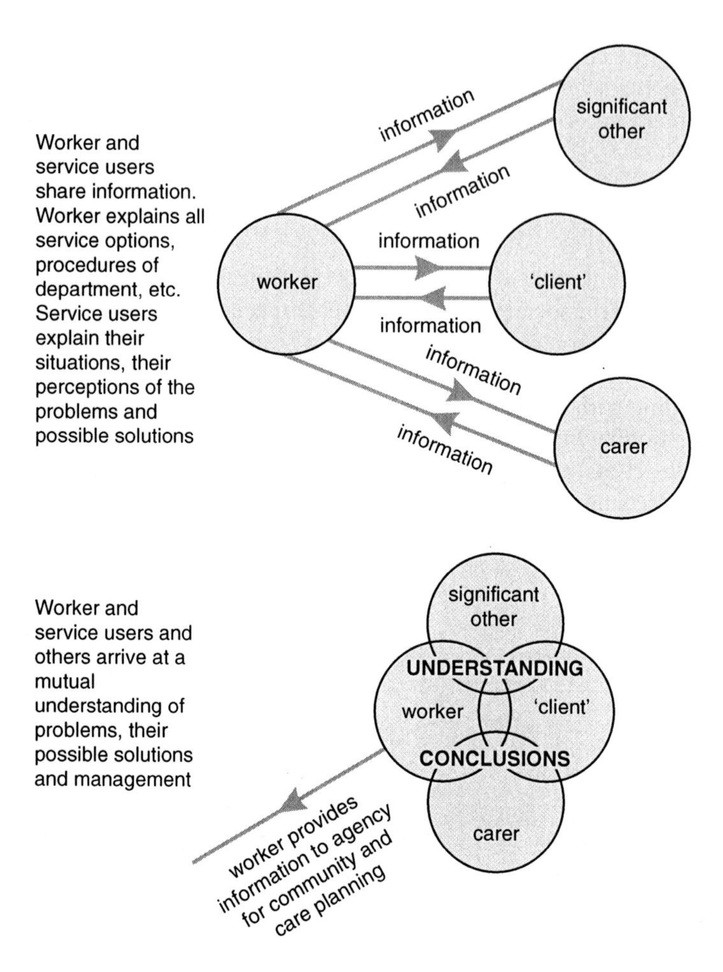

FIGURE 6.2 The Exchange Model

As the diagram indicates, the practitioner's conduct is based on asking questions, processing the answers and using the responses to make a decision on their own about the level and nature of care to be offered. It is a model that reflects the agency objectives, which links client need to pre-set categories and budgets within the agency.

The Exchange Model takes a different approach (Figure 6.2). It focuses on the exchange of information between practitioner and all others involved. The objective is to engage family members and other significant members of a network. It shares some of the characteristics of a family group conference discussed in Chapter 3, where the perception of the situation, the strengths and weaknesses inherent there, the definition of problems and their possible solution derive as much from the family as from the professional. In this model the practitioner is a resource and an enabler, not a conductor of the outcome. Communication across ethnic, racial, class and gender boundaries should be easier because preconceived agency categories and solutions are not subtly framing the interaction.

You may be able to see the strengths of the Exchange Model in relation to working against social exclusion:

- People are able to communicate their own ideas, beliefs and knowledge about their situation and what they need; they are not passive waiting to receive the professional's messages. Dialogue occurs when people interpret messages in accordance with their own assumptions and beliefs. Communication is the convergence of these perspectives; it is central to adult learning and can be achieved only through the exchange of information.
- People are the experts on themselves – not only do they know more about their own situation but they bring a certain degree of control and commitment over their actions that 'expert practitioners' can never instill in them from outside (Smale *et al.* 2000).
- Practitioner expertise centres on the ability to negotiate and conciliate between people who have different perceptions, values, attitudes, expectations, wants and needs. This activity may take place at a time of high stress for users. In this it is similar to the 'political skill' that community leaders, community workers and organisers need to draw on when negotiating around neighbourhood interests.

ACTIVITY 6.1: DANIEL

Daniel Gunn is 58 years old. He has spent recent periods in psychiatric hospitals with what is described as bouts of manic depression. His son and daughter-in-law have just started their own family and although they live in the same city do not feel they can have him living in their household. He appears to have no friends. He was last discharged two months ago. The hospital social worker, failing to secure his going to live with his son, Tom, settled him into a flat of his own on a council estate characterised by a good percentage of households having no work and a high percentage of children living in workless households. For a time after his discharge he kept his out-patient appointments for his medication, but the health service lost contact with him when he stopped attending for these.

When the social worker called he was pleased to have a visitor; the only other person he could remember calling on him after his discharge was a housing officer and a volunteer from a local evangelical church. He told the social worker he had not eaten well in the last couple of days because his disability allowance had run out. He seemed inattentive and the social workers thought he was 'responding to voices'. The social worker decided there was little she could do to resolve his problems while he remained at home and got him reluctantly to agree to go into a residential establishment 'only for a couple of days'.

From the point of view of Mr Gunn what opportunities do you think the practitioner has missed? What mistakes do you think she has made? Were you working with Mr Gunn do you feel that you could place any pressure on his son and daughter-in-law to do more for him? If you were a gatekeeper for local authority resources what further resources would you explore?

COMMUNITY CARE AND COMMUNITY DEVELOPMENT

Increasingly, practitioners are recognising that the social exclusion of adult service users can only be overcome by connecting the objectives of community care with those of community development. They are in fact strongly complementary. The requirements for tackling social exclusion – joined-up action, local approaches, high levels of community participation and explicit attention to inclusion (anti-poverty) have already shifted the emphasis within community care, making it more receptive to community development. As Barr and his colleagues have asserted: 'Methods of community development can help achieve the objectives of progressive community care, whilst engagement with user communities helps community development to realise its vision of inclusiveness' (Barr *et al.* 2001).

A community development framework places the whole matter of community care services and user involvement in a different light. People are motivated to learn, not by the invitation to join a consultation process for existing services but by the desire to solve real problems that beset them. Learning effective skills and the process of practical action becomes the most powerful form of education (Barr *et al.* 1997). Creating communities that support vulnerable adults can best be achieved within a social inclusion framework rather than community care legislation and procedures.

CASE STUDY 9: KINCARDINE, FIFE

Barr and colleagues examined four projects in Scotland that explicitly linked community care with community development. Each revolved around the needs of a group of service users but chose to meet those needs by breaking outside the narrow confines of service provision to embrace aspects of community development.

In the mid-1990s, Fife's Social Work Department was already committed to listening to the community, local participation in service planning and decentralisation, when it thought that some concerted action on behalf of this poor former mining town was necessary. But despite these principles there was a lack of clarity about how to proceed and who would take the lead in the development work. Much of the early part of the initiative was taken up trying to clarify roles and relationships between services to the exclusion of the community.

Direct involvement of the community began in a small way, with the members of the Kincardine Old People's Welfare providing a lunch club and recreational activities for older people. The Council's initial plans were rolled out at a consultation meeting with local residents, but participants found them unnecessarily complex and were in any case much more interested in what they left out, especially the quality of public transport. The Council realised that a more imaginative approach was needed and that the agenda of the community was different from the Social Work Department, although there was overlap with concern for threatened day-care services and patchy home-care services.

For local residents community care was much broader than a specific set of responsibilities or services as the Council had understood them. They wanted better co-ordination of service provision, improved maternity and paediatric services and better public transport. 'Participation' in the context of specific services was also insufficient as residents looked to a more holistic solution. To the credit of the workers involved once they understood where they were going wrong they re-framed their approach in terms of an ongoing dialogue with local people, through both meetings with community organisations and with personal contacts in the community. The social worker brought in a community worker concerned with local community development to work with the community social worker to further expand activity and dialogue. They obtained funding to carry out a surveys of local needs, specifically around day care and support services in the community.

The project developed some imaginative channels for dialogue and participation which are worth emulating. These included:

- Regular and informal meetings – 'Blether over yer denner' – in which members of the Old People's Welfare lunch club met council and other agency staff informally to raise any issues of concern to them.
- Development of community leaders: the 'community' was not an amorphous whole so the recognition and nurturing of leaders who had the backing of specific constituencies was an important resource. These leaders showed evidence of altruism and genuine concern for the situation of other people. But there were also gains for them in terms of their own development. There was little evidence that 'user panels' would have been helpful: their credibility rests on other stakeholders' belief that they have conveyed accurate reflections. The leaders in the project were sometimes users and sometimes not, but all showed a flexible appreciation of the user–leader relationship.
- Vastly increased accessibility of front-line workers: rapid, direct communication was possible and mutual trust could develop. Having skilled and committed community practitioners on the ground willing to listen to the opinions of local people and to act on them paid enormous dividends. They helped connect diverse local concerns with local authority decision making.
- A strong over-arching value framework: the paradox is that a community's care needs can better be realised within a social inclusion framework rather than within the community care legislation. Caring communities is the task for everyone in community planning and not just social work and social service departments.

(Barr *et al.* 2001)

Community development approaches to community care emphasise:

- Focus on disadvantaged people and the redistribution of resources and power. It recognises that users and their carers are disproportionately poor. But the reverse is also true: that in disadvantaged communities there is likely to be large numbers of people with care needs. Moreover given the relationship between ill-health and poverty *people are likely to become care users at relatively younger ages than the national average*. The link between community care and community development brings a recognition that the needs of particular groups such as older people or people with disability are intimately linked to levels of employment and inadequate services like housing, public transport or education (McLeod and Bywater 2000; Barr *et al.* 1997).

- Focus on the neighbourhood and communities of interest. Groups of care users may form communities of interest through their common experiences and needs which prompt them to act on a collective basis. Much of community care is based on the premise that users should be able to participate as fully as they are able; the task of community development is to help develop this participation. The principles of 'normalisation' and citizenship cannot be achieved without the active participation of care groups in the planning, provision and consumption of care services (Barr *et al.* 1997: 3).
- A commitment to helping communities find ways of resolving unmet need through their own and others' resources and to assist them in developing an analysis of their problems. Local citizens become their own service planners. (Kretzman and McKnight 1993).

ACTIVITY 6.2: DEVELOPING CARING COMMUNITIES

Drawing on the case study from Fife, reflect on the scope of your own practice. Do you see the possibility of applying some of the approaches tried in Fife in your work and area? For example, are there opportunities to have very informal discussions with users and officials? Are there potential community leaders that could develop with support? In responding to this challenge draw up a list of those forces that would inhibit you and those that would enable you. Inhibiting factors might include lack of staff commitment, no premises accessible to users and local citizens or an assessment caseload too pressing to free up the time. Enabling factors could include drawing on voluntary agencies for suitable premises, searching out and publicising examples of good practice for team meetings and setting up a small working group to study possible projects.

Community care practitioners need several skills to fuse their work with community development. They need:

To engage with people *in the community in setting aims and objectives*. For example, in the setting-up of a carers' support scheme in a neighbourhood by a social worker with older people, consulting the community by advertising and holding a public meeting in the time-honoured way would likely have a poor response. It is more effective for practitioners to identify ways in which they are already in touch with members of the community through home-care service, low-cost day centres, lunch clubs or contacts with family and relatives. This allows them to pool useful information, to find articulate spokespeople for their interests and engage in lateral thinking around others' ideas. It also initiates discussion with potential partner services – health visitors, GPs and voluntary agencies.

To record methods and review outcomes; community development work has many possible outcomes and draws on a range of resources. In that sense it can be difficult to answer value for money queries or the scepticism of senior management. We address evaluation issues in Chapter 9 but it is important to know now at the outset to keep a record of *who* is involved, for example team colleagues, community leaders, local residents, workers in other agencies and volunteers. It is critical also to note *how* they are involved – their roles, contact (face-to-face, formal or informal meetings, written communications, small house meetings). Any decisions should be recorded, as should how they were made and with whom.

To release individual capacities in the locality by knowing who can do what in specific areas of development work. It is important to understand the difference between needs and deficits on the one hand and strengths and capacities on the other. Building supportive communities emphasises the latter. Use a Skill Information Inventory designed to pinpoint who has what skills; this is not dependent on skills learned on the job or through formal training although these are included too (see Kretzman and McKnight 1993).

ADDRESSING THE EXCLUSION OF USER GROUPS

In this section we examine some of the implications of tackling social exclusion with specific groups of adult service users.

People with disability

People with disability articulately expressed the experience of exclusion long before it became a popular concept. Their discussion and practitioners' responses contribute extensively to our current understanding of exclusion as a process that occurs across a whole range of activities from the labour market, to shopping mobility, to simple access to buildings and across city streets.

Generally, social work in the past based its practice towards people with disability on the basis of 'individual pathology' and meeting individual needs; as we have seen. disability in the Children Act automatically renders a child 'in need'. Disability was defined as a set of deficits and needs, and practitioners approached disabled people and their families holding attitudes that linked disability with dependency and care. For decades services were segregated through special schools, adult training centres, residential establishments and long-stay hospitals. Separate leisure facilities are still common with clubs and special holidays undertaken in groups.

Such segregation underpinned a depth of discriminatory attitudes at work in society at large which held mixtures of distaste, distance, pity and condescension. Disabled people felt the full force of multi-layered exclusion: low income through benefits, exclusion from the labour market, from cultural and intellectual activity and disrupted social networks. They also faced a variety of threats to their very existence. One threat came from the judgement that a potentially disabled foetus can rightfully be aborted while another arose from court-sanctioned euthanasia of those in 'vegetative state'. The latter raised within disabled groups the explicit memory of the National Socialist programme in Germany which undertook the first mass destruction of disabled people (Burleigh 1994).

ACTIVITY 6.3: WHERE DO YOU STAND?

Many disability activists are proud of their disability because it provides them with a channel of understanding different to those of able-bodied society, a powerful network and community, and insights and humanity on which they place great value. Thus within the disability movement and between the movement and mainstream society there are sharp debates as to how far disabilities should be avoided or treated. This is an important issue for you and may involve matters of deep personal or religious value that you will want to contemplate. Work through the following brief scenarios to see where you stand on this issue.

1. A deaf activist who resists having a cochlea implant in his ear which would enable him to hear more effectively. He prizes his capacity for fluent sign language and is a sign language interpreter. He and his wife have two children aged eight and six. Do you think he should have the implant or not? The younger of the children also has a severe hearing impairment which an implant could improve. What would you advise?
2. A woman of 44 is two months pregnant. Her husband, who is five years older, believes very strongly that she should have an amniocentesis to determine whether or not the foetus could have Down's syndrome. If the test should determine that that is the case he thinks strongly the foetus should be aborted. She is not so sure. What would you advise?

Largely through persistent advocacy and argument, dedicated activity and civic protest, disabled people have shaped and communicated a vastly different idea of disability. 'The social model', as it is generally called, focuses on how social attitudes have excluded people with impairments. It is society and not the disabled person that has failed to adjust. In this view disabled people do not need a mobility allowance but a transport system that eliminates the barriers to people with impaired mobility. The way homes are constructed do not cater for the full range of physical capabilities; the world of work is completely geared to maximising profit from the able bodied. Community care plans and needs-led assessment have not overcome the core of disabled people's persistent exclusion, with practitioners often deciding what services to provide with little effort to develop the means of self-assessment (Oliver and Sapaey 1999).

Others are now arguing that the social model of disability should be the basis for a 'mutual model', which could be used as a tool for promoting greater understanding and inclusion by focusing more on the common ground between disabled and

THE SOCIAL MODEL EXPLAINED

In our view, it is society which disables physically impaired people. Disability is something imposed on top of our impairments by the way we are unnecessarily isolated and excluded from full participation in society. To understand this it is necessary to grasp the distinction between the physical impairment and the social situation, called 'disability', of people with such an impairment. Disability [is] the disadvantage or restriction of activity caused by a contemporary social organisation which takes no or little account of people who have physical impairments and thus excludes them from the mainstream of social activities.

(from a statement by the Union of Physically Impaired Against Segregation 1976, quoted in Oliver and Sapey 1999: 22)

non-disabled people. In this perspective impairment and related 'disability' are present throughout society with large numbers of people, including carers, family, friends and colleagues involved. In this view disability in some form is not the 'fate' of a restricted minority but a *development* faced by many millions at some point in their lives, particularly as they grow older (Christie 1999). In this view an agenda for 'mutualism' emerges – re-designing workplaces, services and infrastructures – that has the potential for including the, currently, non-disabled, but also addresses disabling barriers in workplaces and other environments.

Income, benefits and work

Employment rates among disabled people are low at around 40 per cent, and have remained low throughout the years of economic prosperity. In 1999 disabled people made up half of all those who were not employed. One telling statistic is that of those who become disabled while in work, one in six lose their employment in the first year of disablement (Burchardt 2000).

At the same time disabled people consistently report that they would like to work; indeed, one-third assert they are available to start work in a fortnight (Burchardt 2000). But getting work is more difficult for disabled jobseekers and of those that do get work one-third find themselves out of work again by the following year. Disabled people are twice as likely to be long-term unemployed and six times more likely to be out of work and claiming benefit (DfEE 1999). Drawing on the Labour Force Survey (DfEE 1999) certain clear patterns emerge:

- Disabled people account for nearly 20 per cent of the working age population but only 11 per cent of those in employment.
- Disabled people are seven times as likely as non-disabled people to be out of work and claiming benefits.
- Disability levels rise with age so that just under one-third of those in the 50–59 age bracket report a current long-term disability or health problem.

(Christie 1999)

In the Labour government's view work is the single most important channel by which any group may overcome social exclusion, so it is not surprising that it is attempting to raise the levels of employment among disabled people. For example it has introduced the New Deal for Disabled People and Single Gateway projects, which offer individual support for disabled people as they move toward work; other measures include a capacity test assessing what work a disabled person is capable of doing, and a disability income guarantee and disabled working tax credit. Additional assistance is promised for disabled children. Incapacity benefit is now means-tested and eligibility narrowed to those who have worked within last two years (to avoid prolonged spells out of work as in effect early retirement).

Helping disabled people in the transition from benefit to work depends on joint working with local employment services to provide integrated support. In the White Paper *Modernising Social Services* (DoH 1998) social services are explicitly given the task of supporting the employment of disabled people for those who are able to work. Social service departments and local health authorities are to draw up joint investment plans for welfare to work for disabled people. For the social worker in community care full exploration of such a transition becomes an important objective. A number of tasks need to be undertaken:

1. For any disabled person who is assessed for community care the social worker should consider how and in what ways their capacity for work can be maximised; this might include looking at how training centres might be used to enhance particular skills or how the direct-payment scheme could be invoked to allow users to purchase their own training or equipment requirements in preparation for employment.
2. Much closer links with the personal adviser under the New Deal for Disabled People initiative need to be established. As with Connexions, the role of personal adviser extends well beyond the traditional remit of the employment service. Social workers can bring far wider perspectives on community supports, the role of networks and commitments to empowerment that they alone have combined in their professional perspective. The personal advisers are a kind of care manager. They can:
   - assess users' own hopes and goals for employment
   - draw up a plan with the disabled person for realising these goals
   - arrange work preparation or training using local providers
   - help with the job search through promoting or matching a user's capacities with employers, countering employer discrimination and bringing employers into job provision in principle
   - support the user throughout the process and help with personal problems that might impede the move toward work.
3. Assessing the extent of local need, mapping out current provision, noting gaps and developing new approaches and projects are all part of the Joint Investment Plan. The Department of Health clearly expects social service departments to increase the numbers of disabled individuals they support in exploring employment options (DoH 1999).
4. Local rehabilitation, job brokering and job preparation are already undertaken by individual social service departments.

(Thornton 2000)

A range of other partners might assist such as local user and advocacy groups, local rehabilitation providers, supported employment agencies, TECS, or local education authorities. Other service departments such as housing, transport and economic regeneration can also play a useful role (Department of Health 1999). But of course when engaging multiple systems in this way it is essential to remember practice is participant centred and aims at creating confidence and building capacity and skills.

Direct payments

The Community Care (Direct Payments) Act 1996 introduced the concept of direct payments to users in lieu of community care services, allowing people with a variety of disability and care needs to purchase their own support, particularly personal assistants. The act applies equally to people with physical disability, mental health problems or learning difficulties although the take-up is greatest among the first group. It is potentially an extremely radical, culture-changing innovation which should allow each user 'to be their own care manager', as Gerald Smale had long thought should be the case.

Direct payment schemes give disabled people the means to set up their own system of personal assistance with a level of personal oversight and control that is unlikely to be matched by agency provision. For direct payment schemes to work, however, social workers need to develop trust in users' capacity manage things independently *and* trust in them to ask for help when needed. PASS, the personal assistance support scheme run by disabled people themselves, is able to assist individuals with the skills for selecting personal assistants and managing the relationship as an employer.

DIFFICULTIES WITH DIRECT PAYMENT OF PERSONAL ASSISTANTS

Mrs B, in her forties, has a debilitating neurological condition. Her husband cared for her until she was admitted to a care home. That placement proved inappropriate and Mrs. B. wanted to return home with a personal assistant directly paid by themselves. The social worker as care manager then sorted out funds from the local social services department, health authority and the Independent Living Fund. The couple completed various documents covering the agreement for paying an assistant directly. But in seeking a personal assistant Mr and Mrs B were vague about the person specification and job description. The social worker was concerned about the unreasonable level of care tasks being placed on the PA and thought that the conditions of employment might become abusive. The Bs did not appear to understand or take proper responsibility for their duties as employers and seemed to place a higher priority on the flexibility and willingness of PA to fit in with their particular demands.

(George 2001)

INDEPENDENT LIVING FUND

The Independent Living Fund provides funding for domestic and personal care but not for nursing needs or child care.

To be eligible for the ILF, a person must meet the following criteria:

- be aged between 16 and 65
- be receiving the highest rate of Disability Living Allowance (care component)
- be able to live in the community for at least the next six months
- have capital of less than £8000
- be assessed as at risk of entering residential care
- be receiving at least £200 of services per week (including any direct payments).

But the matter is somewhat more complex to implement. To make any scheme workable disabled people need to be involved in all stages. Social workers are still the 'gatekeepers' so that most people become aware of the possibility of direct payments rather than services through their social worker. Moreover they still need a social work assessment to determine whether or not they would be eligible for services – and hence for direct payment. As Smale (1994: 6) has noted: 'Being a customer with money in your pocket is not an insurance against powerlessness. It is difficult for users to make real choices when their past experience of using social services is limited. There is always the tendency for 'people to want what they know rather than know what they want'.

But the culture is changing and control is an increasing prize for disabled people. As one disabled person who employs a personal assistant has said: 'With social services home care I felt like they came in, "did me" and then went off and "did" someone else and I was beholden to them. With direct payments I'm the boss and the employee has a different approach to me as I'm paying them rather than someone else sending them to help a hopeless person' (Dawson 2000).

Dawson (2000) listed the benefits of direct payment in employing personal assistants. Disabled people are enabled to:

- Employ whom they choose.
- Determine the hours of employment.
- Determine the tasks they require the PA to undertake.
- Benefit from the flexibility of the employment relationship which allows them to vary their routines.
- Decrease involvement with professional agencies.

People with learning difficulties

Although by no means complete, as with disability campaigns there have been concerted efforts by advocacy organisations promoting greater participation by people with learning difficulties in community life and employment. This process began before the phrase 'social exclusion' took root in the UK but the objectives are the same. 'Normalisation' and 'social role valorisation' (Wolfensberger 1973) and O'Brien's five accomplishments (1985) opened up the dialogue between 'community' and people with learning difficulties – the sharing of gains by increased community involvement by those with learning difficulties as they learn specific sets of social skills. The de-institutionalisation – the closure of the long-stay hospitals for the 'mentally handicapped' and the old adult training centres where basic, repetitive 'employment' was available in a highly institutional atmosphere – were gradually transformed into 'social education centres'.

There have recently been several important developments in both personal planning and in the kinds of services available to break down this enforced separatism of people with learning difficulties:

- introduction of person-centred planning processes
- adult family placements
- supported employment.

Person-centred planning

There is a growing recognition that people with learning difficulties need a greater range of opportunities to work and pursue interests and leisure activities that are community based and expand their friendship networks. One way of doing this has been through the introduction of a 'person-centred' planning process which has both enabled people to realise more of their aims and goals and developed an effective form of participatory engagement.

The concept of person-centred planning grew out of the UK-wide Changing Days Project which was set up to explore ways of promoting user involvement in choosing and arranging day-to-day activities (including work). Each person with learning difficulties has their own 'planning circle', made up of people he or she has chosen: circle members care about the person and are committed to improving their life by helping them to work out what they want to achieve. Importantly the circles draw on people from outside the service itself thus acting as a change agent for the service culture (Cole *et al.* 2000).

The planning circle focuses only on the interests and personal goals of the user. Because of this overriding individual focus, independent facilitators – rather than service-based personnel – are more effective in establishing and nurturing the circles. Independent facilitators are able to hold more firmly to the principle that the person with learning difficulties is the driving force in the planning process and can negotiate more effectively any possible conflicts with the person's care establishment than if the facilitator were a member of staff.

Within circle discussions it may emerge that many users want to find part-time work. Because most have not worked before, intensive long-term support is required to realise this objective, usually in the form of access to supported employment (see below). Leisure or educational objectives are perhaps easier to pursue although they have implications for carers and for those with whom users are living, such as residential home staff or placement families. Planning circles can lead to more involvement in the community and established friendships with local people. This takes time, however, and requires deliberate action, persistence and creative thinking from within the planning circle itself (ibid.).

Adult family placement

Adult placement means that a vulnerable adult goes either to live or to stay with a family not their own. ('Family' here is used in the widest possible sense and may involve any number of carers in a settled relationship.) The family – often referred to as 'carers' – are themselves usually recruited and supported by some form of adult placement scheme. The general expectation is that the vulnerable person lives as part of the family and the carers are paid a fee in return for providing appropriate support. Such placements are quite distinct from board and lodging arrangements or small group homes. Through them a range of exclusionary barriers can be addressed and overcome, particularly the isolating effects of institutional or semi-institutional living.

Robinson (1996) has outlined the common concerns that have evolved among users and which need to be explicitly addressed in any arrangement. In particular any 'family rules' or norms with which the user is unfamiliar need to be explained prior to placement and, if they are deemed inappropriate for adults on placement, to be acknowledged as such by the carers. The adult on placement should have accommodation and facilities that allow for privacy. Personal keys, access to transport, reasonable levels of weekly allowance and holidays are all of great practical significance and need to be agreed in advance. Having a personal key, for example, means that the person with learning difficulties has some opportunity to make informed decisions on their own about risk and the freedom to act on those decisions (ibid.).

Supported employment

People with learning difficulties have regularly voiced their aspiration to have a real job, yet during the 1990s the daily routine for most were days spent in day centres, training centres or sheltered workshops, segregated from their non-disabled peers and earning negligible wages. The notion of supported employment runs counter to this longstanding practice: a person with learning difficulties is helped by a supported employment agency to find a job, internship or work experience that matches their skills and interests. Social workers and care managers should look closely at this option with their service users and be more energetic in stimulating the provision of supported employment opportunities where none exist.

Supported employment agencies offer a variety of objectives:

- Helping people identify their skills and preferences through the development of vocational profile.
- Job development to find the person's preferred job through contact with employers.

CASE STUDY 10: RICHARD

Richard is in his fifties and lives in a small staffed hostel with five other people who have learning difficulties. He has recently been introduced to a job as a storeman – cleaning, loading and stacking – through supported employment after spending many years attending an adult training centre for five days a week. Following a recent change in the policy of his social services department he no longer earns anything for his attendance at the centre. Richard's IQ is 51. He can write his name and read a few single words while his numeracy enables him to count up to ten. Richard is able to look after himself in all areas of his life, only requiring help to budget and to deal with his benefits and medical appointments. He can cook, launder his clothes and shop independently. When he was at the training centre he was known as a hard and dependable worker who completed his tasks thoroughly.

Now he has left his training centre altogether and is working 39 hours a week as a storeman earning above the minimum wage. By certain identifiable scales his support needs might be thought greater than others with learning difficulties, and his measured IQ is certainly lower than many of his peers in the training centre. But he fitted into his new job well, has high levels of interaction with other employees and regards himself as quite happy.

(adapted from Bass and Drewett 1997)

- Job analysis to find out more about the workplace, co-workers and the support needed in that environment.
- Job support to ensure that both employee and employer receive 'just enough' creative assistance, information and back-up so as not to undermine independence and growth of skills.
- Career support to help people think in the longer term about progression.

(O'Bryan *et al.* 2000)

But there are barriers to supported employment opportunities: access remains difficult for many, funding is precarious and fragmented and the benefit system continues to cause difficulties through its lack of familiarity with the concept.

Practitioners can assist in overcoming such barriers by ensuring that strengths of supported employment are fully understood by other professionals and would-be service partners, including personal advisers, and by identifying supported employment as a key component of better services, especially for young disabled people. Local authorities should include supported employment objectives in all community care plans as a core component, and should ensure that the Connexions service offers job tryout, and assistance with transport. Using direct payments for in work support, to increase a person's productivity, is a further promising step forward (O'Bryan *et al.* 2000).

The key to effective employment is in the support. Once a person is matched to a job, the supported employment agency provides a staff member, known as job trainer or job coach, to accompany the new employee to their new place of work. The job

LEARNING, DISABLED ADULTS AND WORK

Social firms are businesses created to provide training and employment for disabled people and others at disadvantage in the labour market. The London Borough of Ealing has developed a policy on social firms bringing together significant funding through a multi-agency approach. The authority has placed dedicated staff in an employment support unit who work with staff in day centres in social services, the local regeneration partnership, and with voluntary groups (Mencap, Age Concern). The firm, called SuperCare, provides home and garden cleaning and maintenance services for older residents, and ground maintenance and cleaning at sheltered housing units, while another firm, Zoomin video, provides training in video production.

(*Community Care* 18 January 2001)

coach helps the employee to learn how to carry out the various responsibilities of the job. As those responsibilities are mastered the job coach withdraws but continues to keep in touch and to be available if needed. The principle of supported employment works for several groups of would-be jobseekers – those with mental health problems, physical disabilities, sensory impairments and brain injury (Bass and Drewett 1997).

There are generally three stages in the supported employment process:

- Vocational profiling which determines the jobseeker's skills, interest and personality.
- Job development which secures a job that matches the profile and meets an employer's need.
- Job analysis which examines in detail the tasks required in the job and the type of social behaviour valued by the workplace culture.

(ibid.)

For practitioners the importance of supported employment as a means for overcoming the social exclusion experienced by people with learning difficulties cannot be emphasised too strongly. Powerful research has established that the levels of *engagement* (defined as taking part in purposeful activity) in the kinds of activities that users find interesting are raised very significantly above what users had experienced in their previous training centres (ibid.).

Older people

Exclusionary forces gather pace as a person grows older: the older person may be out of the job market or have a precarious hold on it; friends die, children grow up, income falls off; networks thin out and become less responsive. There is growing evidence that personal networks have a protective effect on health and wellbeing at all ages but as they erode so that effect wears off (Sluzki 2000). Other trends also contribute to what might be called a 'new precariousness' for older people living in low-income neighbourhoods; one example is the social polarisation found on public housing estates, where pensioners feel intimidated by large groups of young people. Older people too experience the risks associated with the structural change in the labour market: ill-health and disability are less tolerated. Other contributors to the new precariousness are the shrinking of social provision, the destruction of civility and the degradation of family ties through divorce and marital conflict that affect older people's support networks (see Forrest 2000).

ACTIVITY 6.4: AGEISM ON TELEVISION

Pick the listings for any two nights in a given week between 7 p.m. and midnight. What target audience do you think each programme has in mind? Note the images of older people: what role do they have and how do they interact with the local community? Note also the social content and the meanings that you think each programme conveys and whether it confirms the notion of 'generativity' which Erik Erikson described as the eighth stage of human development (see below).

Social isolation, loneliness and networks

Personal social networks may be stable but the fabric of relationships generally constituted by family members, friends, acquaintances, associates from work and relations that grow out of our participation in formal and informal organisations – social, religious, political, neighbourhood – are ever-evolving. These networks have been described as a 'social cocoon' which constitute 'a key repository of our identity, our history and our sense of fulfillment and satisfaction with life' (Sluzki 2000: 271).

Old age is described by Erik Erikson as beginning at that point where a person has already reached the peak of their accomplishments, or if not is facing stagnation and self-absorption. The senior is in transition to that final stage in which all prior stages are integrated with a sense of validity and appreciation, or if not falling into despair, regret and fear (Erikson 1959). Social networks play an important part in this stage of life. A person's social network tracks the individual lifecycle to a degree with some weakening of social bonds from the death or movement of members, loss of some social roles and tasks often related to retirement. A decrease in the older person's capacity to undertake the social tasks required to maintain network links and a reduction in the opportunities for making new friends or new social ties also affect network ties. On the other hand this trend can be offset by intensification of select friendships, the expansion of social tasks through volunteer work or by re-activitating family tasks (ibid.).

Understanding how old age is socially constructed is an important first step in seeing the process whereby older people are excluded through ageism. The social conventions produce 'invisibility' which presumes a lack of sexual interest, an array of phyical weaknesses and the inability to work. Yet, as Bill Bytheway, reminds us 'old age' has no real scientific basis since there are no clearly identifiable set of physical

THE WOODEN BOWL

In Iran they tell this story about old age:

Once there was a family living in peace and harmony: mother, father and a young boy of about six. Then the father's own aged father came to live with them. All was well for a time until the old man's eating habits grew quite sloppy and eventually declined to a point where he dribbled a lot and dropped his food so that he made a mess at the table and on the floor below his chair. He was unsightly and his mouth had to be wiped occasionally. The old man's son and daughter-in-law were repelled by this; they were convinced they had to do something lest the old man set a bad example for their young son. So they shaped a rough-hewn bowl from a lump of wood and gave him a spoon and made the old man eat with these utensils on a mat in a corner of the eating room.

On the second night of this new arrangement, with the old man eating in his corner, the young boy suddenly jumped from his seat in the middle of the evening meal and ran outside. His parents heard sounds of woodworking, hammering and scraping. 'Whatever are you doing?' they called out to their son. 'Why, I am making bowls for both of you when you are old,' he replied. The old man rejoined the family at the dinner table that very night.

changes that marks a person's entry into old age at a given point in time (Bytheway 1995). Physiologically the body changes and deteriorates in different ways throughout life often with compensating strengths developing at the same time. Despite this, older people are routinely barred from opportunities and services on grounds of age – often with widespread popular agreement – in a discriminatory way that would not be legally acceptable if based on race, gender or disability (ibid.).

As with people with disability and learning difficulties older people have fared poorly out of community care services and in particular the lack of links between social care and health care. One key support is for post-hospital care, but the various resources for this – night sitting, home care, help with transport, shopping, laundry, residential convalescence and companionship – are in short supply. Health and social care departments struggle to liaise: in one study in the mid-1990s 40 per cent of senior patients said that no member of staff had discussed with them the sort of help they might need after leaving hospital (McLeod and Bywater 2000). Another study found that even when elderly patients' care needs are considered after discharge, 'hierarchical and discriminatory practices often deny the the opportunity to shape decisions in their own interests'. The pattern of discrimination, particularly against older women, is pronounced: older people are less likely to be referred for home care, and those over 85 are less likely to be admitted to hospice care, although far more likely to be living alone (McLeod and Bywater 2000: 110, 135).

Barber and Crean's study have added powerful detail to this overall picture. Their research shows that, contrary to their original purpose of guardianship, orders under the Mental Health Act have tripled since the implementation of the NHS and Community Care Act 1990. They found that the orders have generally been made for older women and those with dementia. Despite the intention of community care objectives

JOINT PUBLIC AFFAIRS COMMITTEE FOR OLDER ADULTS

JPAC's Institute for Senior Action in New York City integrates education on effective advocacy and critical ageing policy issues with practical grassroots application. Its aim is to hone the skills of longtime community activists as well as provide a way for recent retirees to become more involved in social action. It explicitly addresses the capacity for 'generativity' which Erik Erikson noted as marking the last of the eight stages of life – old age. JPAC founded a comprehensive ten-week leadership training course which has become a powerful tool for introducing and engaging recent retirees into advocacy activism. Their curriculum serves as an excellent model for all advocacy and community development programmes interested in strengthening local leadership.

The curriculum includes:

- the budget and legislative process at national, regional and municipal level
- voter registration and outreach
- policies, programmes and entitlements for seniors
- organising across the generations and within a multi-cultural community
- fundamentals of fundraising
- techniques of social action
- volunteerism and mentoring
- running an effective meeting
- working with the media
- writing skills and techniques
- conflict resolution
- public speaking with confidence.

(adapted from Epstein *et al.* 2000)

enshrined in legislation half of these orders were for older people in hospital *who were then moved to nursing or a residential care home*. In other words the orders were not used to support people at home but to effect a move from hospital to a social care institution (Barber and Crean 2000).

Elder abuse is also a particular feature of the social exclusion of older people with Pritchard (2000) reporting that victims are often socially isolated. Those who suffer it want informed practical help, especially about leaving abusive situations, and need information on choice and availability of housing, entitlements to benefits, access to joint bank accounts held with the abuser; the concerns are for food and warmth, social contact and support. Frequently the abused older person's history of poverty and hardship in earlier life shapes their basic need simply to have enough food and live in a warm environment.

As so often when user views are probed, the matters that older people want addressed in any home care are both practical and social. Raynes *et al.* (2001) found for example that older people want help to keep home clean, regular carers so that trusting relationships can be built up, notification of what tasks older people can expect carers to undertake, and notification of any changes in carers – so that older people are not opening their doors to strangers. For those under eighty years of age the most important objective was 'helping people to get out': to 'Get away from the four walls'.The assistance there is one of companionship: someone to go for a walk with or take them to shops; to meet others with transport, get out and back to their homes safely without being 'shaken up' (Raynes *et al.* 2001). Researchers also find that older people looked to have some influence on shaping the service. The suggestions made to Raynes and her colleagues included daily contact by a service manger with one user to audit experience, and meetings three times a year between a representative older service user, purchasers and providers, and elected members to hear and record user views.

Involvement and participation of older users in shaping services, as we have noted, is a necessary first step to reducing exclusionary barriers. This is an area of work directly under the influence of practitioners themselves. User groups have been shown to be extremely effective with older people; they are increasingly popular and are found on local, regional and national levels and they often have a formal constitution, with officers and management committee (Carter and Beresford 2000). Their real contribution lies in providing an organisational context in which people gain skills, experience and confidence as they learn to work with others and realise the effectiveness of collective action. In this sense they follow the same kind of path as the community organising discussed in the next chapter: they learn to carry out research, develop a sense of what their interests actually are and, in moving together, exert some influence over their local political environment. Carter and Beresford (2000: 34–5) have noted that, among the strengths of user groups, they:

- offer an effective way of people working out together what they want to do by developing their own agenda
- offer a route for personal development
- offer individuals support and purpose through social contacts and activities.

The strengths of a users' group derive from its independence. Without that it quickly loses its purpose, which is to build up a base of influence and action. The practitioner can certainly facilitate, support and obtain useful resources from her or his agency but at the same time must constantly examine such steps to see that the integrity of the group is not being compromised in an unintended way. The 'iron rule' of community organising applies here too: 'Never do for the people what they can do for themselves. Never.'

But user groups are not universally applicable. Carter and Beresford note that people are often reluctant to get involved, particularly as that involvement can be demanding, and that many groups are under-resourced and have difficulty in attracting members from minority ethnic groups. There are other forms through which older people participate in service development, including user panels which provide views on local services, and user forums which take up a wider range of issues such as pensions, community care charging policies, or employment (Carter and Beresford 2000).

In common with other user groups, older people have developed a strong self-advocacy movement – pressing a political agenda, educating the public and arguing for civil rights. As with all self-advocacy movements a key step forward has been to throw off the passive, medicalised and individualised view of old age as constructed around the social conventions of 'inevitable decline' and 'failing powers'. The introduction of the Human Rights Act into UK law (in October 2000) and awareness of the powerful political activism of self-advocacy groups in the US staffed by older people have offered further impetus to the movement already under way.

Working with HIV/AIDS

Social work with people living with HIV (human immunodeficiency virus) and AIDS (acquired immune deficiency syndrome) means confronting a number of complex barriers. Furley (2000) has noted that there are two parallel sets of phenomena in the exclusion of those with HIV and AIDS. One is the medicalised treatment programmes of HIV infection; the other is social stigma, fear, ignorance and discrimination. He asserts that social work has important roles to play in responding to both – whether through counselling, advocacy, social action or policy development.

We are already able to look back at significant medical advances in the medical treatment of HIV and AIDS, and to improved levels of public awareness at least in the developed countries such as the United Kingdom. These have followed the use of highly active antiretroviral treatment (HAART) which dramatically slows HIV disease progression. But this progress has only added complexity to the social work task. In addition now to needing skills around momentous life events – sexuality, dying, death and bereavement, drug or alcohol abuse – have come additional issues to tackle. These include working with users who are now able to plan for their future, when previously that future had been short term at best, becoming informed of the impact of intricate drug regimes, and helping in returning to work or in job training (Furley 2000). In promoting empowerment the social work practitioner helps people to normalise HIV, and to hold different possibilities for the future. This extends across a broad range of issues, whether reviving aspects of their social and sexual lives or learning to take an active role in their own medical management.

But as with other excluded groups, social stigma and discrimination also play a role in the exclusionary process and require energetic challenge from practitioners and users. At the core of this is physical intimidation and public homophobia. The experiences of gay men reveal a large group of adults excluded through violent victimisation, harassment and discrimination. In one important study in Edinburgh, Morrison and Mackay (2000) found that of their large sample 57 per cent of respondents had experienced some form of harassment in the previous 12 months while one in four had suffered a violent incident over the same period. They also reported that the work place is the setting for a significant amount of victimisation, but many employers fail to recognise gay men as a vulnerable group. The authors concluded that violent victimisation is endemic to the lives of most gay men, the accumulating effect of which is the exclusion of members of the gay community from the services and structures of support available to other groups in society.

Beyond physical intimidation lie the discriminatory attitudes and areas of ignorance that exclude further. For instance, Wolfe (2001) has underlined the everyday difficulties for gays and lesbians in employment and the social relations that build up within the work context. Often there is pressure to remain outside such circles and networks simply because of the implicit heterosexual culture of family and partnership that dominate them, with high levels of anxiety that personal relationships will be uncovered. Wolfe's vivid example is that of the former cabinet minister Peter Mandelson, who was often portrayed in the press as aloof, or walking alone or with his dog. As for HIV/AIDS itself, public attitudes, while changing, still embrace disgust, blame and fear toward the virus and at the same time show levels of 'AIDS fatigue'.

Finally, practitioners should bear in mind the strong evidence to suggest that ethnically diverse families, oppressed by 'race' and socio-economic status, are less likely to seek early treatment and more likely to die sooner (Goicoechea-Balbona 1998). The development of a culturally specific model which aims to explore the shared beliefs and behaviours that prevent families from pursuing medical treatment is another important prong in tackling public ignorance, in this case among would-be users. Such a model would embrace a specific understanding of the cultural community, being worked with, a culturally sensitive approach to assessment and intervention, and the use of key health providers originating within that community (Goicoechea-Balbona 1998).

KEY POINTS

- ❑ Care in community policy and practice has often served to reinforce the exclusion of vulnerable adults; nevertheless, participative forms of assessment can to a degree overcome some of the exclusionary impact of routine, proceduralised forms of care management.
- ❑ Linking care in community objectives to a community development framework creates far greater levels of user control and at the same time develops capacity within communities to tackle other civic tasks.
- ❑ There are specific ways of breaking down the exclusion of particular user groups such as older people, and people with learning difficulties or disability. These include supporting self-advocacy, links with supported employment, promoting networks to overcome loneliness and family placements for adults.

KEY READING

Barr, Drysdale, and Henderson, *Towards Caring Communities: community development and community care* (Pavilion, 1997) effectively links community care with community development and takes you and your colleagues through a number of exercises to underpin their point.

Tony Carter and Peter Beresford in *Age and Change Models of Involvement for Older People* (Joseph Rowntree Foundation, 2000) have produced a short, wonderfully clear guide to inclusive practice, with examples and resources also available in its 45 pages.

Eileen McLeod and Paul Bywaters, *Social Work, Health and Equality* (Routledge, 2000). Social workers have to learn to deliver their services for adults in close relationship with health services; this book provides an excellent grounding for this with a strong emphasis on overcoming exclusion and inequality.

Oliver, M., and Sapey, B., *Social Work with Disabled People,* 2nd edn. (Macmillan, 1999). This is the classic account of the 'social model' of disability, now in a new edition.

Gerry Smale and his colleagues, Graham Tuson, Nina Biehal and Peter Marsh, in *Empowerment, Assessment, Care Management and the Skilled Worker* (National Institute of Social Work, 1993) intertwine the themes of inclusive community care practice with focus always on the 'social situation'.

CHAPTER 7

WORKING WITH DISADVANTAGED NEIGHBOURHOODS

OBJECTIVES

At the end of the chapter you should:

- Understand how specific neighbourhoods become excluded from the relative prosperity and opportunity found elsewhere in the town or region of which they are a part
- Know certain techniques for building up community strengths or 'capacity building' in support of local citizens and organisations determined to shape their own future
- Understand the importance of maximising resident participation in any community development project and how to audit levels of participation
- Be familiar with approaches and strategies that help local services play a key role in reviving such areas, such as creating partnerships and neighbourhood teams.

Increasingly a consensus embracing practitioners, managers and policy makers has realised that social exclusion has a spatial dimension. In neighbourhoods of high deprivation the various components of exclusion reinforce each other so that everyone in that particular area is affected. Services are poor, there is a sense of physical insecurity because of high crime, housing is overcrowded, levels of political participation are low, and employers and commercial outlets leave the area, so there are few jobs; many residents thus rely on benefits. When a whole area is excluded, such as a public housing estate, the most damaging long-term impact is in terms of what sociologists call 'neighbourhood effects' – the decline in the social fabric and loss of control over public space.

This chapter explores the approaches and techniques of working with excluded neighbourhoods, helping to build the structures and capacities on the ground so that local residents can more actively shape and contribute to the renewal of their own localities.

Since the mid-1980s the notion of 'neighbourhood', like 'community', has virtually disappeared from social work concern. This is partly because of the pressure on social workers to focus on risk and protection and partly because of increasing specialisation around groups of users rather than areas. But it is also a result of changing professional values and attitudes: there is distrust of the very notion of 'neighbourhood' and 'community' which are seen as potentially repressive entities.

Tackling social exclusion on a local basis allows social work to redevelop its expertise in community building that historically was always part of its activities dating back to its origins in the work of settlement houses. Unless this reconnection with locality is explored and developed social work will only be further bureaucratised as the local, neighbourhood dimension is lost to other services (Fox Harding 1997).

ACTIVITY 7.1: WHAT IS A NEIGHBOURHOOD?

It is important to reach some understanding of what a 'neighbourhood' is. Write a list of what you consider to be the characteristics of a neighbourhood – not what an ideal neighbourhood should be, but as it is. It may help for you to consider first the areas in which you work, or live, or were brought up. In your understanding of what defines a neighbourhood which of the following is the most important: physical boundaries such as roads, culture or ethnic make-up, social networks and local associations, income levels or housing tenure?

The neighbourhood as the focus for combating exclusion is not the cosy, rosy world evoked in memoirs of working-class districts and mining communities or in the idyllic pictures of suburban living in the 1950s. A neighbourhood may mean nothing more than an area with some sense of physical boundary or other defining limits. In tackling exclusion neighbourhoods become the focus, not because of any belief in a false consensus but because local areas are sites where *multiple strands of exclusion come together*. In fact in your work you will want to uncover any false consensus and recognise local diversity whether in culture, ethnicity, gender or income levels.

Forest and Kearns (1999) provide a convenient summary of a number of studies on neighbourhood effects:

- Decaying or abandoned homes and buildings have a severe negative effect on the morale of residents, providing a major incentive to move elsewhere
- Highly disadvantaged neighbourhoods lack organised activities and community facilities

NEIGHBOURHOOD – A DEFINITION

A neighbourhood is a geographic zone or area which is continuous and surrounds some other point, usually a person's home, and is smaller in size than some other recognised spatial entity, for example a city sector or a city. Neighbourhoods can be defined by individuals, groups of individuals or by organisation and they may be defined for single functions or the overall set of household activities. They do not have precise borders but are judgements about who and what to include in the operational definition.

(adapted from Maclennan 2000: 11)

- Residents do not see themselves as being in control – and what they want is to have influence over regular services rather than special projects
- Neighbourhoods do matter to residents, and it is wrong to characterise disadvantaged areas as lacking social cohesion and interaction which can survive in difficult places.

Socially excluded neighbourhoods in Britain are generally those composed of inner-city public housing flats such as high rises, the decaying owner-occupied or privately rented terraced housing of older cities and the peripheral housing estates that ring many of Britain's urban areas. Even prosperous towns have large council-owned estates which over a period of time have experienced intense deprivation.

Neighbourhoods in decline

What cuts a neighbourhood off from the economic, social and political activity of the city or region within which it is located? Physical layout and the nature of the housing have much to do with it. Social housing (a term which embraces both housing associations who let their property to those in social need and local authority housing) has become a residual service, that is an under-resourced, basic service for those individuals and families who could not find housing in other parts of the housing system (in the main through home-ownership). As a result certain low-income groups are channelled towards specific areas within a local authority area. For example, Ms Rice in Chapter 4 quickly noted there were other lone mothers living near her; that was not the result of coincidence but deliberate housing allocation policy by the local authorities. The consequence is polarisation within housing as the council estates provide for an increased proportion of deprived people and to cater more exclusively for this group (Lee and Murie 1997).

But poor housing is not the only factor. As a result of the concentration of poor people living together the social fabric of the estate – that is the way people relate to each other and the strength of local organisations such as churches or mosques – is also changed. In *Estates On the Edge,* Anne Power provides a good overview of how a range of negative pressures build up within large housing estates.

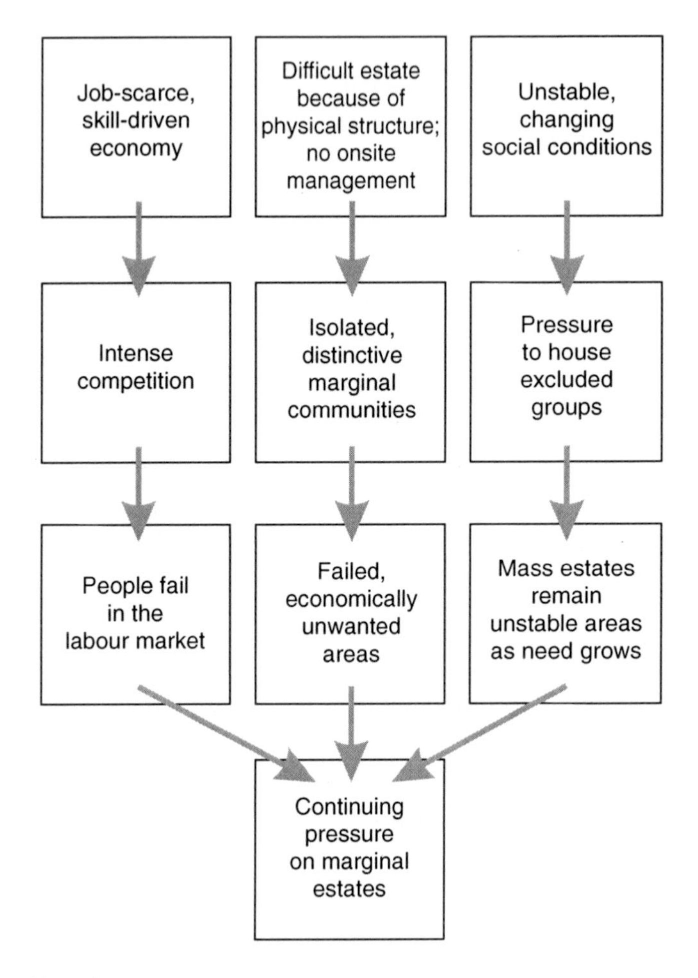

FIGURE 7.1 Negative pressures on mass estates
Source: adapted from Power 1997.

Figure 7.1 shows how:

- Larger economic pressures such as the demands of the labour market for highly skilled people combines with
- Local conditions such as the layout and structure of individual estates (for example with back-alley access to individual houses which facilitates burglary, and no on-site warden or manager) and
- Disrupted social fabric as excluded, relatively impoverished individuals and families take up shorter-term tenancies. These factors result in loss of confidence accumulating, property being abandoned and declining in value, levels of local activity and energy being run down, services being withdrawn, loss of authority and collapsing viability.

(Power 1997; Power and Mumford 2000: 81)

Social capital

It is easier to identify certain aspects of a neighbourhood's exclusion such as poor housing or unemployment. This will show up in data provided by the local authority on the proportion of households where the head of household is not in work, the proportion of households that are overcrowded or the number of households living in temporary accommodation.

But getting an idea of the extent of social cohesion or what is now referred to as 'social capital' for an entire neighbourhood is more difficult. Social capital refers to the accumulated social networks and connections in a given neighbourhood which includes things like the level of activism in civic organisations, the degree of politicical involvement and the vitality of local institutions such as churches or mosques. A number of indicators have been developed that show the extent of social capital in a given area. One such indicator is the proportion of individuals who are not involved in any civic organisation – whether political party, church, mosque or temple, trade union, tenants' association, club or social group. Another is data on community safety, say the total number of burglaries, access to insurance against crime, individuals expressing dissatisfaction with their neighbourhood (Putnam 2001). Also included in an audit of social capital are new organisations associated with environmental activism, local exchange and trading schemes (LETS), credit unions and other participatory initiatives. The concept of social capital now should be integral to its theorising about change.

CAPACITY BUILDING IN NEIGHBOURHOODS

Initiatives for tackling the social exclusion of neighbourhoods have to address both the physical fabric and the social fabric of a local area. Very broadly the objectives of such projects are described as 'regeneration' or neighbourhood renewal. The present government's flagship regeneration programme is the New Deal for Communities in which certain deprived estates construct local partnerships involving all sectors of the locality in order to put together plans for funding to tackle the worst of their social problems (SEU 1998). But the government's strategy goes well beyond this; the publication of *National Strategy for Neighbourhood Renewal* (SEU 2000) outlines a broad range of approaches and measures to restructure the social capital of many of Britain's most deprived estates and provides essential reading for a global understanding of the scale of activity that is now taking place.

As soon as you look closely at the scope of any renewal project you will see how the many threads of social exclusion are being tackled simultaneously. The only way to lift a neighbourhood out of exclusion is to address community safety, educational attainment, local economic development and health inequalities at the same time. For good reason are such strategies called in the US 'comprehensive community initiatives' (Kubisch and Stone 2001).

As a social work practitioner you may find you and your agency are part of a renewal strategy for a particular area. Many of the approaches discussed in earlier chapters play a part in neighbourhood renewal. For example, you may contribute to a community safety plan by working with young offenders, or help to get a Sure Start

CAPACITY BUILDING – ROYDS COMMUNITY ASSOCIATION

The Royds Community Association is now nationally prominent as an example of local citizens developing immense capacity and strategic range within what started out as a small organisation. It was set up in 1993 to regenerate three local authority housing estates in south-west Bradford. Its aim was to build self-sustaining communities with residents centrally involved both in identifying their future needs and in achieving them. The original group included several residents, a person from the private sector and a local authority housing officer.

They spent three years doing their research and preparing plans and proposals before a major bid for urban regeneration funding was made. Now the Royds Board has twenty-two directors, including twelve elected locally. Most of its committees and groups are chaired by local people and assets are controlled by residents. As an indication of how its prowess is viewed the Association is deemed the accountable body for central government monies rather than, as is much more usual, the local authority. Now its objectives include major social, economic and physical development. To be sustainable the Association offers extensive capacity-building training and support for local residents allowing the various communities to be involved in its affairs. A social action programme was launched in 1998 which aims to have more than 100 residents involved in voluntary work on the estates by 2002. One interesting statistic: during the period of their summer programmes youth crime reduced almost to zero.

(Duncan and Thomas 2000; Shaftesbury Society 2000)

scheme off the ground as part of a larger renewal strategy. Equally you, your colleagues and your agency may want to adopt a 'neighbourhood approach' on your own in order to develop closer links with a specific area. Whatever the scale of the project, learning to work within such initiatives, finding roles and clarifying responsibilities for yourself and your service is a challenge but a rewarding one.

The common thread that runs through all neighbourhood renewal is 'community building' or as it is now more frequently called, 'capacity building'. Capacity building means helping a local area develop and strengthen its own organisations, increasing levels of resident participation and engagement, developing local leaders – all with the purpose of strengthening the neighbourhood to take control of its own affairs. Capacity enables local residents and organisations to engage in consultation, planning and implementation of regeneration objectives. It includes training, personal development, mentoring and peer support, based on the principles of empowerment and equality provided they ultimately benefit the neighbourhood (Skinner 1997). If capacity building can be reduced to one phrase it would be 'learning to acquire and to use power and influence to secure certain democratically determined objectives'. Whether a project is a large and complex one, centrally funded under the New Deal for Communities, or a small initiative which you and your colleagues have initiated, such as bringing together a closely worked out joint social and health care plan to a small neighbourhood, capacity building in the area is the prerequisite to its success (Henderson and Thomas 2001).

CAPACITY BUILDING – FRESH LOAF

One of the main concerns of the community in Ferguslie Park is food poverty. This quite simply means that families cannot afford or do not have access to enough food for an active healthy life. The development of out-of-town supermarkets and closure of local shops together with the low level of welfare benefits and lack of transport have made accessing a healthier diet increasingly difficult for growing number of households. FRESH LOAF was formed to maximise local knowledge, skills and resources to address the problems caused by food poverty. The project has brought together a number of groups – Women's Health Group, Diabetic Self Help, Middle Years Group, 50+ Activities and Health Group Elderly Forum, and Women's Food Poverty Group. All members are local people.

The objectives of FRESH LOAF are to:

- Identify problems experienced by low-income households in accessing affordable good-quality food.
- Devise practical ways that communities, relevant agencies and the food industry can work together to address the problems of low income.
- Identify opportunities for job creation through the development of local food economies such as bulk buys.

The group has undertaken a range of activities. It has:

- Collected information on food poverty and become familiar with service agencies' attiitudes and practice and national policies.
- Carried out a community survey to gauge local support and find out what residents wanted.
- Organised public meetings and visited community shops elsewhere in Scotland.
- Proposed a corner shop development within the estate. Because the group had already gained commitments from various agencies to work in partnership it received advice from the Co-op on retailing, while Forward Scotland provided a grant to enable group members to take part in retail and management training.

(The Poverty Alliance, *Action on Poverty and Social Exclusion* n.d.)

Examples of capacity building initiatives include:

- Development of vision and action plans
- Negotiating a written service agreement between the locality and the agencies involved
- Ensuring community representatives chair and occupy the majority of places on partnership boards and other forums

- Resident-led consultation including street meetings, door-to-door surveys and local planning events
- Resourcing and supporting resident involvement in developing new local organisations, such as credit unions, to the point where they manage the project and assets.

CASE STUDY 11: LABO

LABO Housing Association was set up in the mid-1980s to combat local homelessness among local ethnic minorities and has long responded to the needs of local Bengali and Somali women and women-headed households. It has pioneered the concept of 'housing plus' long before that concept became familiar either in the UK or the US.

One of the founders, Myra Garrett, says 'We were always oriented towards women. Other organisations which were dominated by men became riven with messy political divisions – we have avoided that. Women often carry the family, the domestic support – they are the key to well-being. We always tried to get women actively involved' (cited in Short 1999: 9). LABO, with its Sylheti-speaking director Solma Ahmad, has supported families facing racist attacks and Asian women suffering domestic violence, and also offers accommodation to refugees. In all of its activities it facilitates tenant and community participation.

(Short 1999)

Housing plus

Building local capacity and holistic services around housing provision is a community development model that has gained recent credibility. Strong research evidence in the United States shows that social services provided within an organisation that offers low-income housing services as well are accessible and have credibility among tenants and residents (Sullivan 2001). In the UK the equivalent is the 'housing plus' activities undertaken by some housing associations and registered social landlords which have taken on board a range of service activity on top of providing low-cost social housing. Some of these activities include:

- One-stop shops providing access to other services in a local venue
- Employment and training services linked to job experience in construction, maintenance and security undertaken by the housing association itself
- Leisure and activities provision for young people
- Community network development through social activities, meetings and block parties
- Establishing credit unions and providing money advice
- Improved infrastructure through the provision of shops and health care facilities.

(Taylor 2000)

CASE STUDY 12: NEW HORIZONS SAVING AND LOAN SCHEME

This credit union began work among tenants of a housing association in Cambridge. The association ran four residential homes, supported housing projects for teenage parents and adults with learning difficulties together with sheltered housing and a nursery. It has an explicit anti-poverty strategy for its tenants and had found that some of them were being approached by loan sharks asking interest rates of up to 300 per cent.

The development worker faced certain obstacles: tenants were dispersed over a large area, there was little tradition of tenant involvement and numbers were small. Nevertheless the credit union was established after careful research and links with a building society in the city. What is distinctive about this particular credit union is the repeated survey research it undertakes and its willingness to adjust practice and renegotiate procedures very quickly. Thus far they have learned that:

- Their original loan policy had been too traditional and restrictive
- Initial changes removed restrictions but then became too liberal and resulted in arrears
- A new policy now takes a more personal approach and asks more relevant questions on ability to pay.

(Reynolds and Kohler 2001)

Credit unions

But building local capacity happens in many forms. Combating financial exclusion offers one example. Exclusion from access to financial services in deprived neighbourhoods, especially in inner-city areas, is well documented. Local citizens in poor neighbourhoods are vulnerable to loan sharks and other expensive forms of credit: catalogues, hire purchase, local money lenders, store cards and bank or building society overdrafts. Credit unions are one tool for repairing the effects of financial exclusion (Rossiter 1997).

Essentially they are self-help, not-for-profit organisations that encourage members to save regularly, thereby creating funds that can be used to provide other members with low-interest loans. They have grown rapidly since the mid-1990s; there are now over 600 credit unions with assets of £104 million and a total membership of some 200 000.

For example in Birmingham, credit unions cover two-thirds of the city and focus mainly on areas of financial exclusion and deprivation. Their impact is larger than their function because as volunteers become skilled they augment local capacity. Women comprise two-thirds of the membership and lone parents are over-represented as are people in part-time employment and members of the African Caribbean community (Feloy and Payne 1999).

Helping a small group set up a credit union is a good example of a neighbourhood-level intervention in which you can assist. A credit union may begin as an informal group of savers with only a handful of members, but the idea can come from anywhere, including yourself in house meetings or working with tenants' groups or clusters of service users. Some guidelines and characteristics are listed below:

- Any credit union needs to define its network and location boundaries. This requires some thought and local knowledge. For most credit unions choosing an agreed area can take six months.
- Raising money and training requires a number of volunteers. The work of most credit unions is carried out by volunteers and calls for considerable levels of skill, particularly in managing organisations and working in teams. While permanent staff are a great resource, often credit unions' backbone are their volunteers.
- Start-up grants are provided but are usually inadequate for the purposes – insurance, registration fees, printing and equipment.
- Finding low-cost office accommodation is often beyond reach so that all materials, books and equipment have to be taken home by volunteers after each session. Ideally, permanent secure accommodation is required for an office but also to enable confidential discussion among members.
- Election of a board of directors is a necessity. The operation and policy of the credit union are governed by an elected board of directors and various committees. These are usually drawn from the volunteer workforce.

GETTING STARTED IN THE NEIGHBOURHOOD

You and your agency as well as other public and voluntary services have a large role to play in capacity building. To do so there are several steps that will get you closer to a specific neighbourhood, to the point where you and your service are an asset rather than a liability in this process. These are:

- Thinking through your role, your agency's role and your relationship with other prospective partners
- Getting to know the neighbourhood
- Generating maximum levels of participation in developing goals, objectives and plans.

(adapted from Henderson and Thomas 2001; Twelvetrees 1991; Skinner 1997)

Thinking through your role

Before beginning any concerted neighbourhood work you will want to resist the temptation to undertake some form of immediate engagement and think through what your objectives are in the work ahead. The temptation to begin immediately by making an array of contacts and carving a path of your own strewn with suggestions for residents to chew over is strong, especially if you are new to the work or new to a given neighbourhood. It is unlikely however that as part of a larger effort to tackle social exclusion on an estate that you will be given a broad, open-ended brief to do 'community work' without some broad objectives already in place. Regeneration initiatives are often complex projects that extend over a long period of time so you, your team and your agency will want to discuss what your contribution should be and how you can sustain it. You will need to think through in advance what is possible within your existing role and responsibility and also how those roles and responsibilities might be altered to incorporate explicitly some form of neighbourhood involvement.

While it is essential to respond to what local residents are saying they need there is nothing stopping you from thinking out in advance what your expertise and agency activities might contribute in broad terms. These might include:

- Developing the resources of a 'caring community' discussed in Chapter 6
- Working to establish a neighbourhood one-stop shop that brings services such as housing, health and social services together
- Developing a family centre or a community-run after-school club or other form of family support in the neighbourhood
- Helping set up and run a local advice centre
- As a member of a youth offending team, contributing to a neighbourhood safety plan.

But you will also have to step back and think about values and general principles. Are you and your agency really willing to work in partnership and perhaps to let others receive credit for a well-handled project? Will your agency provide funding to local residents' groups even though it means diverting funding from elsewhere? Are you able to merge activities with other service agencies who may be identified as a 'lead body'? How far do you think resident participation and control should go? Are you willing to set aside notions of professional expertise and control to allow residents and their organisations develop their own projects and approaches although they may diverge from your notion of what ought to happen?

For any particular project a broad brief may already have been formulated by your agency, or by a local partnership board. But the basis of your entry into the neighbourhood still requires explanation and negotiation. You will need to know where you fit within the broad outlines of the project or emerging regeneration plan. Explaining what you see as your role and how it fits with the aspirations of local people will be a distinct challenge. The local priest, Bangladeshi youth leader, activist nun, tough-minded pensioner who heads the local tenants' association, the local councillor, the manager of the local women's centre, the committee raising funds for a mosque all have influence and will all want to know what you are about.

Getting to know the neighbourhood

It is essential to become familiar with the area. There are many sources for local research to explore: local newspapers, census data, ward deprivation index. But talking to as many persons and the leaders of local organisations as you can provides the best way of building up a picture of who holds influence and what the effective networks are.

Such research has two effects. It helps orient you in your work but it also helps the neighbourhood because you begin the process of accumulating vital accurate information that is useful in subsequent negotiations with other stakeholders, for project proposals and funding applications. It is surprising how fast you can build up your familiarity with the networks in the neighbourhood. Soon you should be able to put together, for example, a rough neighbourhood network map and a list of local organisations with the names of individuals prominent within them.

Community profiling

You may want to gather much more detailed information because you do not want to be caught out using hearsay or surmise in a crucial meeting with prospective funders or in a neighbourhood forum. You will find that gathering and making sense of local facts and figures will strengthen your arguments and make your objectives more useful to local residents, organisations, service managers and funders.

This level of research has to be carefully planned and before you rush into it there are a number of points which you and your team or group should consider. It can:

- be time-consuming to plan and carry out
- absorb a group's attention and divert time and energy from other main tasks
- produce poor-quality information which you find in the end is unusable
- raise expectations that the findings on their own will lead to change.

If you do require more sophisticated information it may be possible to draw on the research skills of a local college or university who would be eager to join a collaborative effort. If you decide to go ahead ask yourself and your team two key questions:

1 What do we want to find out? The more amorphous or general your objectives the greater the chance of not meeting them. Be clear and opt for specified areas of inquiry: for example, finding out the extent of closure of bank branches (leading to financial exclusion) is an easier task than say the extent of 'dumping' of lone parents into run-down housing.
2 How do you intend to use the information? Will you use the information to:

- lobby within your own or other service organisations to improve the level of provision?
- present to the media or use at a public meeting in order to raise public awareness or support?
- develop better relations with neighbourhood residents and activists who want to move on some issues?

(see Henderson and Thomas 2001; Hawtin *et al.* 1994)

Answer such questions as clearly as you can and you will save yourself a lot of wasted effort. What you intend to do with the information is crucial to the form in which you gather it. In drawing up your research plans there are a few rules to remember:

- Try to keep it simple – a lengthy questionnaire will put residents off. It must be easily understood by all who come in contact with it.
- Make sure that information you want can be easily obtained.
- Collect all relevant information, *especially* that which might run counter to what you expect or want to get out of it.

- Make sure your research methods are sound so that they cannot be easily dismissed. The point is that sooner or later, if the research has any value at all, you will want to use it in negotiations, in advocacy, or to apply pressure whether inside or outside your agency. The information has to be reliable; you can be sure that those with whom you are negotiating will have their own research and will pick up anything that does not support your case.

(Hawtin *et al.* 1994)

Networks for neighbourhoods

Neighbourhoods have their own system of networks with various capacities, strengths and weaknesses and you need to know what these are. 'Informal networks consist of a variety of personal and associational relationships which connect individuals and families in informal but often effective ways' (Gilchrist 1997). They change and expand or contract as they encounter other networks. Informal networks provide an important system for communications although they have loose structures based around shared interests, values and identity. They are profoundly affected by locality because people who are familiar with each other, have common points for meeting or gathering and both facilitate the formation of informal networks. With this should go the realisation that informal networks are 'communicative grapevines' oriented only to certain sections of the neighbourhood; worse, they may also be exclusionary, discriminatory and restrictive (Gilchrist 1997).

Learning to map networks for a neighbourhood is as important as for a family or individual if you are engaging in any form of community development or community social work. These may be built around formal associations or institutions – a mosque, luncheon club, temple or school – or they may be freestanding. Age, gender and social status are all prime determinants for shaping networks in a neighbourhood.

Relational organising

One helpful tool in capacity building is the concept of 'relational organising'. This is patient and long-term work that promotes discussion between neighbourhood workers and individuals. Through it both worker and resident gain a deeper understanding of local issues as they impact on individual families. In relational organising, meetings are small and informal, often no more than between two individuals in a person's home. The intention is to generate on-going dialogue that sustains participation and uncovers issues of concern to local residents. This contrasts with an 'activist' approach that moves directly to mobilise as many residents as possible around a potentially explosive issue.

As issues of concern and urgency emerge they become the common property of the neighbourhood, to be further explored through grassroots consultation, research meetings with officials, academic experts and consultants, and the organisation's own research efforts (Wood 1997). The focus then is to locate where the authority lies to implement a solution to the problem – it may be with corporate officials, city administrators, elected council members or members of the state legislature.

ENSURING PARTICIPATION

OPTIONS FOR PARTICIPATION

- Meetings with residents' groups
- Public meeting
- Individual or household surveys
- 'Planning for real' and community visioning events
- House meetings
- Focus groups and task-oriented forums.

THE IRON RULE

The Citizens Organising Foundation has a single guiding principle known as 'the iron rule': *Never do for the people what people can do for themselves. Never.*

(Jameson 2001)

High levels of participation in neighbourhood projects are essential for several reasons:

- Residents are the major stakeholders of any efforts: there are already active groups with concerns, knowledge and capacities to undertake sustained effort. They experience local problems at first hand and as a whole and not from the point of view of an agency's set tasks. They know the networks and can reach people that agencies cannot (Taylor 1995).
- If residents feel they own regeneration initiatives they are much more likely to be effective. Youth centres are more likely to be used if local young people have had a hand in setting them up. After-school clubs will have greater support if parents have been involved. A jobs training programme will have greater take-up among long-term unemployed if prospective trainees have been brought in alongside employers in setting up the scheme.
- But the most powerful reason has to do with capacity building: unless the area itself is able to ultimately generate the knowledge and skills for residents to run a project themselves, the project will not succeed because it will not last. This is the lesson that thirty years of neighbourhood initiatives has taught us (Burns and Taylor 2000). Deprived neighbourhoods often need a multi-pronged approach to participation. It may be that to engage a seriously demoralised neighbourhood, structured consultation lasting several weeks may be necessary to infom

properly and motivate local residents and organisations while other neighbourhoods may be ready to engage in higher levels of participation immediately.

Developing a vision together

'Vision' essentially means the long-term changes that local people want to see occur in their neighbourhood and will embrace the specific changes to the quality of personal and community life. Vision will have a strongly aspirational, even utopian element to it because it is based partly on what people hope will happen. Because of this factor it has a powerful, motivating role. Vision is important because:

- It sets a clear framework in which activities can be planned and evaluated
- It provides a sense of directions and helps bring people, practitioners and local organisations together
- It inspires people to be creative and dynamic.

(Barr and Hashagen 2000: 29)

The process of defining a vision can be extremely illuminating. It can expose and then address conflicts among the various stakeholders in a project, identify changes in priorities, stimulate all sides to think and debate in public and to examine whether local residents are actually going to be empowered or not (ibid.).

THE VISION OF THE OCEAN ESTATE (STEPNEY)

In ten years' time the Ocean will be a beautiful place in which to live in the heart of London, rich in its culture, education and employment. We will achieve this by:

- Making the Ocean a place to be proud of, placing the community at the heart of the neighbourhood renewal process, taking reponsibility and working with partners to create new and effective ways of harnessing existing and future resources.
- Making the Ocean a place to learn, challenging under-achievement in our whole community, improving educational attainment and investing in our young people, who are the future.
- Making the Ocean a place that works, enhancing pathways to employment for local people and changing employer perceptions ... in the City Fringe and Docklands ...
- Making the Ocean a place that cares, creating an active, healthy and caring community where healthy living builds our ability to participate effectively in every aspect of community life.

(extract from *The Ocean Delivery Plan* 2000)

ACTIVITY 7.2: VISIONING

With a small group of colleagues consider one of the following neighbourhood projects:

- Establishing a neighbourhood forum that includes residents, local practitioners, managers and politicians who will oversee a scheme to co-ordinate health and social care for older people.
- The introduction of an expanded neighbourhood watch scheme to reclaim a derelict public area currently used by drug dealers.
- A project in which you and your team may already be involved.

Then imagine the project in three years' time. What impact would you want the project to have? Does it coincide with or differ from what you think local residents would want? What kind of resources and other inputs will the project need to reach this point. If the project is successful what would be happening then that is not happening now? How could that success be demonstrated to those outside the area? (adapted from Barr and Hashagen 2000).

Community visioning

Developing a vision of what change a project or initiative will achieve is an important step but difficult because it will try to blend the aspirations of all residents and organisations in the area. Community visioning is a way of involving large numbers of adults and young people in a range of discussions about the future. Following the production of discussion guides and widespread publicity the public are invited to submit their ideas, plans and hopes as to how the whole range of community life could be improved. Done well, community visioning involves:

- Rapid progressive learning with and by local people, based on their criteria and categories
- 'Optimal ignorance', using appropriate imprecision and not finding out more than is needed
- Triangulation – using different methods, sources and disciplines, and a range of informants from a range of locations
- Direct contact, face-to-face and in the field
- Seeking out diversity and differences.

(Burton 1997)

ACTIVITY 7.3: LOCAL PARTICIPATION IN VISIONING

Re-read 'The Vision of the Ocean Estate'. What barriers do you think might have inhibited local residents from participating in putting together this vision statement?

Maximising participation

Involving local residents in formulating the vision of a project is one thing; maintaining high levels of participation throughout the length of time required for the formulation of detailed action plans and their implementation is even more difficult.

The often technical nature of developing holistic projects to counter social exclusion of a neighbourhood means that local residents face formidable obstacles to their ongoing participation. These include the inevitable influence that professional expertise retains – not just from education or social services but architects, planners and 'experts' from leisure and transport. Paradoxically then, participation strategies often reinforce professional authority. Other barriers will be particular to the locality.

ACTIVITY 7.4: MAPPING LOCAL BARRIERS TO PARTICIPATION

Burns and Taylor encourage an audit of these barriers to participation.

Example	*Explanation*
Violence, drug use, anti-social behaviour	May deter people from going to meetings
Perception that nothing changes	People may have low expectations of change
Lack of care and pride in community	People do not care enough about their environment
Racism and 'not in my backyard' attitude	Can set different sections of the area against each other and lead to some being excluded
Domination of meetings by individuals or groups	People feel excluded from participating
Poor experiences of participation in past	Previous projects led nowhere and wasted time and energy

With a small group of colleagues map out the local factors which may inhibit long-term participation in an area you are familiar with. Try to list as many as possible – major and minor factors. If you were to start a project in this area, what strategy would you adopt to overcome these barriers?

(adapted from Burns and Taylor 2000: 16)

Audit of participation

A thorough audit of participation in any initiative or project will reveal not only a great deal about the project with which you are involved but will also tell you a lot about how to maximise participation in other projects. Danny Burns and Marilyn Taylor have put together a handbook for assessing the degree and effectiveness of participation that is applicable to virtually all projects. There are several main tools for carrying out an audit of participation:

- Baseline mapping exercises.
- Checklists of activities or approaches that contribute to effective community involvement.
- The questions that need to be asked if community involvement is to be effective.
- Scales to help practitioners and stakeholders to think through the quality and extent of the participation activities they are planning.
- A 'decision trail' to track whether particular matters raised by local residents got into the decision-making arena, how these matters were decided upon and by whom, and finally whether or not they were actually implemented.

(Burns and Taylor 2000)

'Planning for real'

Developing strategies for involving and maintaining high levels of involvement is essential. There are techniques for overcoming this gap and in fact exploiting the differences in perspective and types of expertise. One such is called 'Planning for Real' developed by the Neighbourhood Initiatives Foundation (NIF) and used across the country in a variety of situations.

Its focus is the mutual construction of a 3D model of the locality which provides an initial informal opportunity to involve local people whether school children (especially those aged 7–11), adults or members of a tenants' association. All participants learn something of the history and physical, economic and social development of the area. The pack provided by NIF is on a scale of 1:250; sufficient to allow residents to recognise their own front doors and other landmarks easily. Once the model of the locality is constructed it takes centre stage, giving a bird's-eye view of the neighbourhood. It becomes the common ground and focus for everyone – whether resident or outside expert – to mill around and ponder the future. Its physical centrality has the effect of diminishing confrontation and expression of conflict. Through colour-coded cards participants make suggestions as to what they think ought to happen and they place those cards at the location on the model most associated with that problem. Each card colour represents a different issue area – yellow cards for housing, green cards for the environment, orange cards for crime and safety and so forth. Cards are placed anonymously and no one has to argue for or defend their idea at that point. The only rule is that no one is allowed to move or remove someone else's suggestion cards from the model (NIF 2000).

Soon the model is covered with a range of suggestions. By the end of the event it will be clear to everyone present from the predominance of a particular colour or the accumulation of cards in a particular spot that *that* is what matters most to people and *where*.

This is only the beginning of the 'Planning for Real' process. Small working groups then focus on particular topics such as care services, education or public safety. They collate all the suggestions within their topic, giving each one a priority rating ('now', 'soon' or 'later') with a note as to its location. In this process local knowledge plays an important role, for example in identifying who in the area holds local skills through a

THE OCEAN'S ACTION PLAN

The Ocean Estate's delivery plan under the New Deal for Communities was devised after many weeks of consultation with local residents, including a 'Planning for Real' exercise, meetings of neighbourhood forums, fruitful discussion with the government office in London and regeneration officials at the London Borough of Tower Hamlets. The process was not always smooth but local activists, council officers and residents were determined that the local voice would be heard. In part the plan reads:

What we will achieve

We have developed a comprehensive programme of change. Some of the key activities which we will carry out over the next ten years are:

Neighbourhood renewal

- A Standing on Common Ground programme to prepare the community for management of the neighbourhood renewal process.
- A Neighbourhood Management Model to sustain joined up, localised service delivery in the long term.

Education

- A Community Education Zone to improve educational achievement for nearly 2000 children in local schools to the national average at Key Stages 1, 2, 3 and GCSE.
- An English for a Purpose programme to enable more than 1000 adults to gain English language fluency in order to effectively access education, employment and service provision.

Employment

- A comprehensive Employability Programme to help more than 500 people into work.

Health

- An Improving Services and a Healthy Living programme to enable residents to access high quality integrated health and social care services.

Community safety

- A Tackling Drug Misuse and Connexions Plus initiative of education, diversion and rehabilitation projects designed to improve opportunities for young people and rid our area of anti-social behaviour and drugs.

(Ocean Estate NDC 2000)

survey. This is undertaken by local people starting small – their street or block of flats, perhaps practising on each other first and then moving from house to house. Gradually an action plan for the area emerges: one based on consensus, which is one of the Planning for Real objectives.

ACTIVITY 7.5: WHERE IN THE PROCESS ARE COMMUNITIES INVOLVED? A CHECKLIST

Burns and Taylor (2000) have developed their own ratings scale on which to chart how much influence communities have over particular neighbourhood projects: 9 = lip service – participation amounts to nothing; 8 = consultation around pre-arranged options; 7 = provision of high quality information; 6 = genuine consultation; 5 = community has formal advisory role; 4 = limited delegation of control over decision-making; 3 = substantial delegation of control to community; 2 = community control over all activities within agreed conditions; 1 = community ownership of all assets.

In your team choose a major 'partnership' project in which community participation is emphasised. Using the scale above note the extent of participation in each of the following functions.

- Policy making
- Strategic planning including budget decisions
- Commissioning or deciding who gets funded
- Budgetary control – who has day-to-day responsibility as well as overall accountability
- Managing staff – including appointment, appraisal and training
- Identifying objectives and performance indicators
- Planning individual projects
- Managing individual projects

(Burns and Taylor 2000: 24)

Strengthening neighbourhood leaders

The role of leaders and leadership is crucial to the success of area-based initiatives to overcome social exclusion. One of the major ways of talking to 'the people' is through their leaders. Saul Alinsky, one of the chief architects of community organising, argued that you talk to people through their leaders; if you do not know the leaders you are in the same position as a person trying to telephone another party without knowing the telephone number. ... Talking with these natural leaders is talking with the people' (Alinsky 1969).

Through their rich but at times schematic training in anti-discriminatory and pro-empowerment techniques, social workers may be naturally suspicious of local leaders and potential leaders and not see the fundamental extent to which initiatives rely on them for sustenance and communication. But this reactive position undervalues leaders by and works to undercut local leadership as it asserts itself within partnership structures.

Regeneration projects often presuppose 'communities of place', with the expectation that leaders will speak for it; but the concept of a unified community or neighbourhood with a handful of leaders speaking as community representatives is misleading. The representativeness and accountability of community leaders is limited by the diversity of social groupings and divisions within the area (Purdue *et al.* 2000).

SPREADING INVOLVEMENT

- Get to know the estate and its 'moving spirits'; don't rely solely on initial contacts or the most vocal residents.
- Do not view the estate as one 'community' – find out about the different communities on the estate.
- Remove obvious barriers to involvement – by offering childcare, accessible venues and safe ways of getting involved.
- Provide the information people need to feel able to contribute.
- Start by supporting small-scale and achievable activities that residents identify as important.
- Find ways of involving young people – offer a range of ways to get involved.
- Support existing groups to consult other residents and give them enough time.
- Don't overload the leaders; agree with them how you can help get others involved.
- Respond – nothing works like success.

(Taylor 1995: 17)

Tensions also arise between a first generation of community leaders, often recruited at speed to legitimise a regeneration bid (and given responsibility but not much power) and a second generation which emerges after a period of local capacity building (ibid.). Leaders may occupy formal positions – such as the manager of a Bangladeshi resource centre – or they may be informal, such as a member of a youth club among peers, or among a group of Asian women organising their own IT training.

Think of leaders in terms of their constituencies, organisations and the number of people over whom they have influence. Individual capacity is not the only criterion for leadership; others are the social networks and strength of connections that potential leaders have. It might help to think of different kinds of leader:

- Primary leaders are individuals with a large following who have broad vision and a willingness to work hard on themselves to develop leadership skills
- Secondary leaders have an institutional base of support and an appetite for power but are less broadly focused on the common good

- Tertiary leaders are issue-specific and task-oriented. All levels of leaders are required for a broad-based organisation to become powerful.

(Jameson 2001)

Decide carefully who you think might be an influential leader given time and preparation. Henderson and Thomas (2001) describe someone who can:

- demonstrate real commitment to the purpose of the organisation or project
- feel confident about taking a leadership role
- show awareness of the need to hold the trust and support of local people or organisation members
- be committed to democratic forms of organisation and to including others.

Leaders need support and training. Remember, they have a tough job and often give up large amounts of time and energy for no pay and often little or no power. Expectations of them from the neighbourhood and agency personnel can be huge, however, with blame, accusation and cynicism quickly expressed should they stumble. They need training in civic involvement.

FAITH-BASED WORK IN THE NEIGHBOURHOOD

There is currently a great deal of discussion around 'faith-based services', stimulated in part by the commitment to 'faith-based services' of the new administration in the US and its fainter echo from the Conservative Party on the same theme in the UK. Political tendencies that have no faith in government perhaps have a misconceived faith in faith to deliver! But this should not obscure the vital role that faith communities of all kinds – Islamic, Jewish, Sikh, Catholic, Evangelical Protestant, for example – have played in the past and the important role they still hold. Social work's discomfort in working with such movements and institutions resulted in it keeping its distance from institutions which have strong roots in local communities and a long record of service provision, some of it quite innovatory. This distance arose partly because of social work's strong secularist orientation and, more recently, a deeper appreciation of how many religious institutions restrict and confine the role of women and are hostile to other groups such as gays and lesbians.

Against the perceived negatives of a faith-based project must weigh the evident dedication of religious groups to maintaining some voice, often in the poorest neighbourhoods, and links with some of the most excluded and unwanted individuals. At a time when other institutions no longer maintain a neighbourhood presence churches, mosques, temples and synagogues have maintained their involvement, and they will be there long after the partnership pilot schemes, pilots and projects have all gone. The tenets of faith provide an incredible source of energy – bearing witness, working with the poor and engaging in prophetic action. Other faith-based movements have resulted in huge social and political change in the past: Catholic social doctrine, liberation theology, church action on poverty, Jewish and Islamic dedication to service. Newer ranks to such movements include black majority churches and Pentecostal and independent evangelical institutions. 'Civic life', 'third-way politics' and 'community capacity' do not excite, motivate or agitate people in the same way.

ACTIVITY 7.6: THE DIFFERENCE BETWEEN A FAITH-BASED PROJECT AND A SECULAR PROJECT – CHRISTIAN VALUES IN YOUTH WORK

A youth club operates from a church basement in the midst of a multi-faith community. The youth worker recognises that the project may cause some tensions. From the church perspective there are a number of boundaries that should not be crossed, for example the youth worker should have a Christian background. Deeply held moral convictions by leading members of the congregation mean that there is often unease about homosexuality. In general the church's standards and the personal moral standards of the youth worker do not match those of local young people. Yet the project is open seven days a week until 11 p.m. and has a full complement of volunteers, some of whom are drawn from outside the church. During its opening hours there is always an adult for young people to talk to if they so wish.

What do you think are the main differences between faith-based and secular projects? Would you be willing to enter into a partnership with such a youth project? Here are some pros and cons to think about:

For	*Against*
Embedded in locality, have allegiance	Services confined to one group
Informal and caring – not invasive of autonomy	Many religions restrict women
Motivated by vision, operate on small budgets	Difficult to evaluate impact because of informal styles

CASE STUDY 13: A BLACK MAJORITY CHURCH PROJECT IN LONDON

A family support service has been developed by a charismatic member of the congregation. 'She has lived on the edge and walked beside the people the project services'. She provides a model of 'servant' leadership. The management style is informal. The Management Committee is made up of members who are directly involved in either receiving or providing services. Services are developed after listening to persons who come into the drop-in centre. The time pressures on the leader are immense as she juggles the conflicting claims of those in need, those who require spiritual support and administering the organisation. She has received management training from the Borough and the project is also being mentored by a team from Barnardos who have helped draw up a budget and evaluation plan.

FAITH, VALUES AND COMMUNITY WORK IN AN ISLAMIC CENTRE

'The need for a mosque in the area led to the creation of the Centre on the Medina model of combining faith and community work. The model includes a community meeting place, a centre for learning and a place of refuge for those in need. This model provides a natural blueprint for the relationship between faith and community work'.

The provision of the Centre will therefore be geared to helping people appreciate their own culture and identity and then encouraging work and community life with others. The practical outworking of this is that the Centre will have a community relations forum built into it to begin a dialogue and application on community relations issues. They will also partner with other (non-Muslim) agencies to deliver 'non-spiritual' services that are part of the Centre. The services will be open to all but some will still retain an Islamic value base. The services will also seek to learn from the best practice of different and secular agencies. It will seek to be pluralistic and broad-minded in terms of theology, philosophy and practice.

A significant aim will be to educate people and build up identity while counteracting the attitude of superiority and feeling that one group is better than another and will be honest about the positive and negative aspects of Islamic culture.

(from DETR and Shaftesbury Society 2000)

It is also important to recognise that changes in how doctrine is understood are under way, while at the same time there is a growing understanding of the commonly accepted broader principles and practice of community development toward inclusiveness. Faith institutions are increasingly aware of their shortcomings and recognise that they cannot 'do' community development on their own but must work with partners.

A recent survey by the DETR and Shaftesbury provides some interesting consideration for faith-based work. The survey found that:

- Deeply held moral convictions mean that there is often unease about homosexuality and it is less likely than other factors to be covered in equal opportunities monitoring.
- Faith-based community work continues to be distinctive from secular community development because of its theological foundation and values. This sometimes means that there is a lower level of social action but this does not discount the high quality of caring services provided by faith communities. It may also foster social action as those members who are involved increase their understanding of the community.
- Projects highly value their informality and open personal relationships. There is some apprehension among those involved in faith-based projects that a more

formal management style will distance them from members of their community and they will be perceived by local residents as more bureaucratic in approach.
- Yet projects which adopt a management style that includes regular supervision and line accountability appear to perform better, meet targets and have the capacity to support and train their staff.
- Faith-based community work tends to be broad and have generic goals. A majority of projects surveyed had taken action on between two and six major social problems.

(DETR and Shaftesbury Society 2000)

ACTIVITY 7.7: WHAT IS YOUR RESPONSE?

Aisa is a community-support worker for an early years project. Her parents came from Bangladesh some 12 years ago. They and Aisa are devout Muslims. Four members of the project are developing a model for 'women-centred practice'. Aisa notices that she has certain disagreements with some aspects of that model but keeps these to herself. At one meeting two of these colleagues begin talking about 'the mosque' in ways that Aisa regards as disrespectful and slightly condescending; in particular, they underscore several times how men run the affairs of the mosque and are quite oppressive.

What should Aisa say at this point? Should she discuss the tone of the meeting with her parents? To whom should she turn for support? Should she begin to think about modifying her devotion?

This exercise requires research and some deep thinking. Work in a small group of three: outline the matters which you think collectively you need to have greater knowledge about and arrive at your answers by consensus.

KEY POINTS

- ❑ Neighbourhoods are important arenas for the fight against social exclusion not because they automatically have mystical strengths but because exclusion has a spatial dimension. The concept of social capital is one way of understanding the degree of local social cohesion, although it has its critics as well.
- ❑ The concept of 'capacity building' is crucial if any initiative is to become embedded in the community. It requires the patient building up of human and social capital within the neighbourhood, including investing in local people and local leaders. There are many kinds of capacity building projects – 'housing plus' schemes and credit unions are but two.
- ❑ Conducting local research is critical so that, regardless of the forum in which you are involved, or whether you are arguing for resources inside your own organisation, or simply talking to residents about their neighbourhood, you know what you are talking about with impressive accuracy.

- ❑ Opening up channels for local participation is essential; initiatives are fruitless without it. Maximising that participation and learning to audit the extent of local involvement in your project are critical tools to use.
- ❑ Faith-based community development has been long ignored by social work; some more positive understanding at least is required as it is one form in which 'capacity' still survives in poor urban neighbourhoods.

KEY READING

Burns and Taylor's *Auditing Community Participation: An assessment handbook* (Polity Press, 2000) is an indispensable manual for checking the level of participation by local residents in community projects you may be involved with.

Henderson and Thomas have published a new edition of their book, *Skills in Neighbourhood Work* (Routledge, 2001); it is lengthy but is the best guide to neighbourhood work now available.

Steve Skinner's *Building Community Strengths: A resource book on capacity building* (Community Development Foundation, 1997) is in manual format and full of practical advice on local capacity building.

CHAPTER 8

RACISM AND SOCIAL EXCLUSION

OBJECTIVES

At the end of this chapter, you should be able to:

- Identify the various exclusionary effects that racism causes in the UK
- Understand the concept of institutional racism and the implications it has for social work practice
- Recognise the various ways in which practitioners can combat racism within social work practice, such as anti-bias work with children and young people
- See the links between racism and asylum seekers and how practitioners can develop an inclusionary practice.

Racism is a powerful component of exclusion. Racist concepts and the hate movements founded on them have provided fuel for the mass intimidation of and violence against designated groups of people. Racism was one of the main drivers of the enslavement of Africans and the colonisation of Africa and Asia by European powers over several centuries. It lay behind the destruction of the immense cultural and social achievements by native peoples in the Americas, as well as the genocide of whole peoples in the twentieth century. Although we simply do not have the space to explore its history here, knowing that history is vital to understanding why and in what ways racism is periodically able to rear its head again and again. You can see for

DEFINITIONS

Race is a biological and cultural construct to classify one group of people from another, using such criteria as skin colour, language or customary behaviour. It is also used to denote status and lineage (Burke and Harrison 2001: 282). Racial and ethnic categories vary over time in meaning and importance. Generally they imply a distinction between 'whites' and other minorities of colour (Bobo 1998: 7).

Racism: 'consists of conduct or words or practices which disadvantage or advantage people because of their colour, culture, or ethnic origin. In its more subtle form it is as damaging as in its overt form' (Macpherson 1999: 20).

'Whiteness' – refers to white people's favoured position in the social order relative to other racial groups. It describes the automatic, unmerited advantages and benefits conferred upon ownership of white skin by society. It does not mean that every white person is materially or otherwise more advantaged than black or Asian people.

(from Lawrence 2001)

yourself racist contempt develop in relation to asylum seekers, travellers, immigrants and refugees.

The irony is that 'race' is a bogus concept, nineteenth-century in origin, that is bound up with notions of identity, culture and ethnicity, religion annd language. It is purely a social construct without biological foundation which is why most writers now use the term in inverted commas. It is of course a paradox that on the basis of a false concept you nevertheless have groups and individuals engaged in aggressive action: in other words racists without race.

The disadvantage and social exclusion linked to minority ethnic communities is evident. People from minority ethnic backgrounds are more likely than the rest of the population to:

- Live in poor areas and in poor housing: 56 per cent of those from minority ethnic communities live in the 44 most deprived local authorities in the country; two-thirds live concentrated in the four urban areas of London, West Midlands Greater Manchester and West Yorkshire.
- Be unemployed or have low incomes: over 40 per cent of African Caribbean and Indian people live in households with less than half the average national income compared with 28 per cent of all people nationally. Pakistani and Bangladeshi men have high rates of unemployment and women have low rates of economic activity. In 1998 some 20 per cent of Pakistani and 23 per cent of Bangladeshi people were unemployed. Over 80 per cent of Pakistani and Bangladeshi people live in households with less than half the average national income (Berthoud *et al.* 1997).
- Be young and suffer social exclusion. Forty-three per cent of the Bangladeshi population is under 16 years of age compared with 20 per cent of the white population. Nationally this means that ethnic minority youth are a fast-rising proportion of all of those under 25 – some 7 per cent in the early 1990s; a rate that very likely has

doubled in the last ten years (SEU 2000). Conversely, while 16 per cent of white people are over 65, only 3 per cent of Bangladeshi and Pakistani people are. Ethnic minority young people suffer social exclusion disproportionately:

- Two-fifths of 16-year-olds were not in full-time education or work in 1997 (double the rate of whites of the same age)
- Young African Caribbean men are disproportionately caught up in every stage of the youth offending process
- In 1998 only 29 per cent of Pakistani and black pupils and 33 per cent of Bangladeshi pupils achieved five or more GCSE grades A–C compared with 47 per cent of white pupils
- Black Caribbean and black African children were four to six times more likely to be excluded than other children throughout the mid-1990s, although that figure is now falling
- About half of those using Centrepoint's temporary housing services are black
- In 1991 nearly 20 per cent of the children looked after by local authorities were from a minority ethnic background compared with a national average of 9 per cent.

(SEU 2000)

Tackling social exclusion means combating racism in ways that build capacity and link up responsive and innovative services. It is important to remember that behind the data linking ethnic minority communities to poverty and exclusion there are people with strengths, skills and resilience for dealing with adverse circumstances. By no means do you want to think of people only as victims.

SOCIAL WORK AND ANTI-RACISM

Social work was among the first of the professions to focus on racism as a means of exclusion and to make anti-racism central to its practice. The Central Council for Education and Training in Social Work explicitly brought in a black perspective to its deliberations and worked out a set of competencies for anti-racist practice (CCETSW 1991).

Certain aspects of these policies brought difficulties, however, which arose largely from the Council's categorical and top-down approach (Penketh 2001). Constructive criticism of the Council's approach (for example, Sapey 1997) was not listened to. Indeed criticism of the Council was virtually regarded as part of a 'backlash'. Social work's anti-racism was subsequently subsumed within a broader 'anti-oppressive practice' which had the effect of cementing this attitude – 'if you are not with us you are against us' – across the whole range of work (Pierson 1999).

Looking back one can see that this approach radically inhibited coalition and partnership building. For example social work kept all manner of religious institutions at arm's length as well as individual members of various faiths who wanted to become social workers (Channer 2000). Evangelical churches were criticised for their anti-gay attitudes while mosques were widely perceived to be extreme in their strict subordination of women, with little professional effort exerted in trying to broaden the view of these important constituencies. Equally there was little interest in Whiteness as a concept warranting understanding, and it was seen instead as little more than a seedbed for racist and oppressive thinking. Many questions about how individuals wrestle with values, beliefs and attitude change went unexplored. (Van Soest [1997] provides telling data on a social work training course in the US, built around explicit messages about oppression. She found that the course actually decreased student social workers' sensitivity to and understanding of oppression – quite contrary to the author's hopes.)

This experience is important for the valuable lessons it supplies around coalition building, maintaining public support, working with faith-based institutions around the sensitive and all-important matter of racism. There is now every opportunity to pick up the best from the recent past and join it to new thinking and new developments. More important is the cascade of new thinking in which 'race' becomes less essentialist, while at the same time more fully understood in the context of community initiatives (Stone and Butler 2000).

INSTITUTIONAL RACISM

Institutional racism has long been a concern of social work in relation to its own practice and that of other public agencies, much of which has focused on the ways in which its services and practices produce discriminatory results, but as a concept it has also been used in many different contexts and with a lack of precision. The Macpherson Report into the failure of the Metropolitan Police to apprehend the killers of Stephen Lawrence has brought clarity to our understanding of what it is with the clear intention that its recommendations apply to all public service agencies.

One of the great strengths of the Macpherson Report is that it urges examination of the unintended consequences of the activity of public institutions and service agencies, and provides a new set of instruments with which to judge, monitor and oppose

DEFINITIONS OF INSTITUTIONAL RACISM

The collective failure of an organisation to provide an appropriate and professional service to people because of their colour, culture, or ethnic origin. It can be seen or detected in processes, attitudes and behaviour which amount to discrimination through unwitting prejudice, ignorance, thoughtlessness and racist stereotyping which disadvantage minority ethnic people (Macpherson 1999: para 6.34.)

Institutional racism refers to characteristics of formal political, economic and organisation structures that generate racialised but nevertheless widely legitimised outcomes – outcomes that cannot be traced to obvious racial biases in the practices themselves or to acts of individual racism by staff or officials in these institutions. 'Nevertheless these institutions maintain cultures and practices that, in the end, disregard the particular needs of disadvantaged racial groups or facilitate unequal outcomes for different racial groups.'

(Lawrence 2001: 45; note that the author is no relation to the Lawrence family in the UK).

unwitting racism, as much as the intentional racism of individual officers, are eliminated from their practice.

While the act applies formally only to public authorities it is also clearly intended to apply to private and voluntary organisations and other bodies such as multi-agency partnerships.

TACKLING RACISM IN SOCIAL WORK PRACTICE

In the wake of the renewed discussion around institutional racism and equipped with the knowledge that comes from reflecting on the relationship between racism and social exclusion, social work has a good opportunity to expand its approaches and build stronger coalitions to address racism. Such initiatives will stretch across its own service provision, in the joined-up action with other agencies such as early years work, and within the regeneration and community development projects in which it participates.

Family support services

A number of surveys have consistently revealed the immense gulf between families of minority ethnic communities and social services. Qualitative data from interviews and focus groups and statistical rates of service take-up both present a consistent picture among would-be users from ethnic minority communities. They reveal considerable confusion over the role of social workers and social services, suspicion about social work involvement in general and a lack of awareness of specialist functions, for instance in relation to a disabled child (Modood *et al.* 1997).

School exclusions

Social work agencies have been pinpointed by the Commission for Racial Equality as one of the key instruments in devising collaborative arrangements to reduce the disproportionate number of school exclusions from ethnic minority communities. They have a distinct role to play in providing support for those families with children in need. Local authorities have the duty to ensure that children in their care are reaching their full educational attainment (CRE n.d.).

Creating visible partnerships, particularly with schools, mentors, parents and carers, to reduce school exclusion of minority pupils is also part of the CRE strategy. Drawing on existing community strengths is part of this approach. It should include:

- creating good working relationships with community organisations
- setting up a register of information and relevant local agencies
- developing mentoring programmes to match disaffected pupils with volunteers
- running parent-support groups
- opening schools for community use.

CASE STUDY 14: KWESI MENTORING PROJECT IN BIRMINGHAM

The Kwesi Mentoring Project is run by black men for primary-school-age black boys at risk of school exclusion. When schools agree to work with Kwesi they

- must accept volunteers as part of the school team
- provide information on the pupils they are concerned about
- adopt a 'no blame' approach in relation to the child's behaviour and the family.

Each volunteer matched with a child then commits himself to regularly visiting the school and works in class with the child.

(Kwesi Mentoring Project: The Community Room, Handsworth Wood Boys School, Church Lane, Birmingham)

Anti-bias approaches in early years work

As noted the Macpherson Report underscored the importance of working with young people in addressing racism. Independent data supports this. In Cardiff 50 per cent of racist incidents considered by Race Equality Council involved young people under 16 years old and a quarter of those were incidents involving children between the ages of six and ten. 'Radical thinking and sustained action are needed in order to tackle it head on ... in all organisations *and in particular in the fields of education and family life*' (5; my emphasis).

Racism can have a profound effect on the later development of children through the loss of self-esteem, faltering self-belief and by inhibiting a positive view of the child's own background. For these very basic reasons developing programmes to counter prejudice or bias in children should be another component agency's work with children.

Bias has been defined as an attitude, belief or feeling that results in and helps to justify unfair treatment of an individual or group (Save the Children 2000a). As a term it implies less structure and intensity than its cousins such as racism or homophobia and is probably the more appropriate word to describe the sort of prejudice found among young children. In their study of mostly white primary schools Troyna and Hatcher found that white children deployed a variety of discourses when it came to discussing race. They observed that 'Many children display inconsistent and contradictory repertoires of attitudes, containing both elements of racially egalitarian ideologies and elements of racist ideologies' (1992: 197).

ACTIVITY 8.1: DID YOU HEAR WHAT SHE SAID?

A white mother is riding with her white three-year-old daughter on the upper deck of a bus in central London. Suddenly the daughter turns to her mother and says in a loud voice, 'Mummy, I don't like black people. Do you?'

Write down what you imagine might be the range of responses from that mother and how effective each would be. What would your response be?

Young children will begin to show bias against children different to themselves from as early as two unless they have accurate and positive information. They are certainly aware of differences of gender and ethnicity and begin to develop their self identity and attitude towards others from that age. If we ignore their questions or pretend that differences do not exist or fail to provide sufficient sources models for diversity we simply allow this bias to take root (Save the Children 2000; Siraj-Blatchford 1994). The differences they observe in others – physical impairment or difficulty in communication, difficult behaviour, a learning disability, different cultural background, ethnicity or race – can become the focus of distancing, annoyance and ostracism. They will also absorb how their parents, friends, their friends' parents and local society view and value (or not) other children and adults who may be black, disabled, boy or girl.

ACTIVITY 8.2: WHEN DO CHILDREN START TO LEARN ABOUT DIFFERENCE?

If you work with young children or if liaison with a nursery school or family centre is part of your job discuss with a colleague at what age you think young children start to learn about:

- gender and what being a 'boy' or 'girl' means
- noticing and applying names of colour to skin colour
- the differences between genders and how 'boys' and 'girls' might be different
- physical disabilities
- learning disabilities.

At what age do you think they begin to attach positive or negative values to the above? Think back to when you were a child of comparable age. How do the children's values compare with yours then? And now?

(adapted from Save the Children 2000: 19)

As a social worker you may be working directly with young children in care settings or responsible for advising or otherwise participating in creating positive atmospheres for children in their early years, perhaps with a family centre or family support worker. Either way knowing something about approaches to correcting bias is important to you. Two ways of doing this have been tried and tested: the home corner and story telling.

The home corner

Home corners or real-life play areas are special places where children can play out different roles they have seen in the adult world around them. They both explore those roles in relation to themselves and others their age and help make sense of the world they live in. Using the home corner idea:

- Think about how you could change it so that it reflects the communities the children live in, or others that they might one day live in.
- Decide with children what the home corner should look like, perhaps after looking at some pictures, a walk around the community itself or visits to other neighbourhoods that are different.
- Create a more diverse community by using specific props to build different workplaces, with different kinds of tools and implements so that a diversity of gender and culture (for example in cooking) and physical abilities is represented.

The aim should be to avoid a narrow definition of the typical. To do this simply ask yourself what the home corner would look like from different points of view: girl, boy, person with disability, ethnic, religious or racial group, travellers?

Stories

Stories offer all sorts of opportunities to examine bias and create a broad positive awareness of the many different kinds of people there are and how they may see things in a way that is new. There are many options from story books which promote this vision in addition to making up scenarios, skits or story books with children. The many ways of doing this are considered in several key publications mentioned at the end of this chapter. (For more on the home corner and stories see Save the Children 2000.)

Identity project on 'myself'

This approach based in a nursery run by a local education authority began when staff in the nursery noted a number of pre-schoolers who were struggling with or were unaware of their cultural and racial backgrounds. Essentially the work with parents and children is based on an identity workbook, adapted from Jocelyn Maxime's *Black Like Me* (1994) Children, parents, carers and key workers at the nursery are involved in completing a series of activities that explore the ethnic origins and religion of the children and their parents. The exercise is carried out in the form of regular activity sheets prepared in advance and sent home together with requisite materials for completing them. Where parents had difficulty with reading or comprehension they were able to complete the activity with the help of nursery staff (Sawyerr 1999).

Whiteness and young white people

Failing to understand 'whiteness' is one of social work's great omissions in practice. There was a tendency to treat with suspicion claims by young white people, even those from the disenfranchised poor white youth of excluded urban enclaves. Little was done (and social work is not alone here!) to explore white ethnicity among young people and in part because of this anti-racist approaches ignored the needs and perspectives of white working-class students. In the words of the Burnage Report (MacDonald 1991) into the murder of Ahmed Iqbal Ullah in Manchester, the anti-racist initiatives of the time regarded white youth as 'cultureless, wandering spirits' (cited in Nayak 1999: 178). Ironically, the racism of white working-class youth brings that class scant social advantage. It breeds ever-deeper engagement in psychic conflict and in what young white male racists see as identity-confirming violence. They do not see, however, that every act of violence further cements in place the one-dimensional view of would-be employers that they are a violent, disreputable underclass that should not be let anywhere near the job market.

THE SPECTRE OF WHITENESS

My involvement with radical politics on the left, had taught me to disavow the racial exclusivity of white ethnicity, but never to analyse or try and understand it ... The problem with intellectually disowning English ethnicity was that the left never got around to work out what it was ...

(Rutherford 1997 in Nayak 1999)

There has been a lack of anti-racist initiatives responding to young, white working-class people who, as Nayak (1999) explains, can be agitated and insecure in what their own racial grouping ought to signify, or indeed what Englishness might mean. In the perspective of these earlier anti-racist initiatives whiteness is linked with racist energy but not with the social insecurities of white youth.

Nayak concludes that these descriptions of anti-racist practice suggest that the young white people he interviewed perceive them as a largely proscriptive, often negative set of values with the feeling emerging that white ethnicity was being unfairly regulated. This sense of unfairness he regards as a major obstacle to anti-racist initiatives because it functions as 'a screen which filters out the possibility of some whites fully understanding the meaning of racial harassment, and generates an almost impermeable defensiveness' (Hewitt 1996 cited in ibid.).

A DISCUSSION WITH WHITE YOUTHS ON TYNESIDE

Nicola: And there's these dolls that you're not allowed to 'ave.

Sam: Gollywogs.

Nicola: Aye. And on the news now [it says] every child has gotta have a black doll.

Anoop [the interviewer]: Hold on, are you saying that every child by law has got to have a black doll?

Nicola: Yeah, so they grow to accept black people.

Sam: Y'kna how they've started making black Sindys and that, and Barbies?

James: And black Action Man.

Michelle: Aye, black Action Man!

(from Nayak 1999)

FURTHER CONVERSATIONS WITH WHITE GEORDIE YOUTH

Danielle: Mine parents were born in Germany, cos me nanna used to travel o'er abroad.

Brett: I used to have Italian grandad.

Alan: Me next name's O'Maley and that isn't English.

Nicola: I tell yer I'm English, but I'm part German. My grandad came over as a prisoner of war, he was working over at Belsey Park and my grandma was teaching.

James: Some white people have got black people in their family. Like say my aunty married a black person and had babies.

Michelle: I've got one in my family.

Sam: I'm a quarter Irish, a quarter Scottish, a quarter English and a quarter Italian.

(from Nayak 1999)

Nayak suggests that a more positive strategy for engaging with white ethnicity is required. He found projects around local white identities, drawing on life-history and family-history accounts to be particularly effective. Settings where young people could explore and then tell their family stories, share personal biographies or trace their ethnic and social class lineage provided a way of deconstructing whiteness. Tracing their family past was a means of personalising history, making it relevant to their life experiences to date. Once this is under way, the solidity of the 'Englishness' of the Geordie white youth gives way to the inevitable mix of national origins and ethnicity that emerges (Nayak 1999).

Racist groups are hate groups so another line of engagement is to work with young people around the notion of 'hate', exploring with a group particular topics:

- How hate groups function and how they use vandalism to intimidate whole areas
- How specific laws, such as those prohibiting harassment and trespassing, can be used to forestall the activities of hate groups
- The reasons people join hate groups, such as having low self-esteem.

ACTIVITY 8.3: WORKING WITH YOUNG PEOPLE ON HATE GROUPS

Working with a small group of young people keep track of newspaper articles about the national or local actions of hate groups such as Combat 18, Ku Klux Klan or the British National Party. Which hate groups are there in the area and in what ways are they active? Which ones make the news the most often? Does music play a role in the culture of these groups? Are hate lyrics part of that culture – towards black people, white people or women? Racism and hate groups are prevalent in football and use matches to recruit and to chant racist slogans. Is this the case in your area?

ENGLISH FOOTBALL

Last autumn Andy Frain and Jason Mariner were jailed for seven and six years respectively after undercover television revealed their incitement of persistent football crowd hooliganism. They were 'officers' of Combat 18 and Frain was also an officer of the Ku Klux Klan.

In response to incitements such as this the Football Association is disbanding the English Members Club and intends to rebuild it under strict vetting so that hate activists cannot use it to cover their incitements in the future.

CASE STUDY 15: 'ASIANS IN FOOTBALL'

Mick King is a white English social worker who works in the East End of London near where West Ham United play. He takes football into local schools and parks where his 'Asians in Football' project has conducted over 1000 coaching sessions for nearly 20 000 youngsters in the past year. The scheme costs about £35 000 per year – less than the weekly salary of some professional players – and draws on the enthusiasm of the Bangladeshi children in the area.

Neighbourhood regeneration initiatives

The evidence from numerous studies shows that Black and ethnic minority communities have not benefited equally from previous regeneration initiatives (Pierson *et al.* 2000; Stone and Butler 2000; Lawrence 2001). Partnerships need to look at possible direct and indirect discrimination in their activities. Some local residents may be benefiting from regeneration programmes such as New Deal for Communities while others lose out. Holistic approaches to tackling neighbourhood exclusion have tended to seek ways of collaborating across racial and cultural lines without really taking on the responsibility of pushing for racial group empowerment. In general they have failed to see how the position of specific racial groups shapes community capacities in fundamental ways and the activities they need to undertake to remove or counteract the society's racial hierarchy (Lawrence 2001).

Checklist for joined-up neighbourhood initiatives

The SEU have issued specific guidelines for partnerships engaging in New Deal for Communities regeneration which by implication should apply to most partnership-based activities. They suggest carrying out a 'health check', to see whether the partnership engages in 'institutionally racist' policies or ways of working unintentionally. The aim of such a check is to identify those barriers which stop black and ethnic minority groups from becoming fully involved or benefiting equally from the programme.

ACTIVITY 8.4: CHECKLIST FOR RACE EQUALITY IN REGENERATION ACTIVITY

If you are likely to be involved in a partnership or in joined-up activity to address the social exclusion of a particular area, run through the following checklist devised by the Social Exclusion Unit:

- Are we acting fairly with all groups in the local community?
- Do the services we provide reach all the communities they are meant for, and do they meet their needs?
- Are we applying the same professional standard in every situation?
- Do our activities and processes really include all groups?
- Have you gathered baseline data to help you gain a full understanding of the variety of communities within the area? If your partnership has already conducted its baseline exercise, check whether you need any supplementary information about the status and needs of black and ethnic minority communities?
- Have you put in place an equal opportunities action plan, to guide the implementation of race equality measures?

Other points to consider are:

- Be sure to include explicit objectives and targets for race equality in your delivery plan, to help you measure progress. Publish progress against these objectives and targets in your annual report
- Collect and analyse ethnic monitoring data regularly, to identify possible barriers to opportunities, participation and benefits, and take strategic action
- Adopt ways of working which prompt regular questioning and monitoring of the extent to which your programme and projects embrace black and ethnic minority interests, and keep looking for ways of improving your performance.

(DETR 1999)

REFUGEES AND ASYLUM SEEKERS

The experience of refugees and asylum seekers in the UK is heavily racialised. They face many parallel experiences to that of ethnic minorities: dislocation, powerlessness and discrimination while having few supports to call on and no concerted action from government to reconstruct public opinion. From the moment they arrive they face a volatile and often aggressively hostile local public with racist political sentiment openly engaging in intimidation and local press making accusation of 'bogus claims' and 'a drain on national resources'. There have also been aggravated problems of tension at ferry ports, reported by local newspapers in ways that are often virulently and explicitly racist. As an example you may recall the provocative public reactions to incoming Slovaks and Czech Roma in the summer of 1997.

There are of course major reasons behind the movement of vast numbers of people from poor countries to developed nations, including impoverishment, climatic destruction and internal violence. The impression that refugees, clandestine immigrants and asylum seekers can be easily sorted out between those genuinely persecuted who need a haven, those desperately looking for work and those simply ambitious is erroneous. Whatever their 'category', great numbers of people are prepared to take enormous risks and their movement continues. All developed countries face the issue, although some more than others.

Long-term development facilitated by trade, assistance and debt relief is one answer but meanwhile central government policy has slowly tightened opportunity and wrung compassion out of settlement procedures, responding to what it sees as a strong public current that it is dangerous to attempt to reverse. The current policy in the form of the Immigration and Asylum Act 1999 shows this plainly. It leaves social workers in a difficult position, facing almost impossible dilemmas over how far to engage with the arrangements.

To relieve pressure, ostensibly on social housing in London and areas around the ports, the National Asylum Support Service (NASS) was introduced in April 2000 as part of the Home Office, to replace the asylum teams from local authority social services departments.

NASS's function is to house asylum seekers more evenly throughout the country and to provide for their needs on the most basic level. Renting housing and income maintenance had not been a social work task until now, and could as easily be done on an administrative basis by people with a DSS or Housing background as employing more highly paid social work staff. There has been a frosty relationship between such local authority teams and NASS; they accuse NASS of being too eager to get up and running quickly due to political pressure, ignoring their experience and expertise in the area of booking accommodation. What is worse, they often use accommodation previously rejected by local teams as too squalid (Francis 2001).

DEFINITION OF REFUGEES

The United Nations Convention 1951 defines refugees as those who have to flee their home 'owing to a well-founded fear of being persecuted for reasons of race, religion, nationality, membership of a particular social group or political opinion'. Asylum seekers are defined as people who have had to flee their homes and cross an internationally recognised border in search of a place of refuge and safety.

The Organisation of African Unity have improved these definitions – acknowledging the complexity of racial, ethnic and economic factors, in particular inter-communal violence, cross-border raids and intimidation. The OAU definition reads: 'Refugees include people compelled to leave their home countries by "external aggression or domination" or by events seriously undermining public order.'

(Rutter 1994: 5)

For 'persons subject to immigration control' Section 115 of the Immigration and Asylum Act 1999 removes entitlement to means-tested benefits such as Income Support, income-based Jobseeker's Allowance, housing benefit and council tax benefit, as well as a range of family and disability benefits such as child benefit and disability living allowance. Some exemptions are allowed, however, such as asylum seekers who claimed asylum on arrival before 3 April 2000. Importantly for social workers, provision of family support under Section 17 of the Children Act is not available to a dependent child and members of the child's asylum-seeking family *where adequate accommodation or essential living needs are being provided* under the Act's support system.

The 1999 Act places social workers, care managers and social care officers in an uncomfortable position, because it makes the care in the community function dependent on immigration status and thus requires practitioners to investigate a person's circumstances whether or not their professional code of ethics would suggest otherwise. To put it simply no one subject to immigration control is eligible for care services, including the range of basic services such as day centres for those with mental health problems, social work support for mental disorder, meals on wheels and day-centre places for older people among others.

There is also tension between asylum law and the Children Act, since the consideration of the child's welfare as paramount does not automatically apply in immigration-linked cases. The Home Office does, however, have to consider the matter of the child's welfare when deciding to expel children or parents. As Cohen (2001) reminds us, it is imperative for social workers to write welfare reports that address each of the points in the checklist of the child's welfare contained in the Children Act in cases of deportation. (For more details on the Act consult Steve Cohen's excellent new book cited at the end of this chapter. He also provides a wealth of strategies for exploiting legal loopholes.)

Children

Children make up over 50 per cent of all refugees worldwide; unaccompanied children arrived in significant numbers in Britain, especially London, from the early 1990s onward. At first they came from countries such as Ethiopia and Somalia and subsequently from Kosovo, Algeria, China and Afghanistan. Children are especially vulnerable to violence, have no voice and no independent access to services. Many of the unaccompanied were young people able to demonstrate sufficient independence skills to survive in supported accommodation with the equivalent of Income Support in cash payments from local authority social service departments through Section 17 of the Children Act. That support system was terminated by statute in 1999.

ACTIVITY 8.5: SOCIAL WORK AND THE REFUGEE

You are a care manager. You have an older, frail client who speaks no English and seems disoriented and unfamiliar with even the most basic services in Britain. Her needs have been assessed and she now receives three hours a week of home care. You then receive an anonymous letter saying that she entered the UK without permission. Your line manager says that you must inform the Home Office about this new information. Because of her immigration status, he says, she loses her entitlement to community care supports. What is your response?

(adapted from Cohen 2001)

THE CHILD AS REFUGEE: THE UN SPEAKS

Article 221 of the UN Convention on the Rights of the Child (1989):

'A child who is seeking refugee status or who is considered a refugee ... shall, whether unaccompanied or accompanied by his or her parents or by other person, receive appropriate protection and humanitarian assistance ... including help to trace the parents or other members of the family ... in order to obtain information necessary for unification.'

The UK government entered a reservation to the Convention, so that the rights of refugee children to protection and assistance are diminished. As a result refugee children are no longer protected under the 1989 Children Act and the welfare of the child is not legally the paramount concern for local authorities (Rutter and Hyder 1998; Cohen 2001).Unaccompanied refugee children places local authorities under real pressure in providing basic needs such as safe environment and accommodation; income, heating, food, clothing, opportunities for education and recreation. One way forward is through inter-agency collaboration which combines outreach work, advice and service brokerage.

CASE STUDY 16: THE DEVON MULTI-AGENCY ASYLUM SEEKER'S FORUM

The forum was set up in January 2000 by Devon Social Services Department to receive asylum seekers who were being dispersed under the new arrangements. Members include police, education, health, housing, environmental health, Exeter University, local law firms and voluntary organisations, including Oxfam and the Red Cross.

The forum aims to ensure that within a fortnight every new asylum seeker it accepts will have the offer of legal advice, a health assessment, an appointment with a GP, as well as English tuition at a college of further education if needed.

The forum has also set up a mental health centre where asylum seekers may come to talk about their experiences of loss and trauma. Most of them are in fact from Afghanistan and many have experienced the consequences of violence and severe repression; they now also encounter a large measure of racist reaction in the local community. The forum is, however, building a number of partnerships to foster understanding and integration: volunteers run a clothing store to provide additional clothing – since many arrive only in the clothes they are wearing – and volunteers also give weekly English lessons in addition to those at the college.

('Desperately Seeking Sanctuary' *Community Care* 1–7 March 2001)

Dispersal

NASS is able to place people anywhere in the country, irrespective of their connections (or lack of connections) and to give vouchers to spend in designated shops. They have no way of challenging their 'enforced nomadic status', nor is additional help or support offered. Thus 'the vouchers and accommodation constitutes the British government's implementation of what it considers to be its obligations' (Okitikpi and Aymer 2000). In practice refugees are given little or no information on pathways to further welfare supports and have to make do with *ad hoc* bed and breakfast accommodation with low levels of amenities.

Practice approaches

The skills needed for effective work to reduce the exclusion experienced by refugees and asylum seekers are those needed in the other realms of this work: communication, assessment, resource finding, advocacy, mediation, support and counselling. The ecological model has clear implications for practice by getting you to focus on the relationship with family and community with perhaps school or early years centres as crucial institutional sources of support for children. Although obvious in one way Figure 8.1 may help you to visualise how scanty the network of a refugee actually is.

Early years

It is important to understand the nature of the child's experience and the nature of the culture and religious practices that have shaped that experience before arrival in the UK.

A child's identity and sense of community and belonging are bound up with language. If that language is not present or valued in the community he or she lives in, it will be more difficult for the child to value themselves. Ideally children need to feel secure and become competent in English while retaining their home languages (Rutter and Hyder 1998).

The early years practitioner who speaks only English can still use a range of strategies to achieve this. You can:

- build trust through eye contact
- learn a few words in the child's first language, particularly greetings and forms of address. Their parents or carers will be able to explain how the child indicates they are hungry or need to go to the toilet
- be a good language model yourself – speak slowly but in a normal voice
- remember that children can understand what is said long before they can express themselves in the new language – it is important their environment is language rich
- encourage interaction between children: let them teach you and others some words in their home language, while other children may be able to guide them in English usage
- encourage other family members to have contact with your centre, coming in to tell a story or read a book in their home language

(adapted from Rutter and Hyder 1998)

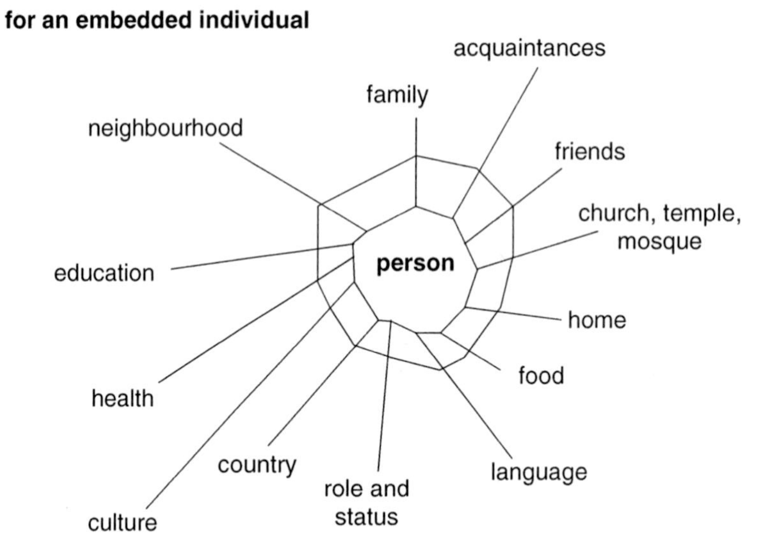

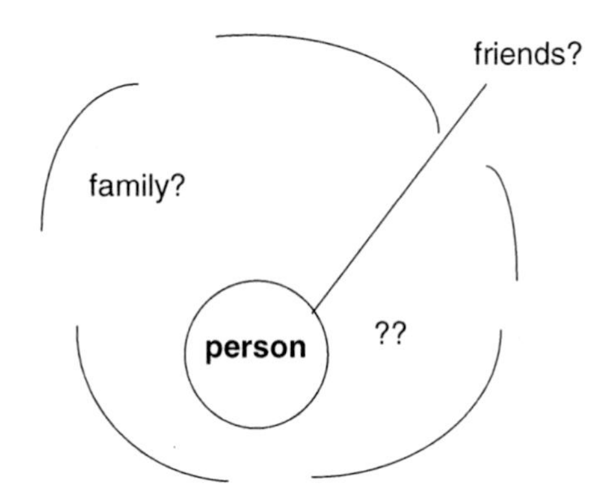

FIGURE 8.1 The web of relationships
Sosusrce: Bolteton and Spafford 1999.

Your agency policy is important since there are many complexities around language to think through. Employing staff with relevant language capacities is important; so is adopting a positive view on bilingualism and not applying pressure to speak English. Children should be enabled to access language through all their senses, including through music, drama and art. (For further practical guidance on early years work with refugee children, Rutter and Hyder have a range of suggestions to follow up, particularly on the importance of play.)

Domestic violence

Women whose immigration status is uncertain experience extreme difficulties in the face of domestic violence. If they are subject to immigration controls they are not eligible for housing assistance, which places them at an immediate and severe disadvantage. Effectively a woman with limited leave to remain faces the dire choice of continuing to live in a situation of domestic violence or risk deportation if she seeks help from a local authority. They fear – rightly – that it is a short step for that authority to inform the Home Office of their change in circumstances and for the Home Office to refuse to take a compassionate approach. A woman who has married a person settled in the UK is in the same predicament. Women asylum seekers may be fleeing domestic violence abroad; new guidelines from the Lord Chancellor's Department ensure that the 'gender aspects' of asylum claims are fully considered.

Fairer, Faster, Firmer (Home Office 1998) acknowledged this predicament: 'in recognition of the dilemma in which victims find themselves ... [for] those who are able to produce satisfactory evidence, such as a relevant court order, conviction or police caution, showing that they have been the victims of domestic violence during the probationary year, will be granted indefinite leave to remain outside the Immigration rules.'

In their comprehensive survey of local authority policy on domestic violence, Thomas and Lebacq note that certain local authorities have developed effective guidelines for practitioners, such as these from Hammersmith and Fulham Domestic Violence Forum:

- Information about services should be targeted at organisations serving a particular ethnic group, including education centres providing language classes for women whose first language is not English, places of worship for all religious groups, housing association newsletters, community groups' newsletters and medical centres: 'It should be remembered that some languages simply do not have words or terms to describe domestic violence.'
- No assumptions should be made about any groups of women, including black women, that lead to those women receiving lower levels of protection than others. Such assumptions may include: that involving a religious leader, elder family member or extended family member is the best way to help; that her immigration status is in doubt; that being abused is an acceptable part of a particular culture.
- All relevant agencies should ensure that their staff are fully aware of the existence and nature of translation and interpreting services that may be needed. Local interpreters should be trained, supervised and supported to understand the particular needs of women experiencing domestic violence.
- Lack of clear immigration status should never prevent women experiencing domestic violence and their children from securing safety and services to support them.

(cited in Thomas and Lebacq 2000)

Building community links

Among the biggest challenges facing practitioners is encouraging links with the community and how to work alongside emerging 'helpers' from within those communities to heighten awareness of refugees' plight and the benefits they can bring to a local area. Practitioners can assist refugees to establish local links by supporting self-help groups. Obtaining funding for local refugee associations to employ a community worker or advice worker has also proven effective (Burgess and Reynolds 1995).

Housing is a key resource in the resettlement of asylum seekers and refugees. This is an area in which refugee community organisations may already be at work, particularly in London, with social housing landlords and others setting up and managing accommodation for refugees. They may start out by managing short-life property from local authorities to which they then add systems of social support. Zetter and Pearl's thorough report (1999) discusses the work of such organisations and the difficulties that emerge in their relations with local authorities and registered social landlords.

While the social work role is uniquely placed to assist refugee families, whether through support or as broker for other services, it has thus far shown some uncertainty as to what precisely it should be. Too often refugee families are treated as if they are in transit, that little needs to be done while they are waiting the outcome of their request for asylum. This, argue Okitikpi and Aymer (2000), is against the spirit of the UN Convention on Human Rights.

CASE STUDY 17: EALING FAMILY HOUSING ASSOCIATION

EFHA is a registered social landlord based in west London, Reading and Oxford. It uses National Lottery funding to employ a development worker whose brief is to create ways of finding work, whether through training, education or work experience. There are points of good practice to consider:

- It has created a partnership with local authority and other voluntary sector agencies.
- It was innovative in seeking National Lottery Funding.
- It responds to government policies around social exclusion including the New Deal for young people, by developing support and training for employment.
- It takes a holistic, Housing-plus approach to the services it offers.

(adapted from Rutter and Hyder 1999: 31–2)

On the other hand, a positive practice is difficult to work out. With the European Union and government essentially abdicating their responsibilities, much is left to local authorities and others working in the field to piece together a strategy on their own. Exclusionary barriers are getting stronger rather than weaker. Refugees and ayslum seekers are placed in increasingly poor accommodation, are more dispersed and isolated with no central strategy in place to integrate them into society. They need education and training packages to give their young people a stake in society. Without a ready counselling and support system those suffering trauma and loss will have only admission to psychiatric hospitals as the first and last resort. Should social workers support those who have had their asylum application turned down when family members are no longer entitled to public funds? Should they 'facilitate' a young person's return home? If so, how?

The political task

Okitikpi and Aymer (2000) argue that there is an unavoidable political task for social workers around the policies of dispersal and detention centres. Current policy constructs an insoluble conflict for practitioners between implementing such procedures (based on repressive and racist political attitudes) and supporting the concept of child welfare, which protects citizen children generally in the UK. The practitioner needs to take part in the political debate by building broad coalitions and raising local awareness of the legal confinements with which refugee families have to cope.

KEY POINTS

- Ethnic minorities suffer social exclusion disproportionately to white people. This is evident in a range of data to do with housing, education, income and other indicators. Racism plays a powerful role in the social exclusion of ethnic minorities and of the areas where they live.
- Social work has a progressive tradition in making anti-racism central to its practice. Nevertheless, in part because of its 'top-down' approach in the past there are ways that it can improve its approach to focus more on building coalitions and partnerships.
- The Macpherson Report on the death of Stephen Lawrence brings the concept of 'institutional racism' into the heart of practice – for social workers as well as all public service agencies.
- There are a number of approaches that social work can develop in its anti-racist practice:
  - in family support services
  - against bias in the early years
  - around 'whiteness' and understanding ethnicity with young white people
  - in neighbourhood regeneration initiatives.
- Refugees and asylum seekers face a highly charged and racialised public context as they enter the UK. Given the legal restrictions they face and the lack of support available to them they constitute the most excluded of all groups. This poses extreme dilemmas for practitioners, who have to choose between two conflicting sets of values. Nevertheless there are niches within which they can begin to construct a positive practice, such as early years work and with refugee community organisations.

KEY READING

S. Cohen's *Immigration Controls, the Family and the Welfare State* (Jessica Kingsley, 2001) provides a detailed account of the legal and societal entanglements that asylum seekers face in the UK; it will soon become the essential text for practitioners.

In her *Tackling Institutional Racism: anti-racist policies and social work education and training* (Policy Press, 2001), Laura Penketh provides a good account of social work's wrestling with anti-racism as a professional objective.

Anti-Bias Approaches in the Early Years, published by Save the Children (2000), provides an excellent introduction to anti-racist work with young children, full of exercises and approaches to use.

CHAPTER 9

SOCIAL WORK AGENCIES AND JOINED-UP ACTION

OBJECTIVES

By the end of the chapter you should be able to:

- Understand the changes in organisational culture and practice required to enable your organisation to attack social exclusion as a core activity
- Develop a set of training needs that you and your colleagues believe will enhance your practice over time
- Explain to colleagues in your organisation the basic principles of the 'neighbourhood management team' as a key way of organising holistic services to tackle exclusion in your area
- Promote the importance of evaluating complex initiatives using approaches such as Best Value reviews and the 'theory of change'.

In the preceding chapters we have discussed the many approaches that you and your colleagues can deploy to reduce the exclusion experienced by users and local areas you work with. You individualy can engage in much valuable work at precisely this level and in the process educate your agency in the means and strategies for tackling social exclusion across a range of fronts. But to make a sustainable contribution in promoting inclusion your agency – whether a large national voluntary organisation, a local authority social service department, small local advice centre or faith-based mission – has to be closely involved in this work. This chapter explains the changes to culture and approaches to practice that agencies have to undertake to engage effectively in a joined-up, local attack on exclusionary barriers for users and citizens alike.

CHANGING CULTURE IN THE ORGANISATION

To tackle social exclusion effectively the culture of social work organisations needs to be fundamentally altered. Organisations fighting social exclusion need to do three things:

- Adopt a neighbourhood orientation in service delivery
- Join up with other agencies to establish holistic services
- Establish dialogue between professionals and local users and residents, providing the latter with channels of influence.

Getting service organisations to do any of this is, however, difficult for the simple reason that bureaucratic and professional cultures are extremely resistant to change. While social service agencies have an undoubted commitment to public welfare, a high degree of probity and a value-base dedicated to promoting inclusion, one of their tacit aims is also to defend and control budgets (Pollitt *et al.* 1999). It is wholly understandable why this should be so: their budget is their oxygen and without it the organisation withers and conditions of employment decline.

But protecting budgets sets in motion behaviour within the organisation that is often cautious, defensive and apprehensive of new initiatives, especially if they hint at loss of sector responsibility and are bent on controlling information, releasing only that which will have favourable budgetary impact. This is one of the main factors in bolstering the 'big silos', in which the major services such as health, education, housing, social services and police have over a long period developed separate cultures, values and management styles. Even in an era of collaboration, say within joint working parties, people act as departmental representatives rather than as 'co-colleagues working towards a common picture' (Wilkinson and Applebee 1999: 33). The big silos in effect have bequeathed us a set of structures, professions, skill mixes and job demarcations for a way of understanding social problems that has long since passed (ibid: 34).

Fitting out an organisation with the perspectives and tools for tackling exclusion is not only a task for senior management. Practitioners themselves have an important role as catalysts in educating and stimulating all levels of their own organisation. While it is important to have senior management behind any initiative – as all textbooks on organisational change stress – it is not a precondition for gearing up your agency to combat exclusion. Within their organisations practitioners should not wait for a message from the top; worry less about where the message comes from and more about getting it across.

A negative consequence of the big silo culture is that issues and social problems are largely seen as 'out there' and 'not down to us', or to do with 'economics – which we have no control over' or 'community development which is not our role' (Wilkinson and Applebee 1999). Overcoming this sense of distance from the deprivation and isolation of social exclusion as experienced by users and local people in poor neighbourhoods is an important step. This is *your* business and that of *your* organisation. If not yours, whose? If not now, when?

Begin in small increments

Building up experience with small initiatives, discussing their impact and the lessons learned within team meetings, assembling data and evaluative material to reflect on, building networks and securing introductions across agencies and in the locality will lay a seedbed in your agency for a practice focused on reducing exclusion. The distinction between 'strong tools' and 'weak tools' helps clarify what roles you might adopt. The former includes matters such as pooled budgets, budgetary incentives, inspections and sanctions, and whole organisation directives which will of necessity require senior management engagement. Soft tools however include persuasion, information, training and learning, building networks, evaluation and changing cultures – the very tools that you, your colleagues and middle managers in the organisation can adopt to facilitate anti-exclusionary practice (6 *et al.* 1999). Building such practice is incremental, moving on from existing approaches and professional relationships step by step in which you:

- begin to relate in different ways to different institutions such as schools, family centres, social housing associations, tenants and residents' association or primary care groups
- respond to different initiatives, such as Best Value or a New Deal for Communities partnership, in a different way
- assemble a different package of services across different agencies and respond to local expressions of what is wanted.

(Taylor 2000)

Waiting for top-down initiatives from within or without your organisation could well be counter-productive. Wilkinson and Applebee note that the single greatest danger with the move toward holistic services is a wave of top-down, corporately-led initiatives which will be complex and time-consuming as senior managers on their own construct partnerships with an emphasis on managing and planning mechanisms. They write: 'Means will become ends. Process improvement will be detached from outcomes and the focus will go internal. The predominating interest will once again be on inputs and top-down indicators of success. In no time we will have an array of indications that purport to measure the effectiveness of partnerships but that are themselves quite disconnected from the real need for partnership on the ground' (Wilkinson and Applebee 1999: 15–16).

Evidence-based practice

Social work has been notoriously eclectic in its attitudes to the specific approaches to practice it adopts. The effectiveness of these approaches has remained relatively unexamined since the 1970s: counselling and 'brief therapy' techniques with crisis intervention, systems intervention, family and group therapies work jostle side by side, leaving the matter to the discretion of individual practitioners. Only task-centred work has had regular and positive evaluation. Sheldon and Chilvers (2001) have uncovered bad habits in the use of evaluative evidence inside social service departments. They found that while nearly 50 per cent of the practitioners had read some 'pertinent literature' in the last two weeks, 20 per cent had read nothing within the last six to twelve months. A full 6 per cent reported that 'it was too long ago to remember' when they last read anything of relevance to their work. The survey uncovered even less practitioner interest in evaluative research.

In fighting social exclusion, it is vital to search out lessons, keep pace with information flows and gather evidence on what works and why. Sheldon and Chilvers make a number of suggestions that agencies can adopt to enhance respect for information and evidence:

- Staff development systems, including supervision, should regularly draw on research to inform decisions about work with users or in projects. Questions should be regularly asked: 'so why are we proceeding in this way?' and 'on what evidence are you making this decision?'.
- Make a range of support facilities available to assist staff in their efforts to keep abreast of relevant research in their field with document supply facilities and summaries of evidence available.
- Practitioner attitudes need to include some personal responsibility for searching out and drawing on evidence of effectiveness.
- Develop collaborative arrangements between social service agencies and local universities and research institutes so that each influences the work of the other through joint seminars and work experience, and so that common purposes around social exclusion practice are understood and mutually interrogated.

(Sheldon and Chilvers 2001)

Practice aimed at combating exclusion is developing fast with an immense range of work now being evaluated and reported on. The information flow is already immense and will prove challenging to social work cultures grown accustomed to slow rates of change in method and disinterested in evidence. To keep abreast with what is going on you can begin with the range of websites outlined in Figure 9.1.

Staff development

In neighbourhood renewal there is no set curriculum for staff development. The various 'cascade' and pyramidal training schemes within organisations – based on a single blueprint which was so useful for the implementation of community care and the Children Act in the early 1990s – will not prove so effective here. The transfer of learning to practice would be negligible since practitioners are only beginning to grapple with the real questions in the field (Wilkinson and Applebee 1999: 138).

A more effective form of training is 'enquiry and action learning' (EAL) which facilitates transferability of knowledge and is more capable of responding to a dynamic field of practice. As practitioners and agencies take their first small steps in, for example, joining up with parents and other agencies to launch a Sure Start programme or a small regeneration partnership the EAL approach becomes an important means of professional development and exploration.

Social work training already has a sound record in developing and applying enquiry and action learning techniques. At its simplest it is based on problems encountered in practice rather than subject-based courses; students work together in small groups on study units that contain scenarios and 'live cases' that come directly from practice. They work on such cases by collectively identifying useful resources, setting learning objectives for themselves, breaking the work down into manageable tasks and reaching decisions about the action to be taken (Cree and Davidson 2000). While developed in relation to work with users EAL is just as

WEBSITES

The number of websites to do with social exclusion is vast. Using Google to search for 'social exclusion' as a term recently yielded no fewer than 267 000 entries. Here are a few ideas to start you off.

- UK government websites are all essential stops. Often publications are available on line in PDF format. Try www.homeoffice.gov.uk/new – once there find 'juvenile offenders' for the relevant approaches to youth offending.
- The Scottish Executive has produced a variety of reports and initiatives which ought to be widely known: www.scotland.gov.uk/
- www.connexions.org.uk/ – for information on the Connexions scheme.
- The Department of Transport, Local Government and the Regions (www.dtlr.gov.uk/) has recently been reorganised. Its web pages often still have the old DETR logo. Try www.regeneration.detr.gov.uk/ for the range of regeneration initiatives for supporting people.
- www.doh.gov.uk/ – for social care, Quality Protects, and the children in need assessment framework among other topics.
- www.dfee.gov.uk/ – for the Department for Education and Employment's thinking on school exclusion.
- www.seu.gov.uk/ – for the policy action reports, guidelines on anti-racism and neighbourhood renewal and much else from the Social Exclusion Unit.
- www.regen.net/users/ – a site that links you to all kinds of regeneration activities plus regular training and conference events.
- www.cre.gov.uk/ – the official site for the Commission on Racial Equality.
- www.jrf.org.uk/ – the home page for the premier research institute in the UK for regeneration, neighbourhood management, housing and social care.
- www.newstartmag.co.uk – the home page for the important weekly on regeneration developments.
- www.community-care.co.uk – the home page of the weekly magazine on social care, social exclusion with the latest news and full article retrieval service.

FIGURE 9.1 Key information sources on the web

appropriate for community development tasks. Other elements of social work training and staff development also lend themselves well to preparing staff for partnership, neighbourhood management and high levels of local participation. These include:

- using reflective diaries
- a strong tradition of regular on-the-job supervision
- an emphasis on using 'critical incident' analysis as a source of reflection for practitioners
- a precise practice teaching curriculum built on adult education principles.

All of the above are powerful tools to help transfer and deepen learning in practice – and will serve social work organisations well in joint training with residents and other services in the complicated multi-task environment that all such partners will face (see Cree and Davidson 2000).

PRINCIPLES OF ACTION LEARNING

- There can be no learning without action and no considered action without sober reflection
- Without learning there can be no real change – for change to work learning has to be greater than the rate of change
- Asking others to change means changing yourself; what Revans (1982) called 'the principle of insufficient mandate'. Managers and practitioners who cannot change their predisposing views of problems during their efforts to treat those problems will never be able to make progress with them.

As a teaching tool in social work, action learning:

- Uses students' or practitioners' previous experience as a learning resource
- Uses 'live' case study material; that is, the practitioner is exposed to the processes and dilemmas that would face them in a poor neighbourhood or in relation to excluded service users
- Adopts active learning approaches in which a process of questioning, listening, investigating, consulting, reflecting and decision-making is undertaken both individually and collaboratively to rehearse a practice in which there are no right answers
- Uses peer learning with the greater proportion of time spent in small groups or in twos or threes where students feel both secure and stretched
- Involves facilitators who listen, clarify, draw out and guide the work of the group, and consultants from outside the process who help students in integrating their understanding with what is happening, and who bring different philosophies, commitments and codes of practice to the student experience.

(Cree and Davidson 2000)

Curriculum for joined-together training

There is no single blueprint for a training curriculum that grounds practitioners in combatting exclusion. It should evolve as the field evolves and ought to model the very forms of partnership that the work itself entails, involving a range of stakeholders. Staff development will nevertheless revolve around the main themes of social exclusion. This means placing emphasis on joined-together services and gearing them toward providing the key means for promoting inclusion, focusing on:

- poverty and raising low income

- holistic approaches to community care and family support services
- improving social networks
- developing participation by local residents.

These apply across the range of initiatives for specific groups of people.

Henderson and Mayo (1998) outline several important principles for any training programme. These include:

1. A training needs analysis, establishing what it is that practitioners, managers and residents as well as other stakeholders need to know, is essential. This could be specific, such as putting together a local response to high levels of truanting, or broader, for example in relation to a neighbourhood regeneration project which will run for several years.
2. Joint and partnership-based training should be undertaken wherever possible. Accessibility is vital. Choosing the time of day or evening to run sessions, weighing up the advantages and disadvantages of weekend and residential courses, ensuring good childcare and adequate means of travel are all important. If local residents are to be involved so is the nature of the publicity issued, what outlets are used and who it is intended for.
3. Confidence – local residents and service users may well feel at a disadvantage in joint training sessions in contrast to practitioners and managers who will be familiar with the format (knowing how to comport themselves when breaking into small groups, for example, or giving a 'report back'). So it is extremely important to offer a range of choices, including women-only and resident-only sessions.
4. Don't assume neighbourhoods are 'empty vessels' – resilience, capacity, skills and the ability to learn quickly are all there among residents.

ACTIVITY 9.1: TRAINING NEEDS ANALYSIS

Assume you have been designated by your organisation to sit on a neighbourhood forum on community safety. The forum itself is linked to a wider regeneration partnership based on a low-income housing estate on the edge of a large city. The partnership is hoping to obtain funding from central government under the New Deal for Communities programme. The plan for community safety, for which the forum will be largely responsible for implementing, reads:

Vision: To make the estate a place that's safe, freer of the fear of crime, drugs and the anti-social behaviour that affects our community.

Strategic approach: Our approach to making the estate a safer place is to move away from reacting to crime and criminality and towards a preventative programme aimed at creating a sustainable safe environment. We do not believe there is a single solution to crime and have developed our neighbourhood strategy accordingly.

'*Tackling youth crime – breaking the cycle*: Breaking the cycle of youth crime demands intervention at a number of levels including involvement of the whole community through education, empowerment and creating an environment where drug dealing and drug use is unacceptable. We will develop parental support and education – actively engaging parents and in particular mothers. This will include work with local schools, faith groups, community organisations and health centres. It will also include a peer-education programme, working with local primary schools on drug education and truanting, developing close links with the Connexions scheme' (text drawn from Ocean Estate NDC 2000).

Discuss with three or four colleagues: what role could you see for yourself and your team within this plan? What training needs do you have to become effective in that role? In answering the second question be as specific as you can and draw up a list of what your training needs are.

Training needs of local citizens

It is important in organisational contexts where certain groups dominate the decision-making processes that other voices be given space to participate in the early stages of capacity building. This can be achieved through the development of smaller focus groups with particular goals such as literacy or vocational training which can then feed into the broader community groups when some capacity is built. The kinds of skills and knowledge local citizens need in order to act include:

- Institutional knowledge, which provides local citizens with an understanding of how services and political machinery work, together with the opportunities and constraints
- Literacy and numeracy skills which provide the platform for more significant roles in decision-making and oversight of projects
- Negotiating skills which enable dialogue with other partners
- Confidence building – particularly for those in groups unable to engage in earlier participatory initiatives through cultural pressures
- Conflict and dispute resolution skills in order to manage the dynamics of community organisations.

(Plummer 2000)

CASE STUDY 18: THE CITIZENS ORGANISING FOUNDATION

The COF is a network of broad-base organisations which runs its own training programme for local activists and leaders. In a week-long series of seminars, discussions and role plays trainees are exposed to the practicalities of mounting a local 'action': from highlighting local issues to identifying and confronting those with the power of redress. The training coincides with a chance to watch a real action in progress: for instance an 'accountability session' when citizens call on their local officials or councillors to agree to particular policy pledges. This provides an opportunity to assess the application of the principles and techniques they have learned in the workshop.

But the purpose of the COF training is also to teach the wider obligations and responsibilities of civic action. Their curriculum has several key learning points:

1. Knowing how to clarify the difference between public and private roles for an individual, and how to conduct yourself and meet your responsibilities with regard to the former, not mixing or confusing the two.
2. Learning to respond to public officials by developing the skills needed to hold your ground in a meeting or negotiating session.
3. The nature of power – that power is both unilateral (that is directive, compelling and coercive) and relational, drawing on the work of Charles Loomer (1976).
4. The skills and conduct for successful 'relational organising' (see Chapter 7) which is built on listening and engagement with residents in small formats such as one-to-one sessions or small house meetings.
5. Applying pressure: how to build countervailing power locally to help in the bargaining with city officials and politicians.
6. The nature and conduct of negotiation – learning to balance conciliation with the application of pressure.

CASE STUDY 19: ASIAN WOMEN LEARNING COMPUTER SKILLS

There are many stereotypes of Asian women held by social workers. On the Estate many women of Bangladeshi origin contributed to the delivery plan by attending meetings and giving voice to their concerns, particularly about drugs and the groups of adolescent Asian youth congregating on the estate. One of the catalysts for this contribution was a women-only course on using computers held once a week above a local youth centre. If you were simply visiting the estate, you might not have seen what was happening; yet in the preparation of the Ocean delivery plan the contribution by Bengali women was evident, and they were given a voice in part through courses like this.

NEIGHBOURHOOD MANAGEMENT

Decentralisation of services comes and goes as a strategy within the history of delivering social work services. One major strand of community social work throughout the 1980s was precisely to 'go local' as the late Roger Hadley (1981) put it. Developing partnerships with local people and organisations, getting to know the neighbourhood intimately, creating easy access points for the public to obtain a service were all part of a well-thought-out 'patch' strategy strongly resembling current initiatives.

Going local was at times not always easy in the 1980s. The notion of joining services together was not thought through, nor had local councils, when they launched sometimes overly ambitious plans to decentralise, always understood the bureaucratic impediments that they were still leaving in place to thwart local popular participation in service development. Finding the appropriate management strategy also proved elusive so that a central core of standards disappeared leaving professionals vulnerable to local politics and uneven, ever-changing service objectives (Hambleton *et al.* 1997). As a consequence high-profile arrangements to decentralise, especially in inner London, were seen to fail.

But with this experience to draw on, and with a greater understanding of how to empower multi-agency front-line teams, reconfiguring services around a neighbourhood agenda has become the decisive element in public services' strategy for tackling exclusion. The concept of 'neighbourhood management' best embraces what these new developments are trying to achieve. Neighbourhood management brings together several threads in the fight against social exclusion:

- local government decentralisation – physical, administrative and political
- inter-agency working and joint planning
- community involvement.

(Taylor 2000: 5).

Neighbourhood management is the most important way of following up the special initiatives to address social exclusion (many of which we have already discussed in this volume), bringing mainstream service budgets and activity to bear on exclusionary barriers.

Key elements of neighbourhood management

The Social Exclusion Unit (2000) has laid out a number of key elements of neighbourhood management which have been backed up by further discussion and research. These are:

- A neighbourhood board involving residents, the local authority, other public agencies, and the voluntary and private sectors to plan and steer a programme of local regeneration.
- A multi-agency team to deliver the plan to address joblessness, community safety, poor housing and poor health, with an emphasis on building human and social capital as a way of overcoming these problems.
- Provision of accessible, integrated services that continually improve the lives of local people.
- Services that place an emphasis in their practice on prevention, drawing on evidence of 'what works'.
- Building capacity through strategies that encourage and prepare residents to participate in strategy development and local control to the maximum that they are able.
- 'Bending' mainstream programmes of the main services so that they routinely target resources in areas of greatest need and in ways which have maximum impact.
- Policies at all levels of government that work to promote neighbourhood management.

(SEU 2000)

What neighbourhood management requires

The development of neighbourhood teams inevitably means a changed relationship between front-line practitioners and management. Neighbourhood teams require devolved budgets (with which social services already has some valuable experience, as does education) to the front line with the teams then held accountable for achieving holistic outcomes that actually show up in the improvement of quality of life and the promotion of inclusion in the locality. This can then lead to pooled budgets in which service agencies and local authority departments look at the combined resources at their disposal and then, after discussion and the creation of jointly agreed action plans, proceed to commission the services required (Taylor 2000: 24).

Of course budgets are the lifeblood of public service organisations and pooling budgets will no doubt be a difficult endeavour especially at the outset when the level of trust between agencies is low. Most commentators acknowledge this and argue that pooled budgets may work best where they remain tied to very specific tasks with predictable goals. As Taylor says 'Any fundamental pooling that involves staff would also encounter problems around salary levels, pensions, working conditions and job security' (ibid: 24).

But these obstacles to pooling resources may yield more quickly than is thought. Budget devolution is one possible step, as is placing a certain proportion of an agency's budget into a fund on which local joined-up projects can draw. (See Taylor 2000, and 6 *et al.* 1999 for further elaboration of this important subject.)

Beyond the vexed question of pooling funds there are other requisites for successful neighbourhood management:

Local one-stop shops from which people can obtain advice for navigating the various service systems and contact, advocates who will speak and work for their objectives as well as access to services themselves – whether family support, social care or housing.

High levels of local participation in determining service strategies and yearly action plans. Neighbourhood forums in particular have become prominent as one way of achieving this. They have a semi-formal role in current regeneration initiatives and in some Best Value reviews, where they are usually organised around particular subjects of local concern, for example young people, community safety or job development. In Stepney the New Deal for Communities project relied extensively on the work of forums to bring its delivery plan together. On the basis of the trust developed in that process the forums' role was formalised; they received their own devolved budgets for implementation of their sector of the plan while remaining accountable to the partnership board.

LEARNING TO EVALUATE EFFECTIVELY

Tackling social exclusion draws on large-scale public efforts intended to be democratic in process while at the same time committed to producing results. These efforts require the support of a wide range of stakeholders, all of whom need to be kept informed of progress and outcomes and to have evidence that their investment – whether of time and energy or funding – is achieving something. Neighbourhood residents in particular need to know whether the promises and hopes extended by particular initiatives are bearing fruit. Effective evaluation through a transparent, trusted and widely understood process is the only way to meet this objective (Hughes and Traynor 2000; Kubisch *et al.* 2001.

There is also another important reason for good evaluation: it guides implementation. Any good programme or agency manager needs formative feedback to inform planning, management and administration, as well as mid-course correction of programmes. But in the creation of new approaches to practice at the neighbourhood level this requirement for sound, effective feedback is particularly acute. As a practitioner you require good evaluation to map against baseline data. Evaluation is a main source of evidence through which you judge your effectiveness and that of your agency.

As with training there is no single blueprint for evaluation format that shows how this should happen. Evaluative structures and activities will inevitably respond to individual neighbourhood circumstances. Although often dressed up in its own language of inputs and outputs, of benchmarks and indicators, of baselines and long-term aims, evaluation is really about one question: is effective work being done?

While the question is straightforward you can see the difficulties in trying to evaluate the kinds of approach and initiative that tackling social exclusion requires. First, there are many different stakeholders in the form of service agencies' managers and practitioners, local politicians, a range of local organisations and their leaders and residents with different interests and commitments. How do they arrive at agreed standards for evaluation? Second, initiatives themselves are complex, with a big social objective – bringing about social change – that calls on a range of actions and resources, the results of which are often difficult to track. How can you identify which input, resource or activity is responsible for any given outcome? Third, initiatives take place over a much longer time frame than the usual techniques are accustomed to handling. How can you link with certainty the outcomes in year four of an initiative to resources put in place in year one? There is presumably some relationship but of course other unplanned factors may have influenced outcomes three years later.

There is one further impediment to effective evaluation: the tension between 'process' and 'product' with which every multi-pronged initiative has to grapple. Process refers to building participative structures, of agreeing the rules of the game for partners, for establishing governance over the initiative, and building trust among collaborating organisations. This takes time and does not easily yield to deadlines. Product refers to the specific outcomes sought – the number of houses re-insulated, or the rise in the percentage of students achieving GCSE passes with grades A–C, or the number of young offenders brought successfully through a local Final Warning scheme. Managers, councillors, funders, even elements of the neighbourhood itself will be more interested in the latter than the former (Kubisch *et al.* 2001). But for local neighbourhoods an excessive emphasis on outcome or product can be disempowering: taking the time to establish participatory channels and to equip residents for governance of a project are all part of the 'process' which can be undermined by tight deadlines and constant emphasis on concrete outputs.

Sadan and Churchman (1997) establish a number of dimensions along which this tension between product and process can be mapped. In each case community empowerment improves as the right-hand side of each spectrum is explored and tested (Figure 9.2). But this makes evaluation, at least in the traditional framework of inputs and outcomes, more difficult.

Directive intervention (product)	*Non-directive intervention (process)*
Service delivery focus	Resident focus
Centralised decision making	Decentralised decision making
Specific task definition	Open-ended task definition
Community as object	Community as subject
Expert practitioner	Reflective practitioner

FIGURE 9.2 'Product' versus 'process'

Source: Sudan and Churchman 1997.

In the sections that follow we examine three different possible frameworks for evaluation.

Achieving better community development

The ABCD model – Achieving Better Community Development – offers perhaps the more straightforward pathway to sound evaluation (Figure 9.3). Within this approach Barr and Hashagen (2000) have incorporated many of the techniques required for evaluating projects with multiple outcomes achieved over time and an important role for services in achieving them.

The ABCD model works on four variables: inputs, processes, outputs and outcomes.

Inputs are the range of resources and tools that are available from within the community or brought in by outside agencies working in support of community development. Such resources move well beyond funding to include:

- people's time, motivation and energy
- skills, knowledge and understanding
- trust within the neighbourhood
- networks
- leadership.

Stakeholders from outside the community bring resources such as a policy framework, expertise and training, additional funding, and co-ordination.

Processes are defined as those actions that need to take place to direct inputs towards specified outcomes. In this framework the central process is one of 'community empowerment' which embraces four components: personal development for individuals, 'positive action' for social justice and social inclusion, community organisation and the effectiveness of community-based groups, and gaining power and influence at local level. This empowerment process can be seen as the way in which inputs are used to develop the ability of the community to achieve change (Barr and Hashagen 2000: 61)

Outputs are the product of community empowerment, the specific actions that relate to economic, social, environmental or political issues of the locality. These outputs may include social service development, a safe and healthy community or increased citizen control over services and political developments.

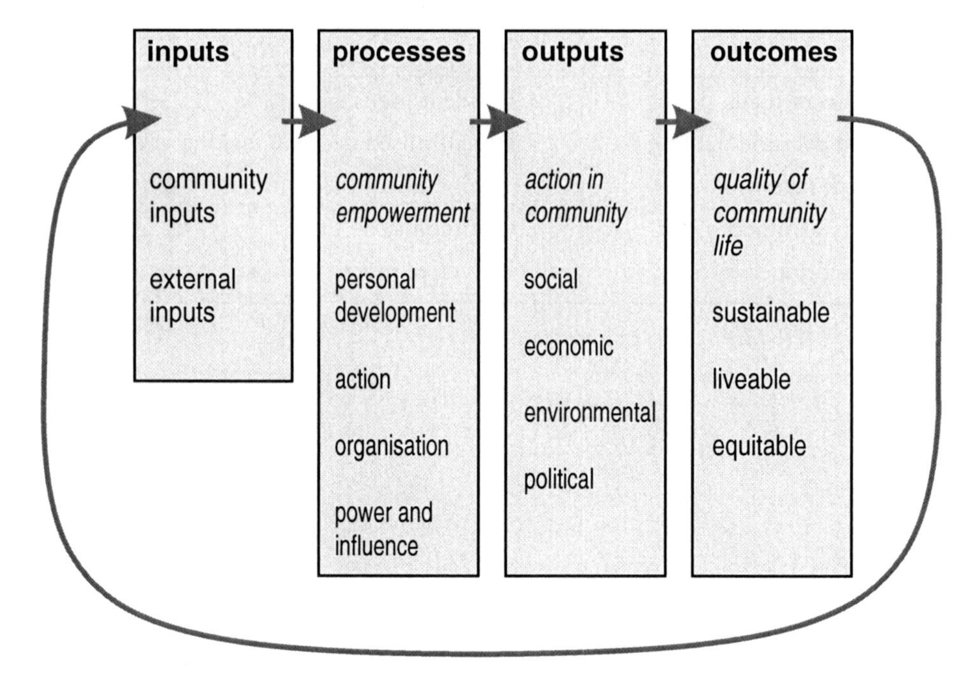

FIGURE 9.3 The ABCD model of evaluation

Source: Barr and Hashagen 2000.

Outcomes are the consequences of the outputs relating to the improvement in the quality of life of the locality.

Evaluation poses critical questions for each stage. What are the inputs to community development activity, and how do they change with the progress of action? How well are the inputs applied to the process of community empowerment? What are the outputs and outcomes? How is empowerment used to influence the quality of community life? (ibid: 62)

To answer such questions some notion of a starting point or baseline has to be established as well as a number of indicators that will provide yardsticks as to what is being achieved. Once a baseline has been established the evaluation task then requires information to be gathered and assessed. Gathering information is the crucial stage requiring advance planning. You need to know what type of information is required, for example whether facts or opinion, and who you want to obtain information from, for example from users, local residents or community representatives. Information can be obtained by:

- Observation, that is having an observer present when key events occur either as a participant–observer or as non-participant.
- Asking questions – through questionnaires, face-to-face interviews, consultations or focus groups. Barr and Hashagen have sound advice as to how to gather information for evaluation:
  - be focused by asking relevant questions about specific activities
  - keep it as simple as possible
  - look for emerging themes by interpreting findings

Key chosen outcome	*Key baseline data*	*Milestones (indicators)*
1 Increase the social and economic strengths of the estate to enable residents to participate fully in the decision making and delivery of local service provision	• 9% of people take part in resident/tenant associations • 10% belong to voluntary/community group • 2% are members of parent/teacher association	By year 3: • Neighbourhood management team in place • Neighbourhood forums in place • 25% increase in participation in local groups and associations
2 Increase levels of involvement in the community from 42% to 55%	• 42% of respondents felt involved in the community as compared with 73% in Tower Hamlets as a whole and 48% at national level	By year 3: • Increase to 45% feeling of involvement in the community
3 Reduce by 60% the number of residents who say that lack of affordable childcare is a barrier to employment	• 29% of working age women identify affordable quality childcare as a barrier to employment (approximately 390 women)	By year 3: • 18% of working age women find lack of affordable childcare a barrier to employment, reducing to 12% by year 6
4 Reduce households with an income less than £10 000 a year to the national average	• 51% of households have an income of less than £10 000 a year as compared with the national average of 34%	By year 3: • 45% of households with an income less than £10,000 a year reducing to 39% in year 6 and 30% in year 10

FIGURE 9.4 Long-term outcomes, baseline data and indicators for making progress from the Ocean Estate's delivery plan

Source: Ocean Estate NDC 2000.

- offer choices and options to those you are seeking information from such as ranking the importance of items
- use innovative techniques such as tapes, photographs, exhibitions, physical representations, diagrams or story telling.

(Barr and Hashogen 2000)

ACTIVITY 9.2: EVALUATING A COMMUNITY RESOURCE CENTRE

Assume you and three other colleagues are evaluating a community resource centre on a low-income housing estate in east London. The centre is housed in a one-storey brick building, built around 1960. It is owned by the the work of local authority but has been leased for a small sum to a consortium of agencies and local residents who have ambitious plans for it. The consortium has worked out a number of objectives that it thinks will provide what local people want from such a centre; it also reflect much of the new thinking around 'neighbourhood renewal'. One set of objectives is to increase the social strengths of the estate by:

- Enabling residents to participate fully in the decision making and delivery of local services.
- Establishing sustainable structures to deliver community services. It wants to do this by increasing community capacity and facilities so that local people can take 'ownership' and leadership of the area, improving communication between the community and service providers to create more responsive services and to develop a neighbourhood management model for those services.

The only member of staff is a part-time caretaker. The resource centre is well used although the activities that take place there do not always seem to further the consortium's objectives. Among the activities that take place within it are the following:

- a luncheon club for older citizens four days a week
- occasional cultural activities for the substantial local Bengali population in the evening
- an after-school club for children up to the age of 14
- a training course in IT skills for women
- a youth club two nights a week
- a venue for local community groups to meet.

With your three colleagues plan a brief evaluation of the centre. Who do you think would be among the principal stakeholders and involved in the evaluation? What and who are the inputs? As far as the set of objectives is concerned what indicators would you look for to measure any progress? What kind of information or data would you need and how would you go about collecting it? How would you present this information to users of the centre and to members of the consortium itself to make it a useful learning tool?

Theory of change

One framework for evaluation of complex initiatives that wrestles precisely with these questions is the 'theory of change'. It has been defined as 'a systematic and cumulative study of the links between activities, outcomes, and contexts of the initiative'. Essentially the theory of change approach asks certain questions of all participants in a project that tackles *exclusion:*

- why is this project going to work?
- what are the theories that in your view will make the project effective and achieve the (often complicated) social objectives that the project aspires to over the time span?

- how will you be able to show the outside world that the project has succeeded?

According to Kubisch and her colleagues the theory of change has several attributes. It:

- outlines the pathway of the initiative by linking the sequences of activity to the longer-term outcomes
- aims to identify the assumptions underlying the activity sequences; 'thus, it integrates a theory of change in outcomes (what will occur) with a theory of change-making (how the changes in outcomes will occur)'
- considers how much change is expected to occur, and when, and the interactions among various types of change
- examines expectations for outcomes in light of available and potential resources (financial, institutional, technical, political)
- is participatory throughout; 'encourages multiple stakeholders to co-construct the theory by drawing upon multiple sources of information, including programme experience, scientifically generated knowledge, and community residents' insights'
- spans the design, implementation and evaluation of the initiative; to do this 'requires specifying, evaluating and then revisiting the pathways of change – that is, the relationship between activities and outcomes – at multiple levels throughout the course of the initiative. Thus, a theory of change can evolve as the initiative incorporates lessons learned over time' (Kubisch *et al.* 2001: 87).

The phrase 'theory of change' means simply making clear and bringing into the open those theories on which the initiative is basing its plans. Theory of change asks 'what are the concepts behind the initiative that enables it to think that the various outcomes identified will be reached over the period of time projected?' Theory of change evaluation asks that projects first establish long-term outcomes and work backwards from these so that intermediate and early outcomes relate to those long-term objectives. Early outcomes are similarly related to intermediate outcomes.

Hughes and Traynor (2000) ask: how is it possible to develop sufficiently rigorous techniques so that credible data can be assembled for appraising outcomes acceptable to all interested parties? How do we arrive at an image of what success will look like?

They find three great virtues of the theory of change approach to evaluation. First the evaluator works from the beginning jointly with all stakeholders – local residents, practitioners, managers, councillors – as they shape up the long-term outcomes of any

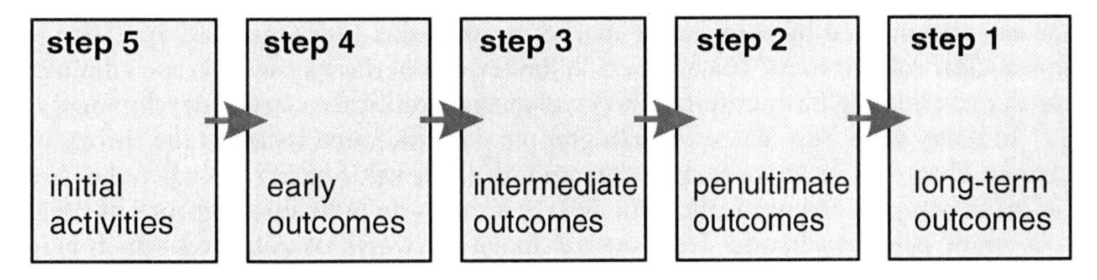

FIGURE 9.5 The theory of change

Source: Hughes and Traynor 2000.

initiative. Second, the very act of doing this helps make explicit what theories are being drawn on to allow stakeholders to have confidence that those outcomes will be reached. Research evidence is important here. For example, family literacy programmes have a demonstrable impact on levels of achievement in school; a tough policy with emphasis on correctional institutions in relation to teenage drug-users has the effect of dragging more young people into criminalised behaviour. Any youth action on social exclusion would want to consider the first element but not the second to ground a project in. Third, the theory of change can blend both process and hard outcomes in framing the first step, that is to say the long-term objectives.

The evaluation by Traynor and Davidson (2000) of the eight community development projects in the Barnardos anti-poverty strategy draws heavily on the theory of change and provides an excellent example of how its framework can be applied.

Using the Best Value framework

The Labour government introduced the Best Value framework in 1997 to replace the compulsory competitive tendering regime (CCT) of the previous Conservative administration. It was clearly seen within central government as a test which could make or break local government.

Best Value obligates local authorities to search continuously to improve quality, effectiveness and efficiency in all of its activities. Unlike CCT, however, it is not simply a value-for-money exercise obtained through canny contracting. Nor should it focus only on individual services and their performance indicators (Wilkinson and Applebee 1999). There are in fact important objectives beyond efficiency that includes developing and promoting holistic service action to tackle exclusion in close consultation with the local community. Richardson (1998) suggests that the Best Value framework:

- moves to a problem focus with emphasis on process rather than structure;
- invests in integrated outcomes while more relaxed about the means to achieve them; and
- facilitates a learning process through incentives to change cultures within the organisation.

(cited in Wilkinson and Applebee 1999)

Thus far there seems to be little awareness of the participative possibilities that Best Value inaugurates; while it retains much of the 'new management' techniques it creates a regulatory regime built on direct dialogue with service agencies and their users while far less encumbered by competitive market mechanisms (Buchanan 2000). There is now a clear role for users' voice in Best Value reviews of the way services are administered, including eligibility criteria. This involvement is critical to service development.

In many ways Best Value reviews grapple with the same issues as the theory of change: How do you arrive at an understanding of the value of services when they are linked in complex arrangements with diverse impacts on individuals, groups of users and whole neighbourhoods? How do you judge the worth of initiatives which may vary highly in their effectiveness and are viewed differently from different perspectives?

Improving the quality of life for local residents requires focusing on outcomes that are holistic and neighbourhood based. Framing Best Value reviews to take account of the big issues in social exclusion – whether improving individual opportunity or raising local capacity or underpinning social cohesion – is a similar evaluative challenge.

Wilkinson and Applebee have developed a benchmarking matrix for Best Value which is designed to clarify the constituent elements of a review which they base on the twin concepts of consultation and participation. Consultation draws out the views and reactions of local people on needs and the capacity of services to meet them as well as prospective service developments for the future. Consultation is the 'transmission belt' so to speak for local knowledge in all of its experiential context that practitioners need to augment their 'programmed knowledge' which is based on past problems. But information elicited through consultation processes often remains detached from service decision-making and users will not know how the information they supply is used.

The matrix aims to highlight the broad dimensions of Best Value benchmarking. No one position is inherently better than any other; that will depend on evidence of what works in implementation of a specific project. One axis distinguishes consultation from participation. Consultation elicits views and opinions about services, user needs and proposed projects.

BEST VALUE IN KENSINGTON AND CHELSEA

The joint inspections by the Audit Commission and Social Services Inspectorate now represent a formidable instrument for the regulation of social care. Their joint report on the Social Services Department in the London Borough of Kensington and Chelsea provides instructive reading for many of the issues facing local authority departments.

In an otherwise positive assessment the report had this to say about the implementation of Best Value in the borough:

> The Authority has responded positively to the Best Value agenda but needs to ensure that it uses best value principles and processes to systematically link key process around ... strategic commissioning and performance management.
>
> [Consultation] needs to be more widespread with services users. The Best Value regime involved interviews with five looked after children, four parents of looked after children and four foster carers only. Consultation was more weighted towards professionals and included 20 staff from Children and Families Services, six primary schools and two secondary schools. Moreover, the staff consultation meetings focused on internal matters such as communication and the Authority's strengths (for example, 'strong leadership', 'potential for creative and flexible approaches') as opposed to ideas for improving services delivered to looked after children.

(From Audit and Social Services Inspectorate: *A Report of the Joint Review of Social Services in the Royal Borough of Kensington and Chelsea* 2001: 65)

	Individual user	*Individual citizens*	*User/target group focus Communities of interest or concern*	*Neighbourhood or local community focus*
Consultation				
Participation				

FIGURE 9.6 A Best Value benchmarking matrix
Source: Wilkinson and Applebee (1999): 128.

The other axis, participation brings local knowledge – the views and reactions of local people – into the decision-making process. It involves closer dialogue with practitioners and some control or influence over the way that that knowledge is used. The other axis of their matrix charts *who* is involved. This includes:

- individual users of services
- individual citizens who are sought for their views on a range of issues and services of local concern
- user groups and communities of interest
- neighbourhood-based organisations which have the whole locality as their area of concern.

The practitioner as change agent

It is tempting to think that you and your colleagues can wait until someone fires the 'time to start tackling social exclusion' gun before taking forward elements of the practice outlined in this book. But that is not a luxury you have. On the contrary your role should be one of catalyst and change agent regardless of your position in the organisation. But to do this you need an understanding of the 'self in the sea of change' to use Gerald Smale's phrase, which is critical to working with the changes in approach, large and small, that tackling social exclusion requires. He frames three important questions that you need to answer, not just about yourself but about your colleagues as well:

1 Are the people you work with active or passive? Will they enthusiastically join, and perhaps lead, innovation or will they resist and have change imposed upon them? Smale reminds us that 'to have the rug pulled out from under you is a very different experience from coming to a decision to reject the old flooring and choose a new carpet' (Smale 1998: 122). In other words imposed or coerced change generates opposition and takes a lot of time to get over.

2 Does the innovation produce a change of identity? The degree of change determines the amount of learning and unlearning that staff will have to do. Tasks will be upgraded and downgraded. Retaining autonomy, respect, dignity in the organisation and breadth of responsibility are all critical factors – often as important as remuneration in a period of change.

3 What do key people win or lose? To understand the impact of change on colleagues and others you work with, for example from other agencies in a prospective partnership, ask *who* is experiencing what aspect of change as a 'gain' or a 'loss'? What can you do to help people recognise real gains and build commitment to the new solutions and new situations?

KEY POINTS

- Tackling social exclusion in collaborative action that has high levels of local participation requires a change of culture and attitudes inside the social service organisation itself. Greater emphasis has to be placed on evidence-based practice, searching out and improving those lines of activity that actually help to tear down exclusionary barriers.
- There is a wave of initiative and project-oriented work currently being taken across the UK which is reflected in many new sources of information whether websites or new journals. It is vital to stay in touch with what is current and to transfer the lessons others have developed to your own work.
- Organisations need to develop effective training and action learning techniques to prepare their practitioners for the range of tasks they will encounter.
- The development of neighbourhood teams which join up services in each locality is a prerequisite for tackling social exclusion.
- Evaluation is the final essential ingredient to good practice: the way it is carried out creates the vital processes for bringing 'local knowledge' to bear on services and gives practitioners and their teams a feedback loop on which to base their ongoing reflection on practice. The ABCD approach, 'theory of change' and Best Value reviews are three ways that acknowledge on the one hand the complexity and scale of the programmes to be evaluated and on the other a process that is plausible and understandable by the range of professionals and public involved.

KEY READING

Marilyn Taylor is always worth reading on participation. In *Top Down meets Bottom Up: Neighbourhood Management*: (Joseph Rowntree Foundation, 2000) she looks at the rationale of local integrated services, giving effective examples.

Gerry Smale's penultimate book before his untimely death, *Managing Change Through Innovation* (The Stationery Office, 1998) argues eloquently for the need of social services organisations to change their culture but does so in a supportive way that builds on existing organisational strengths.

D. Wilkinson and E. Applebee's *Implementing Holistic Government: joined-up action on the ground* (Demos, 1999) lays out an innovative and coherent agenda for the service organisation that aims to integrate its actions with other agencies.

CHAPTER 10

ACTIVITIES

Pointers to the issues

This brief final chapter highlights some of the possible responses to many of the activities set in the book. Not all the activities are covered. Nor do these 'pointers' provide complete answers – they are intended simply to guide the reader toward the critical issues raised.

ACTIVITY 1.2: THE DIFFERENT MEANINGS OF SOCIAL EXCLUSION

The first extract reflects the moral underclass interpretation of social exclusion by a leading exponent, Charles Murray. The clue here is the word 'illegitimacy' – referring to children not born to married couples – and the clear implication that moral codes must be in place to encourage stable families as the basis for community. The second extract by Frank Field, the former minister of welfare reform, notes that welfare must provide incentives for people to maximise their chances to work and not 'buck the system'. It is a good example of the social integrationist perspective. The third extract, by Gary Craig, represents the redistributionist perspective. He emphasises that Britain's real problem is sharp inequality in wealth and policies on social exclusion only divert attention from this central fact.

ACTIVITY 1.3: THINKING ABOUT POVERTY

It is interesting to compare your list with what the public decided in the national survey undertaken by the Office of National Statistics and reported in Gordon *et al.* (2000: 13). The public's view was (figures in brackets are percentages): two pairs of all weather shoes (71), television (56), holiday away from home once a year not with relatives (55), dictionary (53), car (38), carpets in living room (67), microwave (23), daily newspaper (30), regular saving of £10 per month (66), an evening out once a fortnight (37), visits to friends and family (84), visits to the children's school (81), hobby or leisure activity (78), having a telephone (71), small amounts of money to spend on self weekly (59), dressing gown (34), coach or train fare to visit friends and family every three months (38).

ACTIVITY 1.4: REDLINING

Redlining is an extreme example of financial exclusion because it is deliberate 'post-code discrimination'. You may not uncover evidence of such direct discrimination but nevertheless find that the low-income neighbourhood you choose to audit is poorly served. The activity is asking you to conduct a quick audit of financial services. You might begin by noting where banks and cash tills are located and the distance people have to travel to reach them. You might then pinpoint other outlets where local people could cash cheques or giros – if they exist. Finally you might examine how people are able to obtain credit whether buying through catalogues, from a credit union or loan sharks.

ACTIVITY 1.5: REFLECTING ON WHAT SOCIAL WORK CAN CONTRIBUTE TO TACKLING SOCIAL EXCLUSION

From this list social workers do the following when tackling social exclusion: support families, and particularly children, experiencing high levels of conflict; provide services for children whose deprivation is sufficient for them to be assessed as 'in need'; take responsiblity for young people looked after by the local authority reaching educational attainments such as GCSEs and obtaining skills for work and living independently. They also work with older service users to eliminate barriers to their living in the community. For other problems in the list they join with other agencies, for example to reduce crime in a locality through youth offending teams or tackling inequalities in health care.

ACTIVITY 2.1: UNDERSTANDING THE REALITY OF POVERTY

This exercise is simply to get you to think more closely about how totally preoccupying poverty is for those who are poor. What appears to be slack personal habits, disinterest in important commitments, failure to make appointments, lack of concentration – all become more understandable when put in the context of this kind of circumstance. Whether it is a benefits book that is lost or delayed in the post, or a theft of money or an important item for the family like a television needing repair, or a large emergency expenditure, the effect for those on low income can be traumatic.

ACTIVITY 2.2: YOUR BELIEFS ABOUT POVERTY

The important objective of this exercise is to get an idea of the difference between structural and individual factors that may underpin poverty. Structural factors stem from economic, political and social systems which have a heavy influence in the incidence of poor health and creating poverty and deprivation. You could point to some 'individual factors' in Ullah's circumstances that have 'made them poor'. These could include the decision to present themselves as homeless to the Council once the family had been reunited in Britain, as well as smoking which is both expensive and unhealthy. He and his family have also had to contend with deeply embedded social barriers such as his experience as a migrant to Britain in the first place (without family networks), as an industrial worker in what gradually became failing industries (textiles and steel) and facing racial discrimination. Understanding the link between what appear to be personal problems or facets of individual behaviour and such structural factors is critical.

ACTIVITY 2.4: EARLY YEARS BILINGUAL SUPPORT SERVICE

When the service was offering support to a specific child (and its family) who was experiencing behavioural difficulties or suffering from trauma it would be located in the upper right-hand quadrant – that is, a specific service activity offered through direct work with the family. When providing its home–school liaison it could well undertake to negotiate with the school to change the way it responded to refugees, whether in teaching, uniform or curriculum. In this case its intervention would be located in the lower left-hand quadrant as an example of indirect work and change agent activity.

ACTIVITY 3.2: THE HICKEYS

The Hickeys are entitled to the income-based (that is non-contributory) Jobseeker's Allowance, housing benefit, council tax benefit and child benefit. (Remember that working out Income Support and income-based JSA is very similar.) When working out their applicable amount don't forget to take the various premiums into account. It will also be important to ascertain how many hours Mrs Hickey works and what her level of earnings is. Child benefit for the three children will count on the 'income' side of their assessment. The Hickeys are also eligible for housing benefit and council tax benefit but this would not reduce their overall JSA weekly rate. If Mr Hickey defaulted on his fine he could well have it deducted from the family benefit.

ACTIVITY 3.6: PARTNERSHIP – WHO HAS INFLUENCE?

Note: do not forget to include local residents or a local organisation even if their degree of influence is non-existent, that is 0.

ACTIVITY 3.9: HOW MUCH INFLUENCE DO LOCAL RESIDENTS HAVE?

This is a very substantial 'win' for local people in what is regarded as a marginalised and transitory area of London. It is a model of how to proceed to gain an effective voice: soundings of opinion through focus groups, careful research and face-to-face accountability sessions between local people and decision-makers which result in shifting local authority procedures on homelessness.

ACTIVITY 3.12: WHY THE CONTRASTS? THE RIBBLE VALLEY

This is not an easy task and will take some time and research. Basically the exercise asks you to find out how and why Clitheroe has remained heavily white while its neighbouring towns have significant Asian populations. Focus on one part of what is inevitably a complex picture – say, patterns of housing tenure and homeownership or reasons for high levels of deprivation in Burnley but relative prosperity in Clitheroe, or the role of culture in creating 'no-go' areas.

ACTIVITY 4.2: SAFEGUARDING AND PROMOTING THE CHILD'S WELFARE: THE DEPARTMENT OF HEALTH FRAMEWORK

It is important to explore the interaction of each of the three sides of the triangle during any assessment of a child in need. Those factors within 'the family and environment' have the greatest bearing on a family's experiences of social exclusion. This checklist particularly helps illuminate the degree of exclusion particular children will suffer.

ACTIVITY 4.5: MS RICE, RICKY AND ROBERT

This is a complex case because there are no clear-cut guidelines, nor is there a definitive assessment chart to turn to. Of course if you are seriously worried about the children you will need to get in touch with the local authority social services department, or if you work for that department already, go through the 'children in need' assessment procedure from the Department of Health discussed above. Preserve as many choices for her as possible. Her control over decisions is essential. Ther are clearly many other lines of work which you might either want to take on directly or co-ordinate with other voluntary or public services. Some means of bringing the school and family in closer rapport is essential – the ideas around 'family literacy' might be applicable. Connecting Ms Rice with a parent support group (perhaps starting one if there are other parents in similar predicaments) might also be helpful to her and the children. Her friendship with the two Muslim women seems critical and should be reinforced when considering her social networks.

ACTIVITY 5.4: SCHOOL EXCLUSION

You may wish to challenge the decision on permanent exclusion. If so you will need to do some research on how disciplinary matters should be handled when a pupil is statemented. In particular, find out whether statemented pupils can be excluded; this decision probably contravenes those guidelines. You will also need to consult the statutory framework for handling disciplinary matters in the DfEE circular (DfEE 1999) and be familiar with the school's own policy on discipline. Beyond the issue of getting the school to reconsider you may want to consider what your agency might do to promote a less discipline-focused response in the school to statemented children and those with behavioural difficulties.

ACTIVITY 5.5: EXAMINE A GOVERNMENT PRONOUNCEMENT

In some strands of current welfare policy observers have noted a 'new paternalism' which prescribes certain activities and codes of behaviour. Paternalism means a policy of making well-meaning provision for people's needs but giving them no responsibility. More crudely, it means 'we know what is in your best interests'. In this case the government, through its Connexions scheme, sounds as if it intends to make each young person engage in civic good works. Its aims are undoubtedly worthy but if in the actual arrangements of the summer programme, the elements of individual choice and acceptance of responsibility by young people themselves are missing then the programme may only generate resentment. It will do little to teach young people how to have influence within their social environment.

ACTIVITY 5.9: ANTI-SOCIAL BEHAVIOUR IN CHILDREN

The behaviour of these young people presents practitioners with a real dilemma, making it difficult to argue for non-punitive approaches. Local residents are feeling threatened and clearly fed up with their behaviour; the parent of the boys has no interest in exerting any control or responsibility and the local magistrates would not hesitate to place the boys in custody to get them off the streets. In terms of securing diversionary outcomes for these young people much will depend on the groundwork with magistrates that the local youth offending team may have undertaken, as well as the credibility and effectiveness of local programmes around restorative justice.

ACTIVITY 6.1: DANIEL

In using the exchange model with Daniel Gunn the practitioner would focus on the exchange of information between herself and the others involved with him. Much of the work will be in securing the involvement of his son and daughter-in law, the housing officer and the outreach worker from the local church. It may be appropriate to call them altogether for a discussion. The practitioner should strive to establish respect and trust. Dialogue begins on the nature of the problem with the views of Mr Gunn, his son, daughter-in-law all contributing. There may well be some painful moments for Mr Gunn as he realises that for now his own offspring will not be able to look after him day-to-day. The practitioner also explains what it is that her agency might offer in the way of home care (a very limited amount) and information about other services. She asks the son to re-engage the health service on Mr Gunn's behalf. She notes what other people say, brings together some consensus over the effects of Mr Gunn's mental health problems on him, his family and the neighbourhood. She does not steer the discussions but is alert to widening his contacts and supports. For example a little later she stops by the church: she finds it is evangelical with a large proportion of black members, socially conservative with respect to gays and gender roles but has a tenacious service ethos for people who are 'down and out'. Church outreach may in fact be something of a lifeline for the highly isolated Mr Gunn. Gradually the son and daughter-in-law feel that they do not have to shoulder the whole responsibility for looking after him and can see specific ways in which they can contribute to his care and social contacts.

The practitioner is also alert to neighbourhood development. The possibilities here are several. She might try to mobilise small grants for ecumenical outreach, or start a carers' support group. Or she might communicate interest and support to the local tenants association who with their small volunteer staff attempt to visit all new arrivals and periodically assail the housing department for their poor record on repairs and insulation.

ACTIVITY 6.4: AGEISM ON TELEVISION

The images of older people as portrayed in the media are among the most negative of any social group when they appear at all. They are in glaring contrast to the stream of television programmes and print media that concentrate on youth, on images of youth, of youth talking to youth. Ageism is a major barrier to participation by older people in, for example, the labour market, the media, in the consumer market and in obtaining health care. It is so pervasive that at times it is difficult to know where to begin. It helps to start at first principles. Erik Erikson's eight stages of the lifecycle (1994) will remind you how old age grows out of earlier life accomplishments and the importance of older people for society as a whole.

ACTIVITY 7.3: LOCAL PARTICIPATION IN VISIONING

The Ocean Estate's vision was put together after many long hours of discussion and wrangling in both formal and informal meetings of all descriptions. It was not easy to produce the vision statement (Pierson *et al.* 2000). For residents to make their influence felt it required:

- a constant battle with time limits
- needing professional expertise but not letting it gain controlling influence
- overcoming the headstart that the notion of 'partnership' gives agencies and officials who have the time, previous experience and salaried staff to begin work immediately.

At the outset residents felt unprepared and unskilled. But the determination of the local leadership to shape the local vision whether the manager of the Bangladeshi resource centre, the leaders of the mosque and local youth club or the tenants' association overcame those barriers.

ACTIVITY 7.7: WHAT IS YOUR RESPONSE?

Social work does not always see the resourcefulness that faith and faith-based institutions offer its adherents, preferring to focus on their oppressive social attitudes. Oppressiveness undeniably exists particularly in relation to women (all major faiths have struggled to admit women to influential roles within their institutions) and gays and lesbians. But faith-based services also provide reserves of local capacity, a willingness to work with outcasts and the marginalised, and high levels of motivation. Here, Aisa is feeling perhaps she has to choose between her profession and her faith heritage.

It may be that Aisa will have to bring these concerns to the team so that a broader, more inclusive but still woman-centred mission can be talked through.

ACTIVITY 8.2: WHEN DO CHILDREN START TO LEARN ABOUT DIFFERENCE?

In short much earlier than you might imagine. The research that Save the Children (2000) draw on in their report indicates that awareness of difference begins before the child is two.

ACTIVITY 9.1: TRAINING NEEDS ANALYSIS

Your training needs will vary according to your experiences and expertise. In a wider sense this can only be established in close link with other colleagues and even local community groups. There will be specific tasks with which you may need to become familiar such as the drug awareness programme mentioned. If you and your colleagues are feeling disempowered do remember that in this scenario there are multiple points at which you might be able to contribute: parent education, closer liaison with schools, restorative justice programmes and crime awareness with older citizens through day centres. But your needs may be on a more general – though no less important – level such as forming 'joined up' service collaborations or understanding the links between developing community-based resources and tackling specific incidents of youth offending.

ACTIVITY 9.2: EVALUATING A COMMUNITY RESOURCE CENTRE

There is a marked difference between the low level of resources (inputs) and the broad aspirations of the local consortium in this scenario (an old building, a single caretaker for staff – one can only imagine that the budget for the premises is extremely low). But other inputs to do with the community are high: a wide variety of groups use the premises and seem committed to it, and clearly those running the various sessions themselves have technical, organisational and relational skills. From outside the locality the local authority is also a stakeholder.

To measure progress against the stated objectives certain indicators or benchmarks should be agreed. At the moment it would seem that the regular cycle of weekly events do not necessarily move the neighbourhood toward the broad objectives, but you would have to establish this in your information gathering. One set of indicators could be the number of residents who feel involved in their community or levels of volunteering. Another could be to track the amount of fundraising each of the groups undertakes to see if that amount is rising. For both of these you would need baseline data. Perhaps as an evaluator you might offer a suggestion – that a community forum be instituted to look explicitly at progress – or lack of it – towards these objectives. Progress toward setting up a forum could be structured around a given point in time, for example after 3 or 6 months.

BIBLIOGRAPHY

6, P. (1997a) *Holistic Government* London: Demos

—— (1997b) *Escaping Poverty: From safety nets to networks of opportunity* London: Demos

6, P., Leat, D., Seltzer, K. and Stoker, G. (1999) *Governing in the Round: Strategies for holistic government* London: Demos

Alexander, A. (2000) *Mentoring Schemes for Young People – Handbook* Brighton and London: Pavilion and National Children's Bureau

Anastacio, J., Gidley, B., Hart, L., Keith, M., Mayom M. and Kowarzik, U. (2000) *Reflecting Realities: Participants' perspectives on integrated communities and sustainable development* Bristol: Policy Press

Anti-Poverty Alliance (n.d.) *Action on Poverty and Social Exclusion: Case studies and training materials* Glasgow: APA

Arnstein, S. (1969) A ladder of citizen participation *Journal of the American Institute of Planners* 35; 4: 216–24

Audit Commission (1994) *Seen But Not Heard: Co-ordinating community child health and social services for children in need* London: Audit Commission

—— (1996) *Misspent Youth* London: Audit Commission

—— (1999) *Getting the Best from Children's Services* London: Audit Commission

—— (2000) *Getting the Best from Children's Services: Findings from joint reviews of social services 1998/9* London: Audit Commission

Audit Commission and Social Services Inspectorate (2001) *A Report of the Joint Review of Social Services in the Royal Borough of Kensington and Chelsea* London: Audit Commission and Social Services Inspectorate

Bailey R. and Williams, B. (2000) *Inter-Agency Partnerships in Youth Justice* Sheffield: Social Services Monographs

Barber, T. and Crean, J. (2000) Guardianship in the elderly and the Community Care Act: more of the same? *Health Bulletin of the Scottish Office* 58; 6: 471–7

Barr, A. and Hashagen, S. (2000) *Achieving Better Community Development: Trainer's resource pack* London: Community Development Foundation Publications

Barr, A., Drysdale, J. and Henderson, P. (1997) *Towards Caring Communities: Community development and community care* Brighton: Pavilion

Barr, A., Stenhouse, C. and Henderson, P. (2001) *Caring Communities: A challenge for social inclusion* York: Joseph Rowntree Foundation

Bass, M. and Drewett, R. (1997) *Real Work: Supported employment for people with learning difficulties* Sheffield: Social Services Monographs

Bateman, N. (2000) *Advocacy Skills for Health and Social Care Professionals* London: Jessica Kingsley

Becker, S. (1997) *Responding to Poverty* London: Longman

Benioff, S. (1997) *A Second Chance: Developing mentoring and education projects for young people* London: Commission for Racial Equality and Crime Concern

Bentley, T. and Gurumurthy, R. (1999) *Destination Unknown: Engaging with the problems of marginalised youth* London: Demos

Bentley, T. and Oakley, K. (1999) *The Real Deal: What young people really think about government, politics and social exclusion* London: Demos

Beresford, P. and Croft, S. (1993) *Citizen Involvement: A practical guide for change* Basingstoke: Macmillan

Bidmead, C. (1999) Bidding for success: making a Sure Start application *Community Practitioner* 72; 6: 166–7

Biehal, N., Claydon, J. and Byford, S. (2000) *Home or Away? Supporting young people and families* London: National Children's Bureau

Biehal, N., Claydon, J., Stein, M. and Wade, J. (1995) *Moving On: Young people and leaving care schemes* London: HMSO

Biestek, F. (1961) *The Casework Relationship* London: Allen and Unwin

Blue, R. (1994) *Working Together Against Hate Groups* New Jersey: Globe Fearon Educational Publisher/Simon and Shuster

Blytheway, B. (1995) *Ageism* Buckingham: Open University Press

Bobo, L. (1998) Mapping racial attitudes at the century's end: has the color line vanished or merely reconfigured? Paper prepared for the Aspen Roundtable Project on Race and Community Revitalization

Borrie Commission (1994) *Social Justice* London: Institute of Public Policy Research

Braye, S. (2000) Participation and involvement in social care. An overview. In: Kemshall, H. and Littlechild, R. (eds) *User Involvement and Participation in Social Care* London: Jessica Kingsley

—— (2001) Key workers can open doors *Community Care* 3–10 May

Braye, S. and Preston-Shoot, M. (1995) *Empowering Practice in Social Care* Buckingham: Open University Press

Briggs, X., de Souza, X., Mueller, E. and Sullivan, M. (1997) *From Neighbourhood to Community: Evidence on the social effects of community development* New York: New School for Social Research

Bright, J. (1996) Preventing youth crime in high crime areas: towards a strategy *Cambridge Cropwood Roundtable Series* 22: 365–84

Bronfenbrenner, U. (1979) *The Ecology of Human Development* Cambridge MA: Harvard University Press

Bryson, A., Ford, R. and White M. (1997) *Making Work Pay: Lone mothers, employment and well-being* York: Joseph Rowntree Foundation

Burchardt, T. (2000) *Enduring Economic Exclusion: Disabled people, income and work* York: Joseph Rowntree Foundation

Burgess, H. and Reynolds, J. (1995) Preparing for social work with refugees using enquiry and action learning *Social Work Education* 14; 4: 58–73

Burke, B. and Harrison, P. (2001) Race and racism in social work. In: Davies, M. (ed.) *The Blackwell Encyclopaedia of Social Work* Oxford: Blackwell

Burleigh, M. (1994) *Death and Deliverance: 'Euthanasia' in Germany 1900–45* Cambridge: Cambridge University Press

Burns, D. and Taylor, M. (2000) *Auditing Community Participation: An assessment handbook* Bristol: Policy Press

Burton, P. (1997) *Community Visioning: An evaluation of the 'Choices for Bristol' project* Bristol: Policy Press

Cannan, C. (1992) *Changing Families, Changing Welfare: Family centres and the welfare state* London: Harvester Wheatsheaf

Cannan, C. and Warren, C. (1997) *Social Action with Children and Families: A community development approach to child and family welfare* London: Routledge

Carter, T. and Beresford, P. (2000) *Age and Change: Models of involvement for older people* York: Joseph Rowntree Foundation

Catt, H. and Scudamore, P. (1999) *The Power of Networking* London: Kogan Page

Cedersund, E. (1999) Using narratives in social work interaction. In: Jokinen, A., Juhila, K. and Poso, T. (eds) *Constructing Social Work Practices* Aldershot: Ashgate

Chanan, G., (1999) *Local Community Involvement: A handbook for good practice* Dublin: European Foundation for the Improvement of Living and Working Conditions

Channer, Y. (2000) Understanding and managing conflict in the learning process. Christians coming out. In: Cree, V. and Macaulay, C. *Transfer of Learning in Professional and Vocational Education* London: Routledge

Child Poverty Action Group (2000) *Welfare Benefits Handbook 2000/2001* London: CPAG

Christie, I. (with Mensah-Coker, G.) (1999) *An Inclusive Future? Disability, social change and opportunities for greater inclusion by 2010* London: Demos
Citizens Organising Foundation (2000) *Citizens Organising for a Change* Newsletter no.1, Spring
Clark, C. (2000) *Social Work Ethics: Politics, principles and practice* Basingstoke: Macmillan
Cohen, S. (2001) *Immigration Controls, the Family and the Welfare State* London: Jessica Kingsley
Cole, A., McIntosh, B. and Whittaker, A. (2000) *'We Want Our Voices Heard': Developing new lifestyles with disabled people* Bristol: Policy Press
Coleman, J. and Hendry, L. (1999) *The Nature of Adolescence* (3rd edn) London: Routledge
Commission for Racial Equality (n.d.) *School Exclusions and Ethnicity* London: CRE
—— (2001) *CRE's Review of the Race Relations Act 1976: Briefing on the government's response* London: CRE
Cowley, S. (1999) Early interventions: evidence for implementing Sure Start *Community Practitioner* 72: 162–5
Craig, G. (2000) Introduction. In: *Research Matters: Social exclusion special issue* Sutton: Community Care
Cree, V. and Davidson, R. (2000) Enquiry and action learning. A model for transferring learning. In: Cree, V. and Macaulay, C. (2000) *Transfer of Learning in Professional and Vocational Education* London: Routledge
Crime Concern (1999a) *Families in Schools: Best practice approaches for family literacy and positive parenting programmes* Swindon: Crime Concern
—— (1999b) *Reducing Neighbourhood Crime. A manual for action* Swindon: Crime Concern
Dalrymple, J. and Burke, B. (1995) *Anti-Oppressive Practice Social Care and the Law* Buckingham: Open University Press
Darvill, G. and Smale, G. (eds) (1990) *Partners in Empowerment: Networks of innovation in social work* London: National Institute of Social Work
Department of the Environment, Transport and the Regions (1999) *New Deal for Communities: Race equality guidance* London: DETR
Department for Education and Employment (1999a) *Social Inclusion: Pupil support* Circular 10/99 London: DfEE
—— (19999b)*Connexions Strategy Document*
Department of Health (1989) *Caring for People: Community care in the next decade and beyond* London: HMSO
—— (1995) *Looking After Children: Placement plan and assessment and action records* London: HMSO
—— (1999a) *Joint Investment Plans Guidance: Welfare to work for disabled people* London: Health and Social Care Joint Unit
——(1999b) *The Quality Protects Programme: Transforming children's services* Local Authority Circular (LAC(99)33)
—— (2000a) *Framework for the Assessment of Children in Need and their Families* London: The Stationery Office
—— (2000b) *Children (Leaving Care) Act: Regulations and guidance* London: The Stationery Office
Department of Social Security (1999) *Opportunity for All: Tackling poverty and social exclusion* Cm 4445 London: The Stationery Office
Dobson, B., Middleton, S. and Beardsworth, A. (2001) *The Impact of Childhood Disability on Family Life* York: Joseph Rowntree Foundation
Dominelli, L. (1998) Anti-oppressive practice in context. In: Adams, R., Dominelli, L. and Payne, M. *Social Work Themes, Issues and Critical Debates* Basingstoke: Macmillan
Donnellan, C. (1999) *Refugee and Asylum Seekers* Cambridge: Independence
Donovan, N. and Street, C. (1999) *Fit for School: How breakfast clubs meet health, education and childcare needs* London: New Policy Institute
Dowling, M. (1998) *Poverty: A practitioner's guide* Birmingham: Venture Press
—— (1999) *Social Workers and Poverty* Aldershot: Ashgate
Duncan, P. and Thomas, S. (2000) *Neighbourhood Regeneration: Resourcing community involvement* Bristol: Policy Press

Dunst, C., Trivette, C. and Deal, A. (eds) (1994) *Supporting and Strengthening Families* Cambridge MA: Brookline Books
Edgar, B., Doherty, J. and Mina-Coull, A. (1999) *Services for Homeless People* Bristol: Policy Press
European Economic Community (1985) On specific community action to combat poverty *Official Journal of the EEC* 24 February 1985
Fajerman, L., Jarrett, M. and Sutton, F. (2000) *Children as Partners in Planning: A training resource to support consultation with children* London: Save the Children
Family Rights Group (1986) *Promoting links: Keeping children and families in touch* London: FRG
Feloy, M. and Payne, D. (1999) *People Communities and Credit Unions* Birmingham: Birmingham Credit Union Development Agency
Ferguson, R. and Stoutland, S. (1999) Reconceiving the community development field. In: Ferguson, R. F. and Dickens, W. T. *Urban Problems and Community Development* Washington DC: The Brookings Institution
Field, F. (1996) *Stakeholder Welfare* London: Institute of Economic Affairs
Fimister, G. (1988) The organisation of welfare rights work in social services. In: Macpherson, S. and Becker, S. (eds) *Public Issues, Private Pain* London: Insight
Fisher, R., Ury, W. and Patton, B. (1991) *Getting to Yes: Negotiating an agreement without giving in* (revised edn) London: Business Books
Fook, J. (1993) *Radical Casework: A theory of practice* New South Wales: Allen and Unwin
Forrest, R. (2000) The new landscape of precariousness. In: Kennett, P. and Marsh, A. (eds) *Homelessness: Exploring the new terrain* Bristol: Policy Press
Forrest, R. and Kearns, A. (1999) *Joined-Up Places? Social cohesion and neighbourhood regeneration* York: Joseph Rowntree Foundation
Foyer Federation (1993) *Good Practice Handbook* London: Foyer Federation
Fox Harding, L. (1997) Viewpoint social work and community development *Community Care* 7 July 10
Fraser, M., Richman, J. and Galinsky, M. (1999) Risk, protection, and resilience: toward a conceptual framework for social work practice *Social Work Research* 23; 3: 131–44
Fulbright-Anderson, K., Kubisch, A. and Connell, J. (1998) *New Approaches to Evaluating Community Initiatives* vol. 2 Washington DC: The Aspen Institute
Furley, R. (2000) HIV and AIDS: Current issues for the social work role *Social Work Review* 12; 3: 26–8
Geddes, M. (1997) *Partnership against poverty and exclusion? Local regeneration strategies and excluded communites in the UK* Bristol: Policy Press
George, M. (2001) 'Our way or no way' *Community Care* 12–19 July
Germain, C. and Gittermain, A. (1980) *The Life Model of Social Work Practice* New York: Columbia University Press
Gibbons, J. with Thorpe, S. and Wilkinson, P. (1990) *Family Support and Prevention: Studies in local areas* London: National Institute for Social Work
Gilchrist, R. and Jeffs, T. (1995) Foyers: housing solution or folly? *Youth and Policy* 50: 1–12.
Gilligan, R. (2000) Family support issues and prospects. In: Canavan, J., Dolan, P., Pinkerton, J. (eds) *Family Support Direction from Diversity* London: Jessica Kingsley
Giloth, R. P. (1998) *Jobs and Economic Development: Strategies and practice* Newbury Park CA and London: Sage
Glass, N. (1999) Sure Start: The development of an early intervention programme for young children in the United Kingdom *Children and Society* 13; 4: 257–64
Glendinning, C. (2000) Buying independence – using direct payments to bridge the health/social services divide *Welfare Benefits* 7; 6: 10–17
Goicoechea-Balbona, A. (1998) Children with HIV/AIDS and their families. A successful social work intervention based on the culturally specific health care model *Health and Social Work* 23; 1: 61–9
Goldson, B. (2000) Children in need or young offenders? Hardening ideology, organizational change and new challenges for social work with children in trouble *Child and Family Social Work* 5: 255–65
Gordon, D. *et al.* (2000) *Poverty and Social Exclusion in Britain* York: Joseph Rowntree Foundation

Granovetter, M. (1973) The strength of weak ties hypothesis *American Journal of Sociology* 78; 8: 1360–80

Griffiths, R. (1988) *Community Care: Agenda for action* London: HMSO

Hadley, R. and McGrath, M. (1981) *Going Local: Neighbourhood social services* London: Bedford Square Press

Hadley, R., Cooper, M., Dale, P. and Stacy, G. (1987) *A Community Social Worker's Handbook* London: Tavistock

Halliday, S. (2000) Institutional racism in bureaucratic decision-making: a case study in the administration of homelessness law *Journal of Law and Society* 27; 3: 449–71

Hambleton, R., Hoggett, P. and Raazaque, K. (1997) *Freedom within Boundaries: Developing effective approaches to decentralisation* London: Local Government Management Board

Handel, R. (1999) *Building Family Literacy in an Urban Community* New York and London: Teachers College Press

Hardiker, P. (1999) Children still in need, indeed: prevention across five decades. In: Stevenson, O. (ed.) *Child Welfare in the UK* Oxford: Blackwell Science

Harper, K. (1996) *Let's Work Together: Managing children's behaviour. A resource for everyone who works with other people's children* London: Save the Children

Harris, I. (1995) *Messages Men Hear: Constructing masculinities* London: Taylor & Francis

Hastings, A., McArthur, A. and McGregor, A. (1996) *Less than Equal? Community organisations and estate regeneration partnerships* Bristol: Policy Press

Havell, C. (1998) Homelessness: A continual problem for young people in the UK *Childright* July/August 148: 12–14

Hawtin, M., Hughes, G. and Percy-Smith, J. (1994) *Community Profiling: Auditing social needs* Buckingham: Open University Press

Henderson, P. (1997) Community development and children: a contemporary agenda. In: Cannan, C. and Warren, C. (eds) *Social Action with Children and Families: A community development approach to child and family welfare* London: Routledge

Henderson, P. and Mayo, M. (1998) *Training and Education in Urban Regeneration: A framework for participants* Bristol: Policy Press

Henderson, P. and Thomas D. (2001) *Skills in Neighbourhood Work* (3rd edn) London: Routledge

Herbert, G. and Napper, R. (2000) *TIPS: Tried and tested ideas for parent education and support* Lyme Regis: Russell House

Hills, J. (1995) *Joseph Rowntree Inquiry into Income and Wealth* York: Joseph Rowntree Foundation

Holman, B. (1998) Neighbourhoods and exclusion. In: Barry, M. and Hallett, C. (eds) *Social Work and Social Exclusion* Lyme Regis: Russell House

Howarth, C., Kenway, P. and Palmer, G. (2001) *Responsibility For All: A national strategy for social inclusion* London: New Policy Institute and Fabian Society

Hughes, M. and Traynor, T. (2000) Reconciling process and outcome in evaluating community initiatives *Evaluation* 6; 1: 37–49

Jack, G. (2000) Ecological perspectives in assessing children and families. In: Howarth, J. (ed.) *The Child's World: Assessing children in need* London: Jessica Kingsley Publishers

Jack, G. (2000) Social support networks. In: Davies, M. (ed.) *The Blackwell Encyclopaedia of Social Work* Oxford: Blackwell

Jack, G. and Jack, D. (2000) Ecological social work: the application of a systems model of development in context. In: Stepney, P. and Ford, D. (eds) *Social Work Models, Methods and Theories: A framework for practice* Lyme Regis: Russell House

Jackson, S. (1998) Educational success for looked-after children: the social worker's responsibility *Pratice* 10; 4: 47–56

Jackson, S. and Martin, P. (1998) Surviving the care system: education and resilience *Journal of Adolescence* 21: 569–83

Jacobs, J. (1961) *Death and Life of American Cities* New York: Anchor

Jameson, N. (2001) (Director, Citizen's Organising Foundation) personal communication to the author

Jamieson, A. and Owen, S. (2000) *Ambition for Change: Partnerships, children and work* London: National Children's Bureau

Jones, C. (1998) Social work and society. In: Adams, R., Dominelli, L., and Payne, M. (eds) *Social Work Themes, Issues and Critical Debates* Basingstoke: Macmillan
Jordan, B. (1987) *Rethinking Welfare* Oxford: Blackwell
Jordan, B. and Jordan, C. (2000) *Social Work and the Third Way: Tough love as social policy* London: Sage
Kempson, E. and Whyley, C. (1998) *Access to Current Accounts* Bristol: Policy Press
Khan, P. (2000) Asylum-seekers in the UK: implications for social service involvment *Social Work and Social Sciences Review* 8; 2: 116–29
Kretzmann, J. and McKnight, J. (1993) *Building Communities from the Inside Out* Chicago: The Asset-based Community Development Institute
Kubisch, A. and Stone, R. (2001) Comprehensive Community Initiatives: the American experience. In: Pierson, J. and Smith, J. *Rebuilding Community: The policy and practice of urban regeneration* Basingstoke: Palgrave Publishers
Kubisch, A., Connell, J. and Fulbright-Anderson, K. (2001) Evaluating complex community initiatives: theory, measurement and analysis. In: Pierson, J. and Smith, J. *Rebuilding Community: The policy and practice of urban regeneration* Basingstoke: Palgrave Publishers
Langan, M. (1992) Who cares? Women in the mixed economy of care. In: Langan, M. and Day, L. (eds) *Women's Oppression and Social Work: Issues in anti-discriminatory practice* London: Routledge
Langan, M. and Day, L. (1992) *Women's Oppression and Social Work: Issues in anti-discriminatory practice* London: Routledge
Langan, M. and Lee, P. (1989) *Radical Social Work Today* London: Unwin Hyman
Lawrence, K. (2001) Structural racism and comprehensive community initiatives. In: Pierson, J. and Smith, J. (eds) *Rebuilding Community Policy and Practice of Urban Regeneration* London: Palgrave
Lea, J. (2000) The Macpherson Report and the question of institutional racism *The Howard Journal* 39; 3: 219–33
Lee, P. and Murie, A. (1997) *Poverty, Housing Tenure and Social Exclusion* Bristol: Policy Press
Levitas, R. (1998) *The Inclusive Society? Social exclusion and New Labour* Basingstoke: Macmillan
—— (1999) Defining and measuring social exclusion: A critical overview of current proposals *Radical Statistics* 71: 10–27
Lipset, S. (1996) *American Exceptionalism* New York: Norton
Lipsky, M. (1980) *Street Level Bureaucracy* New York: Russell Sage Foundation
Little, M. and Mount, K. (1999) *Prevention and Early Intervention with Children in Need* Aldenshot: Ashgate
Lloyd, E. (1997) The role of the centre in family support. In: Cannan, C. and Warren, C. (eds) *Social Action with Children and Families: A community development approach to child and family welfare* London: Routledge
Luxmoore, N. (2000) *Listening to Young People in School, Youth Work and Counselling* London: Jessica Kingsley
Macdonald, S. (1991) *All Equal Under the Act* London: Race Equality Unit
Maclennan, D. (2000) *Changing Places, Engaging People* York: Joseph Rowntree Foundation
Macpherson, Sir William (1999) *The Stephen Lawrence Inquiry* Cm 4262-I London: The Stationery Office
Madge, N., Burton, S., Howell, S. and Hearn, B. (2000) *9–13: The Forgotten Years?* London: National Children's Bureau
Marsh, P. and Crow, G. (1998) *Family Group Conferences in Child Welfare* Oxford: Blackwell
Marsh, P. and Peel, M. (1999) *Leaving Care in Partnership: Family involvement with care leavers* London: The Stationery Office
Mason, J. and Lewis, H. (1999) *Time to Decide: A guide to supporting young people in public care when making decisions about pregnancy* London: National Children's Bureau
Mayo, M. (1998) Community work. In: Adams, R., Dominelli, L. and Payne, M. (eds) *Social Work Themes, Issues and Critical Debates* Basingstoke: Macmillan
McCabe, A. Lowndes, V. and Skelcher, C. (1997) *Partnerships and Networks: An evaluation and development manual* York: Joseph Rowntree Foundation
McLeod, E. and Bywaters, P. (2000) *Social Work, Health and Equality* London: Routledge
Miller, J. (1996) *Never Too Young: How young children can take responsibility and make decisions. A handbook for early years workers* London: Save the Children

Mitchell, W. and Sloper, P. (2000) *User-Friendly Information for Families with Disabled Children: A guide to good practice* York: Joseph Rowntree Foundation
Moss, P., Petrie, P. and Poland, G. (1999) *Rethinking School: Some international perspectives* Leicester: Youth Work Press and Joseph Rowntree Foundation
Mullender, A. and Ward, D. (1991) *Self-Directed Groupwork: Users take action for empowerment* London: Whiting and Burch
Murray, C. (1996) Underclass: the crisis deepens. In: Lister, R. *Charles Murray and the Underclass: The developing debate* London: Institute of Economic Affairs
Nayak, A. (1999) 'White English ethnicities': racism, anti-racism and student perspectives *Race Ethnicity and Education* 2; 2: 177–202
Neighbourhood Initiatives Foundation (2000) *'Planning for Real' User's Guide* Telford: NIF
O'Bryan, A., Simons, K., Beyer, S. and Grove, B. (2000) *A Framework for Supported Employment* York: Joseph Rowntree Foundation
Ocean Estate NDC (2000) *New Deal for Communities. The Ocean – Tower Hamlets delivery plan, 2000–2010* London: Ocean Estate NDC
O'Flaherty, J. (1995) *Intervention in the Early Years: An evaluation of the High/Scope curriculum* London: National Children's Bureau
Okitikpi, T. and Aymer, C. (2000) The price of safety: refugee children and the challenge for social work *Social Work in Europe* 7; 1: 51–8.
Oliver, M. and Sapey, B. (1999) *Social Work with Disabled People* (2nd edn) Basingstoke: Macmillan
Pahl, R. (2000) *On Friendship* Cambridge: Polity
Park Family Centre *West Cheshire Teenage Parent's Project A Report* Cheshire: Park Family Centre
Parkinson, G. (1970) I give them money. In: Fitzgerald *et al.* (eds) (1977) *Welfare in Action* London: Routledge and Kegan Paul, cited in Dowling 1999
Parton, N. and O'Byrne, P. (2000) *Constructive Social Work: Towards a new practice* Basingstoke: Macmillan
Payne, M. (1997) *Modern Social Work Theory* (2nd edn) Basingstoke: Macmillan
Pearson, G. (1989) Social work and unemployment. In: Langan, M. and Lee, P. (eds) *Radical Social Work Today* London: Unwin Hyman
Penketh, L. (2001) *Tackling Institutional Racism: Anti-racist policies and social work education and training* Bristol: Policy Press
Penrose, J. (2001a) Listening to parents of children excluded from school (unpublished paper)
—— (2001b) Tell me why *Community Care* 15–21 February
—— (2001c) Personal communication to the author
Piachaud, D. and Sutherland, H. (2000) *How Effective is the British Government's Attempt to Reduce Child Poverty?* CASE Paper 38, London: Centre for Analysis of Social Exclusion, London School of Economics
Pierson, J. (1999) Social work and civil society: the mixed legacy of radical anti-oppressive practice. In: Philpot, T. (ed.) *Political Correctness and Social Work* London: Institute of Economic Affairs
Pierson, J., Worley, C. and Smith, J. (2000) *Local Participation and the New Deal for Communities* Stoke-on-Trent: Housing and Community Research Unit, Staffordshire University
Plummer, J. (2000) *Municipalities and Community Participation: A sourcebook for capacity building* London: Earthscan
Pollard, C. (2000) Victims and the Criminal Justice System: a new vision *Criminal Law Review* January, 5–17
Pollitt, C., Gordon, P. and Plamping, D. (1998) *Decentralising Public Service Management* Basingstoke: Macmillan
Power, A. (1997) *Estates on the Edge* Basingstoke: Palgrave Publishers
Power, A. and Mumford (1997) Negative pressures on mass estates. In: Power, A. (ed.) *Estates on the Edge* (1997) Basingstoke: Palgrave Publishers
Power, A. and Tunstall, R. (1995) *Swimming Against the Tide: Progress or polarisation on twenty unpopular estates* York: Joseph Rowntree Foundation
—— (1997) *Dangerous Disorder: Riots and violent disturbances in thirteen areas of Britain, 1991–2* York: Joseph Rowntree Foundation

PRA (Participatory Rural Appraisal) (1999) *Relaxed and Participatory Appraisal: Notes on practical approaches and methods* PRA www.ids.ac.uk/ids/particip

Pratt, J., Plamping, D. and Gordon, P. (1998) *Partnership: Fit for purpose?* London: King's Fund

Prewett, B. (1999) *Short-Term Break, Long-Term Benefit: Family-based care for disabled children and adults* Sheffield: Social Services Monographs

—— (2000) *Committed to Caring: The views of short break carers for children who are 'hard to place'* York: Joseph Rowntree Foundation

Pritchard, J. (2000) *The Needs of Older Women: Services for victims of elder abuse and other abuse* Bristol: Policy Press

Purdue, D., Razzaque, K., Hambleton, R. and Stewart, M. (2000) *Community Leadership in Area Regeneration* Bristol: Policy Press

Putnam, R. (2001) *Bowling Alone: The collapse and revival of American community* London: Simon and Shuster

Puttick, K., (2000a) *Welfare Benefits 2000/2001* Welwyn Garden City: CLT Professional Publishing

—— (2000b) Editorial *Welfare Benefits* 7; 5: 1

Qureshi, T., Berridge, D. and Wenman, H. (2000) *Where to Turn? Family support for South Asian communities – A case study* London: National Children's Bureau

Rahman, M., Palmer, G., Kenway, P. and Howarth, C. (2000) *Monitoring Poverty and Social Exclusion 2000* York: Joseph Rowntree Foundation

Randall, A. (2001) (Birmingham Welfare Rights) Personal communication to the author

Raynes, N., Temple, B., Glenister, C. and Coulthard, L. (2001) *Quality at Home for Older People: Involving service users in defining home care specifications* Bristol: Policy Press

Revans, R. (1982) *The Origins and Growth of Action Learning* Bromley: Chartwell-Bratt, cited in Wilkinson, D. and Applebee, E. *Implementing Holistic Government* London: Demos

Robinson, C. and Simons, K. (1996) *In Safe Hands? Quality and regulation in adult placements for people with learning difficulties* Sheffield: Social Services Monographs

Rogers, H. (2000) Breaking the ice: developing strategies for collaborative working with carers of older people with mental health problems. In: Kemshall, H. and Littlechild R. (eds) *User Involvement and Participation in Social Care: Research informing practice* London: Jessica Kingsley

Rossiter, J. (ed.) (1997) *Financial Exclusion: Can mutuality fill the gap?* London: New Policy Institute

Rutter, J. (1994) *Refugee Children in the Classroom* Stoke-on-Trent: Trentham Books

Rutter, J. and Hyder, T. (1998) *Refugee Children in the Early Years: issues for policy-makers and providers* London: Save the Children and the Refugee Council

Rutter, J. and Jones, C. (1998) *Refugee Education – Mapping the field* Stoke-on-Trent: Trentham Books

Rutter, M., Giller, H. and Hagell, A. (1998) *Anti-Social Behavior by Young People* Cambridge: Cambridge University Press

Sabel, C. (1993) Studied trust: building new forms of cooperation in a volatile economy *Human Relations* 46; 9: 1113–1170

Sadan, E. and Churchman, A. (1997) Process-focused and product focused community planning *Community Development Journal* 32; 1: 3–16

Saleeby, D. (1992) *The Strengths Perspective in Social Work* New York: Longman

Sampson, R. (1999) What 'community' supplies. In: Ferguson, R. F. and Dickens, W. T. (eds) *Urban Problems and Community Development* Washington DC: The Brookings Institution

Save the Children (1998) *All Together Now: Community participation for children and young people* London: Save the Children

—— (2000a) *Anti-Bias Approaches in the Early Years* London: Save the Children

—— (2000b) *We Can Work it Out: Parenting with confidence. A training pack for parenting groups* London: Save the Children

Sawyerr, A. (1999) Identity project on 'myself' with pre-schoolers at a day nursery. In: Barn, R. (ed.) *Working with Black Children and Adolescents in Need* London: British Agencies for Adoption and Fostering

Scott, J. (1998) *Seeing Like a State: How certain schemes to improve the human condition have failed* New Haven and London: Yale University Press

Scott, G., Long, G., Brown, U. and McKenzie, J. (2000) *Women's Issues in Local Partnership Working* Edinburgh: The Stationery Office

Scottish Executive (2001) *Early Education and Childcare Plans 2001–2004: Guidance to partnerships* Edinburgh: Scottish Executive

Scottish Office (1998) *Policy for Promoting Social Inclusion* Edinburgh: Scottish Office

Sennett, R. with Cobb, J. (1993) *Hidden Injuries of Class* New York: Norton and Co.

Shaftesbury Society (2000) *Community Development Work* London: Shaftesbury Society

Sheldon, B. and Chilvers, R. (2001) *Evidence-Based Social Care: A study of prospects and problems* Lyme Regis: Russell House

Shell, R. (1999) *Bargaining for Advantage: Negotiation strategies for reasonable people* London: Penguin

Short, E. (1999) *LABO: Ten years of Housing Plus* London: LABO Housing Association

SEU (Social Exclusion Unit) (1998a) *Rough Sleeping* Cm 4008 London: The Stationery Office

—— (1998b) *Bringing Britain Together: A national strategy for neighbourhood renewal* London: The Stationery Office

—— (1999a) *Teenage Pregnancy* Cm 4342 London: The Stationery Office

—— (1999b) *Bridging the Gap: New opportunities for 16–18-year-olds not in education, employment or training* London: The Stationery Office.

—— (2000) *National Strategy for Neighbourhood Renewal: A framework for consultation* London: Cabinet Office

Siraj-Blatchford, I. (1994) *The Early Years: Laying the foundations for racial equality* Stoke-on-Trent: Trentham Books

Skinner, S. (1997) *Building Community Strengths: A resource book on capacity building* London: Community Development Foundation

Sluzki, C. (2000) Social networks and the elderly: conceptual and clinical issues, and a family consultation *Family Process* 39; 3: 271–284

Smale, G. (1998) *Managing Change Through Innovation* London: The Stationery Office

Smale, G., Tuson, G. and Statham, D. (2000) *Social Work and Social Problems: Working towards social inclusion and social change* Basingstoke: Macmillan

Smale, G., Tuson, G., Ahmad, B., Darvill, G., Domoney, L. and Sainsbury, E. (1994) *Negotiating Care in the Community* London: National Institute of Social Work

Smale, G., Tuson, G., Biehal, N. and Marsh, P. (1993) *Empowerment, Assessment, Care Management and the Skilled Worker* London: HMSO

Smale, G., Tuson, G., Cooper, M., Wardle, M. and Crosbie, D. (1988) *Community Social Work: A Paradigm for Change* London: National Institute for Social Work

Smith, T. (1996) *Family Centres and Bringing Up Young Children* London: HMSO

SSI (Social Service Inspectorate) (1991) *Assessment and Planning in Care Management* London: HMSO

—— (1998) *Removing Barriers for Disabled Children* London: Department of Health

Stein, M. (1997) *What Works in Leaving Care?* Ilford: Barnardos

Stokes, P. and Knight, B. (1997) *Organising a Civil Society* Birmingham: Foundation for Civil Society

Stone, R. and Butler, B. (2000) *Core Issues in Comprehensive Community Building Initiatives: Exploring power and 'race'* Chicago: Chapin Hall Centre for Children, University of Chicago

Street, C. and Kenway, P. (1999) *Food for Thought: Breakfast clubs and their challenges* London: New Policy Institute

Tamkin, P. (2000) Institutional racism: daring to open Pandora's box *Equal Opportunities Review* 92: 19–23

Tanner, D. (1998) Empowerment and care management: swimming against the tide *Health and Social Care in the Community* 6; 6: 447–457

Taylor, M. (1995) *Unleashing the Potential: Bringing residents to the centre of regeneration* York: Joseph Rowntree Foundation

—— (2000) *Top Down Meets Bottom Up: Neighbourhood management*: York: Joseph Rowntree Foundation

Thomas, M. (2001) (Institute of Social Work and Applied Social Studies, Staffordshire University), briefing paper for the author

Thomas, M. and Lebacq, M. (2000) *Beyond Fear: Social work practice and domestic violence* Sheffield: Social Services Monographs

Tosey, P. (2000) Making sense of interventions: stranger in a strange land. In: Wheal, A. (ed.) *Working with Parents Learning from Other People's Experience* Lyme Regis: Russell House

Townsend, P. (1979) *Poverty in the United Kingdom* London: Penguin

Tracy, E. and Whittaker, J. (1990) The social network map: assessing social support in clinical practice *Families in Society: The journal of contemporary human services* October: 461–70

Traynor, T. and Davidson, G. (2000) *'Things Do Change': Evaluation of Barnardos anti-poverty strategy* Paper 3 Ilford: Barnardos

Twelvetrees, A. (1991) *Community Work* (2nd edn) Basingstoke: Macmillan

UN (1995) *The Copenhagen Declaration and Programme of Action for Social Development* New York: UN Department of Publications

Valios, N. (2001) Desperately seeking sanctuary *Community Care* 1–7 March

Van Soest, D. (1996) Impact of social work education on student attitudes and behavior concerning oppression *Journal of Social Work Education* 32;2: 191–202

Vernon, J. and Sinclair, R. (1999) *Maintaining Children in School: The contribution of social services departments* London: National Children's Bureau

Ward, H. (ed.) (1995) *Looking After Children: Research into practice* London: HMSO

Wilcox, D. (1994) *The Guide to Effective Partnership* Brighton: Partnership Books

Wilkinson, D. and Applebee, E. (1999) *Implementing Holistic Government: Joined-up action on the ground* London: Demos

Williamson, H. (ed.) (1995) *Social Action for Young People: Accounts of SCF youth work practice* Lyme Regis: Russell House

Wilson, W. (1996) *When Work Disappears: The world of the new urban poor* New York: Alfred Knopf

Witney, B. (2001) (Social Exclusion Unit, Staffordshire County Council), personal communication to the author

Wolfe, M. (1999) *Debt Advice Handbook* (4th edn) London: Child Poverty Action Group

—— (2001) Personal communication to the author

Wolman, H. and Page, E. (2001) *Learning from the Experience of Others: Policy transfer among local regeneration partnerships* York: Joseph Rowntree Foundation

Wonnacott, J. and Kennedy, M. (2001) A model approach *Community Care* 8–14 March

Wood, R. L. (1997) Social capital and political culture: God meets politics in the inner city *American Behavioural Scientist* 40;5: 595–605

Yorkshire and Humber Regional Development Agency (n.d.) *Active Partners: Benchmarking community participation in regeneration* Leeds: Yorkshire and Humber RDA

Zetter, R. and Pearl, M. (1999) *Managing to Survive: Asylum seekers, refugees and access to social housing* Bristol: Policy Press

INDEX